PERSPECTIVAL METHODOLOGY

Mark Ressler

INCREASINGLY SKEPTICAL PUBLICATIONS

©2025 by Mark Ressler.

All rights reserved.

ISBN 978-1-940551-03-6 (Hardcover)
ISBN 978-1-940551-23-4 (Paperback)
ISBN 978-1-940551-83-8 (Casewrap)
ISBN 978-1-940551-43-2 (PDF)

Contents

Preface   5
   The End of Philosophy 5

1 **Introduction**   19

2 **Progress**   25

3 **Incoherence**   29

4 **Philosophy**   43

5 **Bootstrapping**   55

6 **Naturalism**   67

7 **Inference to the Best Explanation**   81

8 **Reflective Equilibrium**   97

9 **Presuppositions**   113

10 **Phenomenology**   125

11 **Skepticism**   137

12 **Relativism**   145

13 **Error**   161

14 **Explanation**   169

15 **Intuitions**   181

16 **Thought Experiments**   189

17 Necessity	**199**
18 Language	**207**
19 Distinctions	**213**
20 Constraint	**217**
21 Predecessors	**231**
22 Conclusion	**241**
References	**247**

Preface

The End of Philosophy

The notion of the end of philosophy has been contemplated at least since the early nineteenth century. Although there are several senses of an end according to which this notion has been discussed, the two that interest me here are ending as completion and ending as stopping. This contrast is discussed by Martin Heidegger, for example, who himself belongs to the tradition of considering the end of philosophy as completion (Heidegger, 1977, p. 374). Likewise, later Wittgenstein falls into this tradition with his impoverished notion of philosophy as seeking "To shew the fly the way out of the fly-bottle" (Wittgenstein, 2001, p. 87e, sec. 309). Once philosophical problems have been unraveled, and the fly is out of the bottle, so long as philosophy "leaves everything as it is" (Wittgenstein, 2001, p. 42e, sec. 124) with regard to language, then apparently philosophy will have completed its task and does not need to continue.[1]

As completion, the notion of the end of philosophy projects forward to a point at which philosophy will have completed its function, answering all of the questions it sought to answer or possibly showing that such questions need not be answered at all. Like

---

[1] Wittgenstein's intention with his fly-bottle metaphor is clear, but the metaphor is ultimately quite awkward, since one sets a fly-bottle to trap flies which are posing a nuisance. To liberate such flies restores the nuisance, which is metaphorically at odds with Wittgenstein's intention to resolve or to dissolve philosophical problems. Marcuse considered Wittgenstein and similar thinkers to exhibit "academic sado-masochism, self-humiliation, and self-denunciation of the intellectual whose labor does not issue in scientific, technical or like achievements" (Marcuse, 1964, p. 173). For more on the history of those who preached the end of philosophy, see the contributions in (Baynes, Bohman, & McCarthy, 1986).

some religious enthusiasts who claim that the end of the world is immanent, there is a tendency among those who promote the idea of the end of philosophy to claim that this point of completion for philosophy is just beginning, that the end is nigh. As time passes, though, philosophy continues by changing and expanding beyond its previous scope, though perhaps spawning yet another generation of thinkers who will proclaim that philosophy is just about to complete itself by means of whatever philosophical doctrines are prevalent at the time.

By contrast, more recent discussions of the end of philosophy have focused on ending as mere stopping, by arguing that the conception of the function of philosophy is fundamentally mistaken, that philosophy cannot achieve the aims that it has set out for itself and should therefore stop.

Richard Rorty exemplifies this latter conception of the end of philosophy, given his arguments in *Philosophy and the Mirror of Nature*. His stated aim in this book "is to undermine the reader's confidence in 'the mind' as something about which one should have a 'philosophical' view, in 'knowledge' as something about which there ought to be a 'theory' and which has 'foundations,' and in 'philosophy' as it has been conceived since Kant" (Rorty, 1980, p. 7). This aim is pursued by attacking what Rorty considers to be the dominant metaphor under which philosophy has operated throughout the modern era, namely "the mind as a great mirror, containing various representations — some accurate, some not — and capable of being studied by pure, nonempirical methods" (Rorty, 1980, p. 12).

His argument proceeds first by challenging the philosophical notion that the mind is a special sort of glassy essence, referring to a metaphor from Peirce, arguing that this notion arises from the attempt to combine three features of human mental life, namely "separation from the body, non-spatiality, and the grasp of universals", thereby concluding "that if we hold these last three historically distinct notions apart, then we shall no longer be tempted by the notion that knowledge is made possible by a special Glassy Essence which enables human beings to mirror nature" (Rorty, 1980, p. 37). Rather, Rorty argues that the notion of persons without minds is perfectly coherent (Rorty, 1980, pp. 70–127).

Having undermined the traditional notion of the mind, Rorty proceeds to challenge the notion of a theory of knowledge by tracing the development of epistemology in the seventeenth century as a field concerned with representations according to the metaphor of the mind as a mirror of nature. "The moral to be drawn is that if this way of thinking of knowledge is optional, then so is epistemology, and so is philosophy as it has been understood itself since the middle of the last century" (Rorty, 1980, p. 136). He supports the arguments of Wilfrid Sellars and Willard Van Orman Quine against the notion of privileged representations that can be taken as foundational elements in a theory of knowledge, thereby claiming that there is nothing for epistemology to be without the notion of privileged representations (Rorty, 1980, pp. 209–212). To those who think that there might be some successor discipline to epistemology once the reliance on privileged representations is abandoned, Rorty argues against this possibility with regard to two proposed successor disciplines: empirical psychology (Rorty, 1980, pp. 213–256) and philosophy of language (Rorty, 1980, pp. 257–311).

Rather than seeking a successor to epistemology, Rorty espouses a hermeneutical approach to understanding the world, proposing that the philosopher play the role of an informed dilettante rather than a cultural overseer (Rorty, 1980, p. 317). Instead of critiquing other disciplines on the basis of incorrigible knowledge gained by special philosophical methods, the philosopher would simply facilitate dialogue between various disciplines. The role of philosophy would be to provide edification, rather than discovering truths (Rorty, 1980, pp. 360–379), but he offers some consolation to professional philosophers by acknowledging that "the need for teachers who have read the great dead philosophers is quite enough to ensure that there will be philosophy departments as long as there are universities" (Rorty, 1980, p. 393).

Nevertheless, Rorty denies that philosophy will come to an end, since some field will continue to be called "philosophy" even if his arguments against the guiding metaphor of philosophy succeed (Rorty, 1980, p. 394), namely philosophy would continue as hermeneutics and edification. Yet some may think that if that is all that philosophy could hope to be, then perhaps the field simply ought to come to an end, rather than mutating into something so weak and unambitious.

Rorty claims to have learned from his teachers "that a 'philosophical problem' was a product of the unconscious adoption of assumptions built into the vocabulary in which the problem was stated — assumptions which were to be questioned before the problem itself was taken seriously" (Rorty, 1980, p. xiii). Indeed, his arguments against the metaphor of the mirror of nature represents an effort to uncover the assumptions and presuppositions behind the problems of the nature of the mind and of knowledge. Yet the very problematic nature of this metaphor could likewise be taken to be a separate problem that itself might be a product of the adoption of certain assumptions. The arguments demonstrating that this metaphor is faulty would also rely on a number of presuppositions, and Rorty does not spend any time examining the assumptions that support his own arguments. Rather, he ultimately seems to rely on the alleged incommensurability between the discourse of traditional epistemology and that of hermeneutics, an incommensurability that appears specifically to support taking a hermeneutic approach. However, it is not clear whether the very allegation of such incommensurability might also rely on certain assumptions that Rorty has not adequately investigated.

Furthermore, Rorty notes that Ludwig Wittgenstein, Martin Heidegger, and John Dewey each abandoned their early constructive efforts at epistemology in favor of a later therapeutic approach, and these general therapeutic approaches inspires Rorty's hermeneutical conception of philosophy as edification. Yet one might agree with Rorty's critique of traditional epistemology and still not agree with him that all that remains for philosophy is to provide therapy or edification. To jump to that conclusion would represent a failure to imagine further alternatives for philosophy. Even if empirical psychology and philosophy of language fail to provide a successor field to epistemology, these two instances of failure do not demonstrate that every proposed successor to epistemology will fail, particularly successors that may not yet have been imagined.[2]

Indeed, Rorty suggests that some future genius may revital-

---

[2] It is not clear that Rorty is reading Dewey well in this regard. Dewey writes that "An empirical method ... is not an insurance device nor a mechanical antiseptic. It inspires the mind with courage and vitality to create new ideals and values in the face of the perplexities of a new world" (Dewey, 1958, p. x). Indeed, Dewey does thus challenge a quest for epistemic certainty, but his preferred creative approach hardly seems merely therapeutic: "The failures of philosophy have come from lack of confidence in the directive powers that inhere in experience, if men have but the wit and courage to follow them" (Dewey, 1958, p. x). Kitcher also appears to be following Rorty's uncourageous reading of Dewey (Kitcher, 2023).

ize the metaphor of a mirror of nature into systematic epistemology (Rorty, 1980, p. 393). Yet he does not consider the possibility that epistemology may be revitalized on the basis of a different metaphor. Even if philosophers may have explicitly endorsed the metaphor of a mirror of nature in the past, this does not mean that their work may not be reinterpreted under a different metaphor, one that may not be as faulty as the mirror metaphor. Moreover, Rorty does not consider the possibility that traditional epistemology might be revitalized without relying on any metaphors whatsoever.

These considerations suggest to me that Rorty may have quit philosophy too soon, along with Wittgenstein and Heidegger before him, since it is not clear that there is something fundamentally wrong with philosophy in itself, rather than with various pictures of what philosophy should be. Or rather, since these philosophers seem not to have had the strength of imagination to find a way through the problems with traditional philosophy that each of them uncovered, perhaps it is just as well that they had quit. Perhaps they should have quit earlier. Yet their failure to imagine a way forward does not indicate that there is no way forward at all. Instead, it indicates to me that better philosophers than these must arise if philosophy is to move forward.

More recently, François Laruelle has proposed something he calls "non-philosophy" on analogy to non-Euclidean geometry (Laruelle, 2013b, p. 2), also claiming that the relationship between philosophy and non-philosophy is analogous to that between special and general relativity (Laruelle, 2013b, p. 100), although he never clarifies the boundary conditions under which non-philosophy would reduce to philosophy under this latter analogy. While Laruelle does not typically use the phrase "end of philosophy" directly in the context of non-philosophy, he does use the phrase "let the dead bury their dead" (Laruelle, 2013b, p. 211) (Laruelle, 2013a, p. 76) in the context of seeking an exit out of philosophy (Laruelle, 2013a, pp. 92, 193),[3] and claims philosophy to

---

[3] He likewise refers to a positivist caricature as "philosophy is dead; the science of philosophy can replace it ..." (Laruelle, 2013b, p. 29), as well as deconstructionist efforts "to put philosophy in relation with its death" (Laruelle, 2013b, p. 203). At one point, he attempts a distinction between the end of philosophy and the end times of philosophy (Laruelle, 2012, p. 15), but does not actually explain the distinction.

be non-philosophy's "principle adversary" calling it "the most devious and greatest sham" (Laruelle, 2012, p. 217).

Indeed, Laruelle presents the idea of the end of philosophy as a problem:

> Philosophies do not live, they survive, are born, disappear, and are reborn in order to vanish almost at the same moment. Either philosophies die from not dying, or they do not die from continually dying, not containing a sufficient amount of reality to disappear for good. The end or death of philosophy is the greatest trap, tricking us into maintaining its will to survive. (Laruelle, 2012, p. 11)

For Laruelle, philosophy is "beyond life and death" (Laruelle, 2013b, p. 29). Non-philosophers must not abandon philosophy (Laruelle, 2017, p. 118), because "there will always be philosophy" (Laruelle, 2017, p. 228). Rather, non-philosophers should renounce the question of the death of philosophy (Laruelle, 2017, p. 20), because non-philosophy is not intended to annul philosophy (Laruelle, 2017, p. 298), but rather to safeguard it (Laruelle, 2013a, p. 76).

Yet if non-philosophy is properly analogous to non-Euclidean geometry, then there ought to be something analogous to Euclid's fifth postulate in philosophy that non-philosophy denies, such that non-philosophy ought more properly to be called "non-X philosophy", where the X signifies this philosophical postulate or assumption that non-philosophy rejects.[4]

Laruelle describes this key assumption of philosophy whose denial forms the basis for non-philosophy in three different ways:

Philosophical Decision according to which coherence is achieved by philosophical "representation supposed to be constitutive of the real", grounded in "the very nature of the narrative of the philosophical text, which already seems to be referred to the real, not only in order to describe it but also in order to transform it" (Laruelle, 2013b, p. 6). See also (Laruelle, 2013b, p. 49). Defined in (Laruelle, 2013a, pp. 116–118).

---

[4]Laruelle eventually acknowledges this point, later renaming non-philosophy to "non-standard philosophy" (Laruelle, 2013a, p. 16), which lacks the provocative impact of "non-philosophy".

The Principle of Sufficient Philosophy "It states that philosophy suffices for the real and for the thought of the real and thus that it is unsurpassable like the real itself" (Laruelle, 2013b, p. 98). See also (Laruelle, 2013b, p. 12).

The Heraclitean Postulate "which says that for a given term there corresponds one contrary term and one alone" (Laruelle, 2013b, p. 104).

The last way is compared specifically to Euclid's fifth postulate (Laruelle, 2013b, p. 104), and Laruelle links these three ways together in a statement of non-philosophy as forming "more universal practices of philosophy":

> For whichever phenomenon, one should be able to propose a multiplicity of equivalent interpretations, a multiplicity which is no longer simply unitary but "dualitary" and such that it escapes from the Principle of sufficient philosophy; as infinity of equivalent philosophical decisions for the same phenomenon to be interpreted. (Laruelle, 2013b, p. 107)

Yet while it appears clear enough how Philosophical Decision relates to the Principle of Sufficient Philosophy, it is not clear how the alleged Heraclitean Postulate relates to either of these. Just because someone might accept one and only one contrary term for a given term, that does not imply anything regarding "the real" without additional assumptions concerning the relationship of terms to "the real" whose explication itself is not at all clear.

More importantly, it is not clear that any philosopher endorses or presupposes Philosophical Decision, the Principle of Sufficient Philosophy, or the Heraclitean Postulate, let alone that all of philosophy can be characterized as presupposing these three.[5] Laruelle cites Parmenides in support of Philosophical Decision and the Principle of Sufficient Philosophy (Laruelle, 2013b, p. 51) (Laruelle,

---

[5] Doubtless Laruelle was thinking primarily in terms of the French philosophy as practiced when he wrote, about which I am not fully informed. If indeed that French philosophy could fairly be characterized by these presuppositions, then so much the worse for that philosophy. In that case, Laruelle would still be guilty of mistaking the part for the whole.

2017, p. 173) (Laruelle, 2013a, p. 118), but this attribution represents a poor, overly facile interpretation of Parmenides. The reference in the description of Philosophical Decision to transforming the real clearly invokes the claim of Marx and Engels that "The philosophers have only *interpreted* the world in various ways; the point is to *change* it" (Marx & Engels, 1976, p. 5). Yet this quotation does not even support the charge that Marx and Engels endorse Philosophical Decision or the Principle of Sufficient Philosophy, let alone the philosophers that they reference. Of course, there are so few fragments of Heraclitus available to determine his meta-philosophy, and even Protagoras' slogan "Man is the measure of all things" admits a sufficient range of interpretation that it cannot definitively be cited in support of Laruelle's claims. These few philosophers represent a very small minority of philosophers even in the Western tradition, such that Laruelle's attribution of Philosophical Decision, the Principle of Sufficient Philosophy, and the Heraclitean Postulate to *all* of philosophy is manifestly unsupported, with the result that Laruelle's arguments in favor of non-philosophy seem little more than an extended straw man argument.

Beyond the identification of what non-philosophy opposes, there is no shortage of positive characterizations in Laruelle's writings of what non-philosophy is supposed to be:

- "Non-philosophy will be nothing other than what the real experience of thought, what we call vision-in-One, takes from Philosophy" (Laruelle, 2013b, p. 11).

- "Non-philosophy is the authentic, not alienated, concept of 'popular philosophy' and of anti-vulgarization" (Laruelle, 2013b, p. 28).[6]

- "'Non-philosophy' is therefore an ensemble of representations that can be read in two ways or can receive two simultaneous usages" (Laruelle, 2013b, p. 240).

---

[6]Rather comically, Laruelle continues to claim "Philosophy can only really become 'for all' or 'popular' by becoming non-philosophy" (Laruelle, 2013b, p. 28), as though he expected masses of people to be discussing "vision-in-One" and "force-(of)-thought" in coffee shops. However, he later claims, "Non-philosophy is not then a *popular philosophy* (Fichte)" (Laruelle, 2017, p. 296). Apparently, the use of 'popular philosophy' in scare quotes must refer to some undefined non-philosophical conception of popularity.

- "Non-philosophy is the object of a transcendental induction and deduction from the real-One (or the force-(of)-thought) in the field of experience insofar as it is constituted from now on by philosophy and regional knowings" (Laruelle, 2017, p. 7).

- "Non-philosophy is the universal dictionary of philosophies; the transcendental idiom in terms of thought which relates to them" (Laruelle, 2017, p. 14).

- "Non-philosophy as first science is the manifestation of the essence-(of)-philosophy of philosophy and identically of the essence-(of)-science of science, which is to say the aprioristico-transcendental identify of each of these opposing terms..." (Laruelle, 2017, p. 51).

- "Non-philosophy is, then, the radical phenomenal fulfillment of intra-philosophical maxims or injunctions..." (Laruelle, 2017, p. 63).

- "Consequently, non-philosophy is very exactly, through the force-(of)-thought, a *transcendental cloning and a dualysis of the philosophical materials*" (Laruelle, 2017, p. 186).

- "With the vision-in-One, non-philosophy is the experience of the passage from philosophical teleology to a science-thought" (Laruelle, 2017, p. 230).

- "Non-philosophy is the matrix of disciplines of the type called 'unified theory' which each time manifest the 'simple' a priori correlation of philosophy and a region" (Laruelle, 2017, p. 283).

- "Non-philosophy is a transcendental theory of human multitudes and of the manner in which humans of-the-last-instance are in-body..." (Laruelle, 2013a, pp. 46–47).

- "Non-philosophy is an attempt at a reply to perhaps the most determining if not unique question of science fiction and gnosis: *should we save humanity?* and *What do we mean by humanity?*" (Laruelle, 2012, p. 3).

- "What, in the end, is non-philosophy? It is the style of radicality enacted against the absolute, the style of minimality against satiety, the style of uni-laterality against convertibility, the style of heresy against conformity" (Laruelle, 2012, p. 13).

- "Non-philosophy is thus Man as the utopian identity of the philosophical form of the World, a utopia destined to transform it" (Laruelle, 2012, p. 17).

- "More generally, non-philosophy is *a complex thought composed of a multitude of aspects, which is to say, unilateral interpretations, of a philosophical origin, but reduced by their determination-in-the-last-instance*" (Laruelle, 2012, p. 22).

Even if one understands the opaque jargon rampant in these characterizations, it is not clear of any two such characterizations how they could characterize the same thing, let alone all of these characterizations taken together. Consequently, it might be better simply to refer to Laruelle's dictionary definition of non-philosophy:

> Autonomous and specific discipline of an identically scientific and philosophical type that describes — in-the-last-instance according to the One-real and by means of philosophy and of science considered as material — on the one hand force (of) thought or the existing-Stranger-subject, and on the other hand the object of force (of) thought, which is the identity (of) world-thought. (Laruelle, 2013a, p. 98)

Unfortunately, this definition does not appear to have been definitive, since Laruelle later provides yet another definition with new jargon that does not clearly align to the previous definition or to any of his characterizations of non-philosophy:

> This is why we will define non-philosophy rather as *an immanent thought whose arrival determines-in-the-last-Humaneity or according-to-the-Future the (non-) relation of practice and theory.* Non-philosophy is thought made into an ultimatum. (Laruelle, 2012, p. 149)

In any case, what is apparent from all of these characterizations and definitions is that non-philosophy is a practice fundamentally directed toward objects of its own devising.

Superficially, non-philosophy is characterized by excessive reference to neo-Platonic terms like *the One* and *the Dyad* in addition to more commonplace high level abstractions such as *the Real*, *Being*, and *the Other*, liberally connected by notions of *transcendence* and *immanence*. As apparent in the characterizations and definitions of non-philosophy previously cited, non-philosophy is heavy in jargon and neologisms, requiring a dictionary of terminology (Laruelle, 2013a) that not only circularly defines this terminology in terms of that same jargon, but conveniently redefines a dictionary (Laruelle, 2013a, pp. 23–34) and definition (Laruelle, 2013a, pp. 45–46) in non-philosophical terms to forestall any criticism of the dictionary. This jargon relies heavily on gratuitous punctuation, not only the familiar pattern of hyphenation, both joining separate words as in "vision-in-One", and splitting single words such as "Uni-verse", but also parenthesis of some prepositions or prefixes, as in "force-(of)-thought" and "(non-) One".[7]

What would characterize non-philosophy more specifically is the adherence to six rules (Laruelle, 2013b, pp. 129–158), which involve taking existing philosophy as mere material, mixing it up, optionally combining it with other materials such as pictures and poetry under certain conditions, then performing successive operations ultimately leading to something called "vision-in-One".[8] Later presentations of non-philosophy do not emphasize these near-alchemical rules, but focus more on principles, axioms, and theorems (Laruelle, 2013b, pp. 79–96) (Laruelle, 2017, pp. 139–153, 224–227); however, these axioms and theorems do not function as logical axioms or theorems such that anything can be deduced from them, since as expected Laruelle has redefined axioms and theorems in a non-philosophical sense (Laruelle, 2012, pp. 30–31).

With regard to these rules, it is unclear what would consti-

---

[7] All of which is given non-philosophical rationale (Laruelle, 2012, p. 75), apparently comprehensible only to a non-philosopher.

[8] Clearly I do not understand these alleged rules, but this abbreviated summary of the rules is not intended as a parody to misrepresent or to ridicule non-philosophy. I think I have provided a fair description of the rules according to terms that Laruelle himself uses. It is not necessary to ridicule Laruelle; it is sufficient to quote him.

tute following or failing to follow the rules. Indeed, Laruelle himself questions the meaning of following rules with regard to non-philosophy (Laruelle, 2017, p. 191), but his answer to this question seems elusive if one is not already non-philosopher. Predictably, the answer involves a specifically non-philosophical conception of rules (Laruelle, 2012, pp. 54–55).

One wonders whether merely adopting the non-philosophical jargon is sufficient to qualify as non-philosophy. Interestingly, since Laruelle's death, it is now possible to train a system of artificial intelligence against Laruelle's texts as well as those of other non-philosophers, such that new texts could be generated in the style of non-philosophers. Would this qualify as genuine non-philosophy? It is likely that those who are not non-philosophers would be unable to tell the difference. Could non-philosophers themselves tell the difference between authentic and inauthentic non-philosophy? The potential consequences of such artificial non-philosophy would be interesting. If artificial non-philosophy were accepted as authentic non-philosophy, would that mean that a machine could attain vision-in-One so easily? If it is not, but no one could tell the difference, then what is the value of authentic non-philosophy?

More fundamentally, there is a question not merely of whether non-philosophy can deliver what it promises, but what non-philosophy promises in the first place. Indeed, Laruelle poses a series of questions that non-philosophy is supposed to answer, such as "How do we no longer comment on the forgetting of philosophy while playing the perpetual game of suspicion on its behalf?" (Laruelle, 2013b, p. 5); yet the aim of non-philosophy appears elusive unless one is willing simply to take the piece of jargon "vision-in-One" as sufficient. Laruelle himself seems almost intent on undermining any value of non-philosophy:

- "Non-philosophy is *de jure* badly formed ..." (Laruelle, 2017, p. 41).

- "Non-philosophical thought is not comprehensible in a epistemological-experimental manner ..." (Laruelle, 2017, p. 101).

- "We cannot judge the reality of non-philosophical thought

by its effectivity; by its manner of being-given by local realizations" (Laruelle, 2017, pp. 193–194).

- "Non-philosophy has no identifiable effect outside of its immanent exercise ... " (Laruelle, 2017, p. 230).

- "What is the point of 'non-philosophy'? ... non-philosophy has no effect *within* the empirical, and none *within* philosophy and only transforms our relation to philosophy and to regional knowings ... " (Laruelle, 2017, p. 289).

Perhaps the main attraction to non-philosophy is that it enables one to continue to write and to talk about philosophy without being bound by its standards of logic and rationality. Laruelle frequently claims that non-philosophy is rigorous, even more rigorous than philosophy, but inevitably this involves defining a special sense of rigor solely in non-philosophical terms.

Given that Laruelle grounds non-philosophy on an attribution of presuppositions to philosophy that appears to be completely unsupported, such as the Principle of Sufficient Philosophy, it is difficult not to see non-philosophy primarily as an instance of Nietzschean *ressentiment* (Nietzsche, 1994, p. 21). Too weak to practice philosophy effectively, the non-philosopher brands philosophical strength as evil, then proceeds to valorize that weakness as good. Substituting punctuation for clarity, blunt assertion for arguments, allusion for engagement, the non-philosopher constructs a practice that protects all of these weaknesses from criticism, by redefining the terms on which their evaluation depends, like 'definition', 'rule', and 'rigor'.

While Laruelle is quick to accuse philosophy of certain presuppositions, it is not clear whether he devoted any thought to the presuppositions of non-philosophy itself. His reflections on a Husserlian paradigm appear restricted to the consideration of Husserl's phrase "philosophy as a rigorous science" (Laruelle, 2017, pp. 59–63) rather than Husserl's concern for presuppositions, as though mere invocation of "transcendence" or "immanence" alleviates any concern with presuppositions. Yet there are so many gaps between his assertions that only a large number of presuppositions can connect them, and no amount of non-philosophical redefinition can brush them away. Given such presuppositions, one might seek a non-non-philosophy that could transcend them, and the resolution of the double negative in this case could simply demand a return to philosophy, but to a better philosophy, on philosophy's own terms.

Let the quitters quit who cannot see a way forward for philosophy. This book is not for them.

Chapter 1

Introduction

This is a study of philosophical methodology. It is a normative study, namely an investigation of what methodology should be used in the practice of philosophy. Immediately, though, a problem emerges: What methodology should be employed in this philosophical investigation of methodology?

Suppose that I select a methodology at random and proceed to investigate the question of philosophical method according to that method. If the result of the investigation is an affirmation of the same methodology according to which I conducted the investigation, then it would appear that the investigation was merely reiterating the methodology that guided it, particularly if every methodology behaved in this manner.

The situation would scarcely be better if every methodology yielded a different methodology than itself, unless every methodology yielded the same methodology, including that same methodology. Yet philosophy has had a long history in which many methodologies have been proposed and critiqued, so if such a methodological convergence were possible, it seems that it already should have occurred. At present there is a wide range of methods or techniques available to philosophers to deploy at their convenience. This methodological plurality does not appear to trouble philosophers much, but rather is often seen as a manifestation of the richness of philosophical resources at the disposal of modern philosophers.[1]

---

[1] Presented explicitly as such in (Baggini & Fosl, 2020), for example. See Chapter 19 of (Ressler, 2024) for reflections on philosophies as technologies.

If this methodological plurality did trouble philosophers, there are a number of standard responses that might be adopted:

Pragmatism One might see this plurality not as a liability, but as a strength. If the point of philosophy is to solve problems, then having multiple methodologies at one's disposal can only provide benefit, so long as one or more of those methods can actually provide a solution to some problem and every problem can be solved by some method. It does not matter practically that there is no single methodology that can solve all problems.

Communitarianism One might see philosophy primarily in terms of a practice of a community of philosophers, each of which has its own methods. So long as one practices the methodology appropriate to the community in which one belongs, it does not matter that other communities practice according to different methodologies.

Relativism One might simply accept the relativism of philosophical theories to the methodologies that generated them as a fundamental feature of philosophy or of theories in general, beyond any association of methods to communities of philosophers or inquirers.

Skepticism One might go further and see the relativism of philosophical methodologies as an indication that philosophical inquiry cannot strictly occur, if any alleged inquiry merely reiterates what is already inherent in the methods that one adopts in advance. What appears to be inquiry is only the manifestation of philosophical prejudices.

Yet even in these responses, one can see the influence of certain methodological presuppositions. While the responses are certainly consistent with those presuppositions, this consistency merely reinforces the problem.

Meno poses a skeptical challenge to the possibility of inquiry to Socrates:

> But how will you look for something when you don't in the least know what it is? How on earth are you going

to set up something you don't know as the object of your search? To put it another way, even if you come right up against it, how will you know that what you have found is the thing you didn't know? (Plato, 1961, p. 363, 80d)

Meno's challenge concerns the objects of inquiry, and more recently many philosophers have acknowledged that some objects are theory-dependent. When the object of inquiry is the methodology according to which those theories are developed, Meno's problem appears compounded.[2]

Kant claims that there cannot be a general criterion of truth (Kant, 1965, pp. 97–98). In questioning the methodology according to which one investigates philosophical methodology it seems that I am looking for a criterion for a criterion, again compounding the problem.

There are some responses that may alleviate the severity of this problem, but I prefer to retain the problem in its hardest form, since the greatest progress in philosophy often comes from facing such hard problems directly. In fact, the history of philosophical progress can be seen precisely as the history of methodological innovation. Yet the notion of progress in philosophy itself has been challenged. Consequently, the question of philosophical progress requires investigation as well.

This study will develop this line of thought in greater detail. What will be proposed is not a new philosophical methodology to replace all the others, but rather a meta-methodology to coordinate among them. According to this proposal, the presuppositions of methodologies and their resulting philosophical positions will be used to triangulate new positions, thus transforming the problem surrounding philosophical presuppositions into a methodological asset. This is a fundamentally perspectival approach, respecting prior perspectives for the insights they provide, while recognizing their limitations as perspectives. The argument

---

[2]See (Umphrey, 1990). This study forms a response to Umphrey's concerns with zetetic skepticism, in effect transforming skepticism about inquiry into a form of inquiry that embodies skepticism, though grounded in a more productive conception of skepticism. See Chapter 11 for more reflections on skepticism. See also (Bacon, 1902, p. 19, Aphorism XXXVII) for a similar reaction to skepticism.

of this study is that the valorization of such perspectives as such need not devolve into pointless relativism or debilitating skepticism, but represents a distinct philosophical strength.

Consequently, this study will not present a survey of historical or contemporary philosophical methodologies. Such surveys are available elsewhere.[3] Rather, this study will follow a particular line of inquiry in search of a constructive response to the apparent problem of the relativity of philosophical methods and their results to presuppositions. Some contemporary questions concerning methodology will be considered in the course of this inquiry, though not all of them, and the focus will remain on the problem identified here.

Nor will this study engage critically with much recent work on philosophical methodology. The reason is simply that I take a significantly different perspective toward methodology in this study than others, such that there is little to be said directly in response to other thinkers on the topic without abandoning my perspective and adopting theirs. For example, Timothy Williamson claims that "we cannot prove, from a starting point a sufficiently radical skeptic would accept, that those ways of thinking are truth-conducive.... That is the skeptic's problem, not ours" (Williamson, 2007, p. 3). By contrast, this study embraces the skeptic's problem, and seeks to show that this perspective can be highly productive.

Consistent with the proposal that results from this study, the perspective adopted in this study can eventually subsume other methodological perspectives, but the perspective adopted here is not best appreciated by paying close attention to the most current reflections on methodology. Rather, a more broadly historical approach will better reveal the motives for adopting the perspective of this study, as well as the opportunities that it pursues.

If Grice is correct that "By and large the greatest philosophers have been the greatest, and the most self-conscious, methodologists; indeed, I am tempted to regard this fact as primarily accounting for their greatness as philosophers" (Grice, 1986, p. 66), then indeed this study aims for such greatness. The measure of its success will not be gauged merely by its ambitions, of course, but by the subsequent progress in philosophy that it enables. Yet

---

[3] See (Cappelen, Gendler, & Hawthorne, 2016), (D'Oro & Overgaard, 2017), and (Horvath, Koch, & Titelbaum, 2025).

philosophical progress was previously acknowledged to be a problematic notion, so it will be appropriate to start a methodological inquiry there.

Chapter 2

Progress

Very likely most contemporary philosophers have heard the same complaint from scientists or scholars working in other fields: Philosophy never seems to make any progress. Nothing in philosophy ever seems to be settled definitively. The same philosophical issues that troubled the ancients still trouble contemporary philosophers. The same arguments are rehashed again and again. Many centuries of wrangling over these issues have produced a large bulk of writing that appears to be growing exponentially; yet philosophy seems to have very few concrete results to show for all of this wasted ink.

Nothing in philosophy ever appears to die off. It seems that there is no philosophical position however bizarre or even incoherent that does not eventually gain new adherents as those positions are revised and modified to overcome past criticism, only to generate new criticisms. Thus old ideas come back from time to time in the form of *neo-doctrine*, such as neo-Platonism or neo-Meinongianism, for example. Yet it is not clear whether much significant progress has really been made over the old ideas in their new incarnations.

So philosophers continue to pore over ancient texts, arguing endlessly over competing interpretations over what those dead philosophers really thought. Some attempt to revive those dead thoughts by trying to patch what was broken in them, often producing thereby nothing but a ragged patchwork. Perhaps some very few among them actually produce genuine innovations, truly new ways of thinking about old issues, but soon enough these innovations inevitably fall into trouble, either by lapsing into the same problems that plagued the older ways of thinking or by generating new sets of problems. Ultimately, philosophy seems just to generate one failed system of thought after another.[1]

It is not my intention to argue against this criticism of philosophy by identifying some particular set of ideas that have been developed over the history of philosophy and arguing that they have definitively settled some philosophical problem or other. Perhaps there are some such ideas that constitute genuine progress in philosophy. However, I am willing to accept provisionally the idea that philosophy *seems* merely to represent an accumulation of ideas and positions, none of which are ever definitively refuted. What I would challenge is the criticism that this situation fails to represent progress. I suggest that progress in philosophy consists precisely in this proliferation of diverse views and theories, at least in part. Moreover, further progress in philosophy would consist in the generation of even more views and theories.[2]

Yet I would not suggest thereby that philosophy is nothing more than a kaleidoscope of ideas, designed merely to entertain idle thinkers or to confuse inquiring students. I do think that something is missing in the practice of philosophy. However, what is missing is not something that would necessarily settle any particular philosophical issue definitively, as some scientists claim that science has settled many of its scientific issues. I think that the nature of philosophy is notably different from the nature of science in a way that allows that most if not all of the issues in philosophy should remain open. Still, this perpetual openness in philosophy does not preclude progress. Rather, progress would need to be understood differently from the notion of settling some issue or another definitively.

It is, I think, a question of methodology. Science has apparently settled down into a fairly stable general methodology, or at least a general consensus on how science is to be practiced.[3] How-

---

[1] See (Lawler, Dellsén, & Norton, 2025) for an overview of the question of philosophical progress and responses.

[2] See (Ortega y Gasset, 1984, pp. 27–28). Mironov also acknowledges this notion of progress, but challenges "Is this development necessarily progressive, however?" (Mironov, 2013, p. 10). The remainder of this book will explain how this can be progressive. I in turn challenge whether Mironov's conception of progression within organic unity is sufficient.

[3] Even if Thomas Kuhn is right that specific paradigms of science may change

ever, part of the apparent problem in philosophy is that along with the proliferation of ideas and views, philosophy also clearly accumulates a diversity of methodologies. Perhaps not all of those methodologies continue to be practiced by contemporary philosophers, but not all contemporary philosophers practice the same methodology. Yet I would argue that what is missing in philosophy is not a single methodology that all philosophers must practice. Rather, I claim that what is missing is a fully adequate meta-methodology to coordinate the wide array of ideas and methods that philosophy has been accumulating in the course of its history.

This study presents the method of perspectival reduction precisely as such a meta-methodology. It seeks to motivate this method though a consideration of philosophical methodology in general by asking what methodology is proper to philosophy, and it proceeds in this consideration through an examination of some of the contemporary methods in philosophical practice. This examination does not seek to critique any of these methods to demonstrate that some are worthy of wide adoption within philosophy while others should be abandoned. Rather, it seeks to identify the presuppositions of those methods. It is from the question of the relation of those presuppositions to philosophical theory that the method of perspectival reduction emerges.

There is a clear sense in which the general method of perspectival reduction can demonstrate progress in philosophy, though it does not claim to be able to settle any philosophical issue definitively. This progress depends critically upon the proliferation of other philosophical methodologies and theories, a proliferation which some have considered to represent a criticism of philosophy. Perspectival reduction functions as a meta-methodology on other philosophical methodologies by coordinating the results of the application of various methods according to the presuppositions of those methods and their resulting philosophical theories. With the addition of new methodologies into this meta-methodology, an increasingly better understanding of philosophical topics should emerge, precisely because those additional methodologies provide new perspectives on those topics and thereby enable an increas-

---

over time (Kuhn, 1996), the general consensus of scientists concerning the role of experimentation and quantification in science seems to persist throughout these changes as a general methodology, at least from the time of the emergence of science as an independent discipline.

ingly more complete account of those topics. This increase in coordinated perspectives is what constitutes progress with regard to the proposed meta-methodology for philosophy.

Of course, the development of the method of perspectival reduction proceeds on the provisional acceptance of the claim that nothing is ever settled definitively in philosophy. Many philosophers would likely challenge this acceptance. Even if no philosophical issue has yet been settled definitely, and if for every issue there are several rival theories competing for acceptance, this does not mean that every theory that has ever been proposed for an issue is still a plausible candidate for acceptance. It might be claimed that, at the very least, philosophy has made progress by demonstrating that some theories cannot possibly be adequate to a particular issue, and that those theories are inadequate precisely because they are incoherent. So the presence of incoherence arguments in philosophy would appear to constitute one kind of progress that could be demonstrated on philosophy's behalf.

Yet I would challenge this claim. Not only do I not think that the identification of incoherence arguments constitutes definitive progress within philosophy, but I think that those arguments may stand in the way of philosophical progress. Incoherence arguments tend to close off certain ways of thinking, namely those ways that are claimed to be incoherent or that lead to incoherence. However, I would argue that the effort to find coherence within apparently incoherent positions has an instrumental value in expanding the intellectual resources of philosophy. The following chapter develops this challenge.

Chapter 3

Incoherence

I have become increasingly suspicious of incoherence arguments — those arguments which purport to demonstrate that a particular philosophical position or theory should be rejected because it is ultimately incoherent in some way. I am not convinced that any incoherence argument demonstrates that an apparently incoherent position should be rejected. I suspect that such arguments merely pose challenges to be solved with regard to the position. It is the nature of those challenges that lead me to suspect that there is a peculiar instrumental value in such apparently incoherent positions. In short, I propose not only that apparently incoherent positions should not be rejected on the grounds of their putative incoherence, but that such positions should become the focus of increased research, since they represent unique opportunities for philosophy to expand.[1]

The target of the charge of incoherence in these arguments is certain philosophical positions or theories, rather than speech, behavior or beliefs, which are also sometimes considered to be incoherent. If incoherence is supposed to be a fatal flaw in a theory, then coherence must be a general virtue of theories, and it is important to consider why it should be a virtue. The root meaning of the word 'coherence' expresses a quality of sticking together. Why should this stickiness be a virtue? I think the virtue lies in the sense of unity that coherence implies, as suggested by G. F. Stout

---

[1] "Whereas contradictions are a source of discomfiture to the systematizer, the experimental thinker often perceives in them points of departure from which the fundamentally discordant character of our present situation becomes for the first time really capable of diagnosis and investigation" (Mannheim, 1960, p. 48).

in an early response to the coherence theory of truth: "Coherence as a test of truth rests (1) on the Law of Contradiction, and (2) on the Unity of the Universe" (Stout, 1908, pp. 30–31). Since the universe as a unified whole appears to hold together, so should any adequate theory purporting to describe or to explain that universe or any part thereof, and according to Stout, one way that theories stick together is by avoiding contradictions. So coherence as a virtue represents the unity both in the subject matter to be explained and in the theory that explains it. Moreover, it would seem that a theory that does not stick together and therefore flies apart is ultimately not a theory at all.

Of course, British Idealists such as Harold Joachim to whom Stout was responding make it clear that mere logical consistency or validity was not sufficient for the kind of coherence that they considered vital to the nature of truth, particularly if coherence is "confused with the 'consistency' of formal logic" (Joachim, 1906, pp. 76). As F. H. Bradley argues, truth requires both coherence and comprehensiveness (Bradley, 1914, pp. 202–203, 214). However, the notion of coherence that figures into incoherence arguments need not be strong enough to establish truth according to some formulation of a coherence theory of truth. It appears to be some weaker notion of coherence that incoherent positions lack, such that incoherence arguments seek to establish not only that those positions are false, but also that they are not even candidates for truth since the positions cannot hold themselves together.

I think there are two conceptions of coherence upon which incoherence arguments typically rely: (1) argumentative consistency, and (2) systematicity. My claim for these two rests on the basis of an examination of various conceptions of coherence that figure in philosophical arguments, and a determination of which of these conceptions yield sufficiently feasible conceptions of incoherence by their negations that could support a rejection of an apparently incoherent position by means of an incoherence argument. Some conceptions of incoherence merely indicate that the argument for a position is inadequate or incomplete, for example, not that the position cannot hold itself together. I omit this preparatory study of specific incoherence arguments here in the interest of avoiding tedium.

Consider first the conception of incoherence as a failure of argumentative consistency. This conception is linked strongly to the notion of self-refutation. If a coherent position is one that supports a consistent argument on its behalf, a incoherent position could be one that refutes itself. Indeed the charge of self-refutation often features strongly in incoherence arguments. Although the notion of self-refutation seems to represent an insuperable obstacle to the establishment of a viable philosophical position, I nevertheless have doubts concerning whether such self-refutation arguments ultimately succeed.[2]

John Passmore identifies three kinds of self-refutation: absolute, pragmatic, and *ad hominem*. Ignoring the last kind, which is directed against individual people, rather than positions or accounts, there are two ways to show that a position refutes itself: "Formally, the proposition *p* is absolutely self-refuting, if to assert *p* is equivalent to asserting *both p and not-p*" (Passmore, 1961, p. 60). Pragmatic self-refutation occurs when "...somebody has put forward a thesis while at the same time apparently engaging in a procedure which, according to his thesis, is impossible, e.g. he appears to speak the words 'I cannot speak'" (Passmore, 1961, p. 80). Additionally, John Mackie has provided a formal analysis of these kinds of self-refutation, showing how the refutation can be logically demonstrated and identifying the formal conditions under which each kind of self-refutation applies (Mackie, 1964). Given these analyses and others that have followed, it might appear that there are no grounds for doubting the success of incoherence arguments based upon self-refutation, once that self-refutation is adequately demonstrated.

Passmore's account of absolute self-refutation, like Stout's conception of coherence, rests upon the principle of non-contradiction. The appearance of internal contradictions within a philosophical position may indeed be an unwelcome discovery. However, it seems that at least some philosophical positions accused of being incoherent explicitly countenance the kind of contradictions that characterize absolute self-refutation according to Passmore, most notably the doctrine of dialethism, according to which there are true contradictions.[3] Contradictions in these cases are not awkward, unwelcome consequences of a poorly considered

---

[2] My suspicions about incoherence arguments developed from an examination of the charges of self-refutation and incoherence against relativism (Ressler, 2013).

[3] See (Priest, 2006).

position. Rather, the contradictions are precisely part of what is being claimed in the position. To hold contradictions to be fatal to these sorts of philosophical positions would appear to beg the question against them.

With regard to Mackie's formal analysis, comparable considerations apply. Mackie's formal analysis relies upon classical formal logic. So if the results of this analysis were applied to philosophical positions that explicitly reject classical logic, positions that might advocate intuitionist or relevance logics, for example, the claim of self-refutation would thus seem to beg the question, since the claim of self-refutation is based upon logic that the position explicitly rejects. Interpretive charity requires imputing to a position interpretations according to which most of its statements come out true, including interpretations of the logic according to which the position operates. Even if a position does not explicitly reject classical logic, it might be shown later that the position would appear more viable under an alternative, non-classical logic. Furthermore, even if an existing non-classical logic is not available according to which a philosophical position might seem sensible, it may be the case that a new logic might later be devised to make sense of the position.

These considerations point to a reason for suspicion of incoherence arguments. If an incoherence argument proceeds on the basis of classical logical analysis, for example, but there is an existing non-classical logic that makes sense of the position that is the target of such an argument, then I claim that the fault lies with the failure of the incoherence argument to apply existing resources to the problem, not with the apparently incoherent position. Yet suppose that no existing system of logic is available to make sense of an apparently incoherent position. In this case the incoherence argument would appear to be justified. However, suppose now that a new system of logic were developed later according to which the apparently incoherent position would not be incoherent at all. I suggest that in this case, the problem lies with the lack of imaginative resources deployed in the incoherence argument, the lack of imagination to devise an adequate system of logic that could make sense of the position, not with the apparently incoherent position itself. So there seem to be grounds for a suspicion that incoherence arguments represent a failure to imagine ways in which the apparently incoherent position can be coherent. There may be reasons to reject the position on the grounds of the inapplicability of the logic that supports it, but those reasons would no longer constitute an incoherence argument under this conception of incoherence.

It would be premature to claim at this point that these suspicions apply to all incoherence arguments, that they all represent a failure of imagination, since the previous considerations apply primarily to what Passmore calls absolute self-refutation and to a formal analysis of pragmatic self-refutation. There are other approaches to pragmatic self-refutation that do not rely specifically upon purely logical considerations that must still be considered. I think two general strategies for demonstrating pragmatic self-refutation can be identified: (1) showing that the position undermines its own foundations, and (2) showing that the position fails to meet its own standards.

As an example of a position undermining its own foundations, consider a *reductio ad absurdum* argument against relativism offered by Harvey Siegel, who notes that radical relativism claims that there is no neutral framework for theory evaluation. Yet if relativism is correct, then there must be some justification for the position and therefore some neutral framework according to which it can be judged to be correct. So if relativism is correct, the means by which it can be established as being correct effectively undermine the foundations of relativism itself, and therefore "relativism of the sort we have been considering collapses into incoherence" (Siegel, 1984, p. 367).

One problem with this argument as given and with arguments of this sort in general, it appears to me, is establishing precisely what is to count as foundational in any given philosophical position. I have already appealed earlier to interpretive charity in attributing a logical system to a position. The application of interpretive charity in this case would demand that if a position seems incoherent on the attribution of a certain foundational claim, then perhaps that foundational claim should not be attributed to the position. If relativism appears incoherent on the assumption that there is no neutral framework for theory evaluation, then interpretive charity would suggest that relativism may not require this assumption. Perhaps some proponent of relativism may have explicitly made such an assumption, but the incoherence argument would then merely address this careless assumption on the part of one proponent of relativism, not the tenability of relativism itself. The problem then becomes how to understand a form of relativism, even radical relativism, in which there might indeed be a neutral framework of theory evaluation. The incoherence argument does not examine this possibility, but merely accepts the problematic assumption of no neutral framework as given.

Another problem lies in working out the consequences of the position in question, assuming that the identification of foundational assumptions is correct. If relativism does require there to be no neutral framework for theory evaluation, then does the assertion of the correctness of relativism really require such a neutral framework? It would appear so if correctness is understood in an absolute sense, namely that correctness cannot be relativized, but an adherent of radical relativism would clearly not accept a conception of correctness in this absolute sense. Interpretive charity would thus appear to require the rejection of the understanding of correctness as absolute correctness. The problem then becomes how to understand how a position can be only relatively correct in some meaningful way as asserted by some proponent. Again, the incoherence argument stated above does not examine this possibility, but merely accepts the problematic understanding of correctness.

Both problems point to a common pattern according to which incoherence arguments of this form rely on certain assumptions that are not further explored, where the position in question might be understood to be coherent upon further exploration of alternative assumptions. However, there are indeed stronger self-refutation arguments than the one cited from Siegel that attempt to close this gap by posing destructive dilemmas for a philosophical position. According to this pattern of argument, the position under evaluation must accept one alternative or another, but either alternative leads to incoherence. Therefore, the position is incoherent. Indeed, Siegel himself has already presented such a stronger destructive dilemma against relativism in an earlier argument than the one previously cited, based on whether relativism is defended nonrelativistically or relativistically: "In short, to defend relativism is to defend it nonrelativistically, which is to give it up; to 'defend' it relativistically is not to defend it at all" (Siegel, 1986, p. 231).

Yet here too I think the same kinds of problems resurface. Perhaps there are ways of understanding the position such that still more alternatives are viable, ways that the argument does not consider in the dilemma it presents. Perhaps the assumption that the alternatives are exhaustive is mistaken, and that there is some other alternative according to which the position is coherent. Even if the dilemma is framed in terms of a direct contradiction, such as that either relativism requires neutral frameworks or it does not, further distinctions may show that there is an alternative that may require neutral frameworks in some sense and not in another, or that may permit relativistic defense of relativism in one sense and not in another. The incoherence argument only works when such alternatives are no longer explored, and the deployment of an incoherence argument seems to indicate the limits of imagination in failing to identify such alternatives, not necessarily the absolute failure of the apparently incoherent position. So again, an incoherence argument appears to pose a challenge, but it is not clear that such arguments always demonstrate that the challenge cannot be met, merely that they have not in fact been met by whomever deploys the incoherence argument.

The other strategy for demonstrating pragmatic self-refutation is to show that a position fails to meet its own standards. This pattern might be seen as a species of the previous strategy of undermining the foundations of a position, where the foundations in question are not necessarily substantive assumptions, but epistemic standards that the position applies. Perhaps the most notorious instance of this strategy is the argument against logical positivism, which relies upon the principle of verifiability to determine the meaningfulness of statements. It was eventually noted that the positivist statement asserting the principle of verifiability was not verifiable according to any formulation presented by logical positivism and therefore was meaningless according to its own standards.

More importantly for a discussion of incoherence, consider an example from J. M. Fritzman in an article entitled "Against Coherence" in which he argues that the coherence theory of justification is incoherent. Briefly, he states his argument as follows: "Coherentism claims that it is impossible to criticize, evaluate, or justify beliefs from a perspective external to the belief set. Not only is it possible to adopt an external point of view, but it is also necessary. Since coherentism denies this, it is incoherent" (Fritzman, 1992, p. 186). One reason that Fritzman gives for the necessity of an external point of view is that the evaluation of beliefs occurs at a metalinguistic level, which is by definition outside of the level of the linguistic system that it discusses (Fritzman, 1992, p. 187).

This strategy for demonstrating incoherence may seem more secure than the strategy of showing that a position undermines its own foundational assumptions, at least insofar as a position may explicitly outline the standards that it applies. Of course, if those standards are merely extrapolated by the incoherence argument as being putatively inherent in the position criticized, then there is a question whether that position truly entails those standards used against it in the argument. Again, interpretive charity would suggest that if the extrapolated standards lead to incoherence, then perhaps those standards should not properly be attributed to the position. Yet even if a position explicitly states the standards that it demands and that are not met by the position itself, it is not clear whether the position has merely been formulated carelessly, or whether the position is simply untenable under any formulation. What emerges from the incoherence argument is a challenge to reformulate the apparently incoherent position. The apparent failure of a position to meet its own standards may pose a more difficult challenge than that posed by the apparent undermining of a position's own foundations. For example, Fritzman's argument poses the challenge of formulating a coherence theory of justification that spans metalinguistic levels. Yet it is not clear to me that the incoherence argument in question demonstrates that the problem cannot be solved. Rather, the argument appears to take the very existence of the problem itself to be conclusive against the target position.

For these reasons, incoherence arguments by self-refutation seem suspicious to me, since the positions they target appear to pose challenging philosophical problems to be solved, but the incoherence arguments merely take those problems to be fatal to the position, rather than exploring ways to meet the challenges those problems pose. In this context, consider the argument of Michael Stack against certain self-refutation arguments, in particular, arguments that claim that a position is false because arguments are offered for it on the basis of something that the position itself rejects. One example that he gives is the case of the skeptic who denies rational belief. As the self-refutation argument typically proceeds, if the skeptic fails to argue for his position, then he can safely be ignored, but if he argues for his position, he relies on the possibility of rational justification for beliefs and therefore refutes himself (Stack, 1983, p. 328). Stack notes that most self-refutation arguments of this sort are deployed to preserve traditional doctrines, such as the intuition that there is knowledge and justification. His claim is that tradition-preserving arguments on the basis of self-refutation misconstrue positions that challenge traditional doctrines by failing to recognize that the arguments that appear to refute themselves in this way are in fact *reductio ad absurdum* arguments against the traditional positions. If the skeptic argues for his position, it is because he aims to convince someone who does accept rational argument as valid, and if rational argument can be used effectively to challenge rational argument, then the problem would appear to lie with rational argument, not with skepticism. Once the problems with rational argument are noted by means of the argument, the skeptic can discard the argument for skepticism and its presumption of the validity of rational argumentation, as in Sextus Empiricus' metaphor of the ladder that is discarded once it is used to ascend (Sextus Empiricus, 2005, p. 183).[4]

Stack's suspicions concerning self-refutation arguments align very well with mine against incoherence arguments. Tradition tends both to constrain imagination as well as to enable it. Imagination requires a pre-existing stock of images, concepts, and ideas as a source on which to operate. The various techniques of imagination operate by playing with, modifying, and even flatly denying existing ideas, as described by Nelson Goodman as ways of worldmaking (Goodman, 1978, pp. 7–17), for example, rather than producing new ideas from out of the void. Yet that very tradition can also constrain imagination when those ideas become so entrenched that some people refuse even to suppose that the ideas could possibly be denied coherently. It seems to me that a blunt refusal to play with certain ideas lies at the heart of incoherence arguments in general.

I think the question of philosophical imagination likewise underlies suspicions concerning the second conception of incoherence, namely lack of systematicity. The notion of coherence involved in this case appears to derive from Hegel through the British

---

[4]Note that I intentionally do not credit this metaphor to Wittgenstein, who merely used it without providing proper citations (Wittgenstein, 1922, p. 189).

Idealists, for whom the notion of a system was vitally important. If a position is so disorganized or is dependent on such a fragile foundation that no system can even be assembled, then it would indeed appear to be an incoherent position. The problem is not that the system in question falls apart, but that it cannot even come together in the first place, which would certainly be a serious criticism of a position.

An example of this kind of incoherence argument can be found notably in Richard Fumerton's article "The Incoherence of Coherence Theories". Fumerton points out two alleged conceptual regresses faced by the coherence theory of truth. The first concerns the relata of coherence, namely what must cohere with what. According to Fumerton, what makes a proposition true according to coherentism is that it coheres with a set of propositions that is believed. Yet what makes it true that this set of propositions is believed? Presumably that it coheres with some other set of propositions that is believed, and so forth, thereby falling into a regress (Fumerton, 1994, p. 94). The second regress concerns the facts about the coherence relations themselves that hold between propositions. What makes the propositions about the coherence relations true? Presumably it will be their coherence with other propositions. Yet there are propositions about this new coherence relation that will likewise be true on the basis of other coherence relations, and so forth (Fumerton, 1994, p. 96). These conceptual regresses indicate that a coherence theory of truth cannot even get off the ground, that it cannot properly be systematized in order to provide an explanatory account of truth.

Incoherence of this sort is properly directed against any possible systematization of a position, not merely a particular actual systematization. If one proposed systematization fails, that failure by itself does not show that all systematizations must fail. Yet here again I think the same basic considerations about failure of imagination apply as those noted with regard to self-refutation. The charge of incoherence by failure of systematicity can be refuted most effectively by producing a system. For example, with regard to another kind of argument, the core of the argument for intelligent design is that certain living species are irreducibly complex, meaning that they are too complex for the process of natural selection to explain them. In my terms, the claim is that certain species cannot be explained by any system of natural forces that does not include intentionality of design. The response from evolutionary biologists is that they already have such an explanatory system, but that proponents of intelligent design neither bother to learn the system in its entirety nor to understand the evidence for that system. So insofar as intelligent design seems to rely on an incoherence argument by lack of systematicity, the development of an explanatory system without intentionality of design on the part of evolutionary biologists would appear effectively to refute the incoherence argument.

With regard to incoherence arguments in philosophy, I think the most notable example of a challenge to a charge of failure of systematicity is Graham Priest's dialethic logic (Priest, 2006). Because the principle of non-contradiction is so firmly embedded in human thought, it has been considered incoherent to deny the principle, particularly in such a way as to suggest that there might be true contradictions. This incoherence would seem to be grounded in a failure of systematicity, according to which it might be thought that no system that allowed that there might be true contradictions could even get off the ground, let alone hold together, since contradictions are precisely the sort of thing that tear systems apart, as suggested by Stout's comment cited earlier. Priest's response is to produce such a system and to show how it can hold together. Regardless of what one might think of Priest's arguments for his claims that specific contradictions hold true in the world, the formulation of his dialethic system shows that the idea is not incoherent, where incoherence is understood as failure of systematicity, and where the charge of incoherence appears ultimately to be grounded in an inability to imagine or to understand a dialethic system.

With regard to Fumerton's argument, then, there seems to be inherent in his argument a challenge to provide a system for the coherence theory of truth, one that can be formulated in such a way as to avoid the kinds of regresses that he points out. Though Fumerton claims that the first kind of regress is effective against any formulation of the coherence theory of truth (Fumerton, 1994, pp. 95–96), I am not convinced. It may be effective against coherence theories of truth that make the same assumptions that Fumerton makes in his analysis, particularly the assumption that a coherence theory must talk about the relata of coherence (Fumerton, 1994, p. 96), but I am not certain that there can be no formulation of a coherence theory of truth on different assumptions that still counts as a coherence theory of truth.

What Fumerton's argument appears to rely on is a foundationalist pattern of reasoning, though not necessarily an explicit foundationalist theory of truth. The pattern is that the coherence of any single proposition is established on the basis of something else that is already established. With this assumed pattern of argument, Fumerton's conceptual regresses may seem compelling. However, I claim that the problem with this assumption is that a coherence theory of truth should properly reject this foundationalist pattern of reasoning in favor of a more consonant holistic pattern. The truth or coherence of any single proposition is not separately established on the basis of something already established, but rather, every true proposition is established as coherent together and at once. The systematicity of coherentism would be established by the existence of a set of propositions that is a coherent set, according to some operative conception of coherence. So the coherence theory need never eventually address coherence in terms of relata, in terms of a relational property held between individual propositions and something else, as Fumerton claims, but rather, coherence should be understood as a property of an entire set of propositions.[5] There may be an epistemic problem in how to identify such a set, a problem that Nicholas Rescher attempts to address (Rescher, 1973), but it is not clear that there is a metaphysical problem with coherentism in the way that Fumerton claims. The two conceptual regresses he poses are problems only for formulations of a coherence theory of truth that are formulated explicitly using a foundationalist approach, whereas I have suggested that coherence theories should more properly adopt a holistic approach.

I doubt that many will be fully persuaded by my discussion thus far, and may not be persuaded by what I will claim next. Firstly, my arguments have a distinctly *ad hominem* flavor, by suggesting that the plausibility of incoherence arguments is grounded in the failure of imagination of the individual philosophers who offer them. I have attempted to be careful to phrase my argument in terms of suspicions and grounds for suspicion, rather than claiming to have demonstrated that incoherence arguments are always faulty or even incoherent and that the fault lies with those who of-

---

[5] As Harold Joachim claims in (Joachim, 1906, pp. 72–73).

fer them. Yet it might be thought that these kinds of suspicions do not even represent a proper subject for philosophical discussion.

Secondly, and perhaps more importantly, none of my criticisms here seem to extend any farther than effectively pointing out the fallibility of incoherence arguments. Yes, anyone offering a given incoherence argument or any other kind of argument may fail to imagine alternatives that might undermine the argument. The history of philosophy and science is filled with such cases, and it appears unreasonable to demand of any philosopher to see beyond the horizon, so to speak. All that we philosophers can do is simply to offer arguments as honestly as possible according to our best available conceptual resources. Our philosophical descendants will be in a better position to evaluate our arguments, given their expanded resources.

And with this I agree. In fact, my own arguments here may be fallible on precisely the same grounds that I use to criticize incoherence arguments, as doubtless some readers have been burning to point out. Perhaps I have not been able to imagine a conception of coherence and incoherence beyond those that I have discussed earlier that would make incoherence arguments decisive. Perhaps I have not been able to imagine how self-refutation and failure of systematicity can be deployed to defeat any possible reformulation of an apparently incoherent position. In short, this discussion is just as fallible as any of the incoherence arguments to which I direct my suspicion and therefore should seem equally suspect.

Of course, pointing out that all arguments are fallible does not tend to increase confidence in any of them, whether in incoherence arguments or my suspicions against them. What I would point out here, though, is a distinct difference in attitude between those who are satisfied with incoherence arguments and those who may be suspicious of them. If I am satisfied with an incoherence argument, I will not continue to explore the incoherent position to seek alternatives to make the position work. After all, if the position is indeed incoherent, then such exploration would be senseless. If I do continue with the exploration, then this would suggest that I am not satisfied with the incoherence argument after all. By contrast, if I am suspicious of the incoherence argument, I would tend to understand the apparent incoherence as simply posing a problem to be solved, a problem requiring more philosophical imagination than had been applied in the incoherence argument itself. The charge of incoherence leveled by some incoherence argument would thus represent an incentive to investigate the issue beyond the bounds set by the incoherence argument. Thus it seems that satisfaction with incoherence arguments tends to stifle further research, whereas suspicion with such arguments tends to foster it.

Yet an incoherence argument might be understood rather to indicate that the target of the argument is a conceptual dead end such that further investigation might practically be a waste of time. Why spend valuable time trying to fix an apparently incoherent position when there are more promising positions available to be patched up? To the contrary, I suggest that apparently incoherent positions have a particular instrumental value over putatively more coherent positions, and this value lies precisely in requiring greater imagination applied to the solution of the philosophical problems they aim to address, greater imagination than what is required for more traditional, coherent, and comfortable positions.

I am hardly the first to make such a suggestion. Fritzman himself, after arguing for the incoherence of coherence, argues against coherence as a general virtue, framing his argument in a historical context: "Beliefs which now are incoherent may be made coherent by the introduction of a new idea, or perspective, which reconciles or synthesizes them" (Fritzman, 1992, p. 188). Furthermore, Fritzman cites Paul Feyerabend, who contends notoriously that knowledge does not converge toward some ideal final theory, but represents an expansion of incompatible competing theories (Feyerabend, 2010, pp. 15–16). Of course there is an uncomfortable tension in Fritzman's arguments, since if new ideas can make apparently incoherent beliefs coherent, then Fritzman's own incoherence argument may suffer the same fate, with the result that coherence is reaffirmed as a virtue. Comparable tensions have been noted with Feyerabend's position when applied to itself. So it is at the risk of falling into similar problems myself that I proceed to argue for the instrumental value of apparently incoherent positions. I think nevertheless that I can make a good case. I will frame this discussion against the background of a particular conception of the nature of philosophy in the next chapter, and a further consideration of this conception of philosophy will lead to the question of which methodology is proper to this or any other conception of philosophy.

Chapter 4

Philosophy

Philosophy progresses according to the conception of philosophy held by philosophers. Under a narrow conception, philosophy may indeed provide some detailed analysis within a correspondingly narrow scope, an exhaustive investigation of a single concept, for example. Yet if more is to be expected from philosophy, it would seem that the conception of philosophy must be broadened, and broadened across a wider range of philosophers.

Unfortunately, it seems that little or nothing is expected of philosophy today, at least by those outside the circle of professional philosophers.[1] Philosophy if understood at all is likely to be considered nothing more than a pleasant pastime, like solving a crossword puzzle on a Sunday afternoon.[2] More likely, though, philosophy tends to be misunderstood and confused with new-age pseudo-science or merely the proposal of bizarre ideas.

Even among professional philosophers, it seems impossible to reach a consensus concerning the nature of philosophy itself. Consider the following list of conceptions of philosophy that have been espoused by various philosophers over its history:

---

[1] See for example, ("Essay: What (If Anything) to Expect from Today's Philosophers", 1966). This essay was written before I was born. It appears that not much journalistic notice of philosophy has been taken outside of philosophical circles since then, besides ancillary developments such as philosophical counseling, so indeed it would seem that not much is being expected from today's philosophers at all.

[2] Unfortunately, it appears that some philosophers themselves have contributed to this perception. Ludwig Wittgenstein seems to be the primary culprit, at least in Anglo-American circles, given his conception of philosophy as aiming merely at solving puzzles, with others trailing in his wake.

- the servant of theology
- the queen of the sciences
- the handmaiden of sciences
- pre-scientific knowledge
- the discipline of disciplines
- the systematizer of knowledge
- the search for definitions
- the analysis of the structure of thought
- conceptual analysis
- *a priori* analysis
- the search for necessary truths
- the search for general truths
- the mediator between judgments of fact and value
- the critic of abstractions
- the study of possibility as such
- the study of unsolvable problems

These conceptions are not necessarily distinct, and some represent narrower conceptions of philosophy than others. Of particular interest are those conceptions of philosophy that concern the relation between philosophy and science. The success of modern science more than anything else seems to have affected the conception of philosophy, constricting that conception proportionately as the sciences have expanded, leaving such apparently worthless scraps that one wonders whether it is worth pursuing philosophy at all, at least from the perspective of the sciences.

By contrast, Aristotle held a very broad conception of philosophy as knowledge of truth (Aristotle, 1984, p. 1570, 993b20). Of course, philosophy as conceived by Aristotle includes what now falls under the scope of science. However, I suggest that a return to

Aristotle's broad scope of philosophy would be entirely appropriate, despite the great advances in science that appear to threaten the value of philosophy.

The success of science led to what Daniel Wilson calls "a crisis of confidence" (Wilson, 1987, p. 235) in philosophy during the late nineteenth and early twentieth centuries, at least in the United States. The issue was whether philosophy should become more like the sciences in its methodologies and in the specialization of its concerns. Yet if philosophy and the sciences were to share methodologies, then it would seem that only the subject matters of the two disciplines could properly distinguish them, which would raise the question of what the proper subject matter of philosophy is or should be. There is the traditional broad classification of philosophical subject matters into ethics, metaphysics and epistemology. However, if philosophy were to adopt the methods of the sciences, some of the traditional concerns that fall under these classifications would need to be abandoned, notably much of metaphysics, since these concerns are not adequately addressed by the scientific method. Yet other conceptions of the proper subject matter of philosophy have arisen to prominence over the last century, under the ascendancy of linguistic approaches to philosophy, such as the conception that philosophy is concerned with *a priori* or necessary statements, as noted in the list of conceptions given above.

I do not share these more recent conceptions of philosophy, and I think that it is misleading to seek the subject matter of philosophy primarily in contradistinction to the subject matter of the sciences, since philosophy predates modern science. Nor do I think that philosophy should be characterized according to any particular methodological trend, as with linguistically oriented philosophical methodologies, since those particular methodologies have not always characterized the practice of philosophy in the past, and will likely not in the future. I suggest a different conception of philosophy, one grounded in its history or even prehistory, a conception that was held by William James (James, 1911, pp. 3–28), among others.[3]

It has been a long time since anyone has called philosophy the queen of the sciences. The image of philosophy ruling over

---

[3] For example, see (Ortega y Gasset, 1960, pp. 76–80).

the sciences seems ludicrous now, and given the ascendancy of science in modern society, this demotion in rank and prestige for philosophy would appear to justify a crisis of confidence. Yet if not queen of the sciences, philosophy is surely the mother of the sciences, since the early history of philosophy included what is now recognized as the subject matter of the sciences, as seen most notably in the work of Aristotle. At one time, the sciences were known as natural philosophy before becoming functionally independent of philosophy. Psychology only became independent of philosophy in the late nineteenth century. This trend toward independence again raises the question of what should be the proper relation of philosophy to the sciences, if indeed philosophy has any role to play beyond understanding and articulating what science is doing.

I suggest understanding the break of the sciences from philosophy in terms of the model of specialization within the sciences. As sciences progress, the increasingly detailed problem sets that need to be solved make it impractical for individual scientists to work in the whole of science, or even the whole of a broad field of science such as physics. Therefore physics becomes specialized as thermodynamics, fluid dynamics, quantum mechanics, and so forth. This does not mean that physics itself is nothing more than an aggregate of specializations, though. The role of physics in general lies in unifying the results of the specialized branches of physics. Sometimes those results across specializations are unified quite easily, but other times they raise conflicts or anomalies, which pose further problem sets in the affected specializations. Insofar as an individual physicist working in a specialized field seeks to unify those specialized results with results in other specializations, that physicist practices general physics, in addition to any primary specializations.

Accordingly I suggest that the relation between philosophy and the sciences can be understood comparably in terms of specialization. What is the subject matter of philosophy? Since the sciences and other rational disciplines have historically branched off from philosophy, it would seem that the subject matter of the sciences is a subset of the subject matter of philosophy. I therefore claim that the subject matter of philosophy is *anything subject to rational inquiry*. When a field of philosophy gains sufficient unity in terms of its methods and range of concerns, it specializes as an independent branch of study, as a science or other discipline. What is the role of philosophy, then? I suggest that philosophy should study everything not specialized into a separate science or discipline, as well as unifying that study with the results from the specialized disciplines, and unifying the results from the specialized disciplines with each other.[4] Insofar as an individual scientist seeks to unify the results of a branch of science with disciplines other than science, that scientist engages the subject as a philosopher, not as a specialized scientist. After all, where this unifying function extends beyond the sciences, it thereby extends beyond the methods of the sciences and therefore cannot be considered strictly part of scientific practice.[5]

This conception of philosophy does not reinstate philosophy as the queen of the sciences, since science remains autonomous in its specialization. However, it identifies a function that philosophy serves in relation to the sciences and other disciplines in terms of unifying and reconciling these disciplines. Yet what is relevant here to the discussion of apparently incoherent positions from the previous chapter is not this unifying function of philosophy, but rather what remains out of the totality of what is subject to rational inquiry once the subject matters of the sciences and other disciplines have been subtracted. I suggest that this remnant falls to philosophy to study, since other disciplines delineate and restrict their subject matter and their methods away from this remnant as a result of specialization in order to focus on specific problems in specific ways. Philosophy in general is not subject to such restrictions. Of this remnant that falls to philosophy, some fields have been fairly clearly defined, such as the traditional philosophical concerns with ethics, metaphysics, and epistemology, and of course these fields themselves have become further specialized just as in-

---

[4]The conception of philosophy as the critic of abstractions is due to Alfred North Whitehead (Whitehead, 1925, p. 126), where the abstractions in questions are most importantly the abstractions of the various sciences. Accordingly, Whitehead's conception of philosophy captures part of the broad conception of philosophy outlined here, though not all of it.

[5]Comparable conceptions of philosophy are held by Edmund Husserl (Husserl, 1965, pp. 134–136) and Bryan Magee (Magee, 2009), who also cites Bertrand Russell as holding a similarly broad conception in (Russell, 1912). Additionally, Keith Lehrer endorses much the same conception of philosophy in relation to the sciences as I have presented (Lehrer, 1974, p. 7), as does (Sellars, 1991, pp. 7–8), and (Rosenberg, 2015, p. 2).

dividual sciences have become specialized.

Yet what I would ask here is whether these previously identified philosophic fields and the scientific and other disciplines together exhaust the totality of what is subject to rational inquiry? Can one merely enumerate all the known disciplines and sciences and philosophical fields and claim that all knowledge falls into one of these categories, or are there unexplored recesses of the remnants out of the totality of potential knowledge once these known disciplines are subtracted? If there are unexplored recesses, the sciences and other disciplines will not discover them, since by definition these recesses fall outside of their delineated subject matters and methodologies. Therefore, philosophy would seem to be the only discipline in which these recesses could be explored, at least rationally. Yet insofar as philosophy itself has delineated particular subject matters such as ethics and epistemology, focusing strictly on these pre-existing subject matters would appear likewise to fail to discover any new subject matter.[6]

Here is where I claim that apparently incoherent positions gain their instrumental value. Sensible solutions to traditional philosophical problems gain their sensibility by remaining within comfortable intellectual boundaries. Challenging solutions test those boundaries. Yet apparently incoherent solutions tend to break those boundaries completely. If there is any new intellectual discipline to be discovered, I propose that it will be discovered by focusing on these apparently incoherent positions and by attempting to make sense out of apparent nonsense. The rationale behind this proposal derives precisely from my suspicions concerning incoherence arguments, namely that they seem to represent a failure to imagine what would be required to make a putatively incoherent position appear perfectly coherent. The imaginative demands of philosophers researching apparently incoherent positions may need to extend far beyond the comfortable intellectual boundaries that characterize putatively more sensible positions, possibly thereby extending into intellectual regions not encompassed by any existing discipline. In order to explore such regions, new methodologies would need to be devised, methodologies different from those of any existing scientific or philosophical

---

[6]Alexis Meinong refers to "sciences which do not yet exist, but should exist" (Meinong, 1960, p. 100). In the same way I am contemplating branches of philosophy that do not yet exist, but should, if knowledge is to become complete.

discipline. By contrast, by holding to more sensible positions, a philosopher would likely remain within very comfortable intellectual boundaries, use methodologies that are already well known, and remain firmly within the bounds of existing disciplines.

An initial problem may be framed within an existing field of science or philosophy, but a solution to that problem may require the recognition of a new field altogether, with new ways of thinking and new methodologies. And here is where I think philosophy stands to gain value with regard to other disciplines. The philosophical function of unifying disparate branches of knowledge certainly has an important role to play in the overall scheme of knowledge, but more importantly, new philosophical ideas have the potential to revolutionize any number of other disciplines as well as the sciences. Such is the power of good ideas. Rather than aping the methods of the sciences and envying their success and prestige, I suggest that philosophy should recognize its unique position with regard to knowledge as a whole and should aim beyond its current bounds to explore the potential realm of knowledge more completely. My suggestion is that apparently incoherent positions represent a unique locus for study whereby the limits of knowledge can be tested and possibly expanded. Those positions themselves may not turn out to be feasible in the end, but my proposal is that exploring those positions beyond the current bounds of common sense has an instrumental value in enabling new philosophical ideas and discoveries.

I think it is worth citing one example of an apparently incoherent position that was later recognized not only as coherent, but as important. The example is well known and perhaps well worn, but I think it bears repeating in this context. It comes not from within philosophy, but from mathematics and geometry. The status of Euclid's parallel postulate as a postulate had bothered geometers for centuries. Part of what bothered them was that it seemed clearly incoherent that two lines should intersect if the interior angles formed by another line crossing these two were equal to two right angles. If that were so, then it seemed as though space would either explode hyperbolically or implode elliptically. Because of this apparent incoherence, some geometers thought that the parallel postulate could be proved as a theorem from the remaining postulates and axioms of Euclid's system. Yet in the early nineteenth century, János Bolyai and Nikolai Lobachevsky published treatises based on a denial of the parallel postulate and thereby opened up the field of non-Euclidean geometry. Here, as with my prior discussion of the conception of coherence as systematicity in the previous chapter, it appears that the clearest way to challenge the perception that denying the parallel postulate was incoherent is to produce a system denying it. The new field of non-Euclidean geometry became significant enough as a theoretical branch of geometry, but it became much more important with the application of a particular non-Euclidean geometry within relativity physics. What this new field of geometry required was someone with sufficient imagination to see how an apparently incoherent idea could work after all. If this can happen in mathematics, it seems likely that it can happen in philosophy as well.[7]

The conception of philosophy outlined here constitutes a very broad conception,[8] one in which there is certainly room for progress, specifically by the possibility of expanding philosophy beyond its known sub-disciplines. Yet even with a sufficiently broad conception of philosophy, and perhaps precisely because of the breadth of the conception, it is not clear how philosophy should proceed. I have suggested that focusing on apparently incoherent positions is one way to expand the intellectual resources that get applied to philosophical problems, but it is not clear precisely how this should be done. Using traditional philosophical methods would seem merely to demonstrate the incoherence of these positions, without gaining anything new. It appears, then, that new methods would need to be applied within philosophy, if any progress is to be expected.

It might be thought that whatever methods the sciences use should provide a model for a methodology within philosophy, given the development of a broad conception of philosophy on the basis of an analogy with the process of specialization within the

---

[7]What I would characterize as Laruelle's failures to establish non-Philosophy on analogy to non-Euclidean geometry, as described in the Preface, suggest that the endeavor entails considerable risk. Yet Larelle appears to go wrong at the start, precisely by virtue of his problematic conception of what philosophy is, whereas a broader conception of philosophy leads in a distinctly different direction, as the remainder of this book aims to demonstrate.

[8]Note that precisely by virtue of its breadth, this conception subsumes all other conceptions of philosophy, such as those listed at the beginning of this chapter. Anything investigated according to those other conception of philosophy will also be investigated by this broad conception, though not exclusively so.

sciences. However, the analogy seems to break down at this point, since science in general has methodological presuppositions that do not necessarily apply to all branches of knowledge.[9] Perhaps it would be better to say that the analogy indicates that the methodology of philosophy should subsume and reconcile the methodology of science with the methodologies of other disciplines, but that the methods of philosophy cannot be limited to the methods of the sciences.

To introduce the problem concerning the methodology of philosophy as I understand it, I propose the following rough characterizations of existing methods: first philosophy, last philosophy, and median philosophy. I do not intend these characterizations to represent a rigid system of categories into which the work of any given philosopher must neatly fit. They merely represent a rough way to understand the ways in which philosophy has been practiced as a means for introducing the approach to philosophical methodology that I take in this study.

The notion of *first philosophy* appears to originate with Aristotle's metaphysics as the study of first causes, the fundamental nature of being, substances, and theology.[10] Yet what interests me here is not the ontological conception of first philosophy as held by Aristotle, but the epistemological conception as typified by René Descartes. In the exposition of his rules, Descartes notes that "all things can be arranged serially in various groups, not in so far as they can be referred to some ontological genus (such as the categories in which philosophers divide things), but in so far as some things can be known on the basis of others" (Descartes, 1985c, p. 21). First philosophy therefore represents a search for the fundamental items of knowledge on the basis of which everything else can be known. Since Descartes recognizes only intuition and deduction as the two activities of the intellect according to which anything can be known (Descartes, 1985c, p. 14), and since deduction can proceed only on the basis of premises that are already known, if there is any knowledge at all, there must be some foundational piece of knowledge apprehended by intuition. The knowledge that he is a thinking being serves this foundational role

---

[9] See for example the classic discussion of the metaphysical presuppositions of science in (Burtt, 1925).

[10] For an extensive textual examination of the concept of first philosophy held by Aristotle, see (Reale, 1980).

for Descartes (Descartes, 1985a, p. 127), (Descartes, 1985b, p. 18), though this foundational grounding has been severely challenged.

The notion of first philosophy is no longer widely accepted as a viable approach to philosophy. Not only is it unclear how Descartes' particular fundamental piece of knowledge could be capable of generating every other piece of knowledge, but there does not seem to be any other piece or pieces of knowledge that could serve this fundamental role. Furthermore, doubts have arisen concerning the epistemology of intuition and deduction upon which Descartes claims for first philosophy rests. Perhaps the path to knowledge is not as linear as Descartes thought it was, but takes a broader, more holistic route.[11]

Given a fundamental piece of knowledge according to first philosophy, as well as a suitable form of deduction, every other piece of knowledge would follow, yielding a complete system. Yet some philosophers have sought to reach this end state of knowledge without starting from a first philosophy. Accordingly, what might be called *last philosophy* seeks to identify a final state of philosophy, even if the beginnings remain in question. This final state may represent some piece of theological revelation, but it may just as likely represent a particularly high level of philosophical abstraction. I think Hegel best typifies this kind of last philosophy, by demanding that the foundational categories of knowledge be examined before they are employed (Hegel, 1969, p. 41), and then arguing that absolute truth must be a result of this examination (Hegel, 1969, p. 70). The recognition of the absolute as an end state thereby brings with it the recognition of the proper starting point, which ultimately coincides with the end: "The essential requirement for the science of logic is not so much that the beginning be a pure immediacy, but rather that the whole of the science be within itself a circle in which the first is also the last and the last is also the first" (Hegel, 1969, p. 71). Wittgenstein's later work likewise seems to represent a form of last philosophy, given his claim that philosophy "leaves everything as it is" (Wittgenstein, 2001, p. 42e, sec. 124). "Since everything lies open to view there is nothing to explain" (Wittgenstein, 2001, p. 43e, sec. 126). Thus the end state of philosophy for Wittgenstein appears to be given by what is already before us.

---

[11] For instance, see the discussion in (Bosanquet, 1920).

Like first philosophy, last philosophy has fallen into disfavor among practicing philosophers. Perhaps it is because pronouncements of a final state of philosophy seem more like oracular revelations than solid philosophy. If there is an argument presented for a final state of philosophy, that argument will rely on premises or presuppositions that may be called into question. If there is no argument for this final state, then there would appear to be no reason to accept it. Indeed, how can the end state of philosophy be known until it is actually reached? If the end state of philosophy could be identified with a suitable level of precision, then it would seem that philosophy itself must soon reach that end, since all that would remain would be to connect the existing faulty state of knowledge with that end state. Yet philosophy is not finished quite yet, despite various pronouncements of the end of philosophy, as noted in the Preface.[12]

Rather, contemporary philosophy would appear to be best characterized by what might be called *median philosophy*, or philosophy from the middle. Unsure equally of its foundations and of its final state, philosophy nevertheless goes onward. The contemporary problem of philosophical methodology is therefore to show how philosophy can go forward in this middle state without merely flailing about uselessly. If philosophy cannot find its way forward in this state, then perhaps philosophy is well and truly at its end, not by virtue of achieving its proper end, but by virtue of insufficient strength to reach whatever end philosophy may have.

Yet there are philosophical methods currently available that seek to navigate this middle state, and there seems to be the potential for developing still more methods. In the chapters that follow, this study will examine several such methods for philosophy from the middle, namely philosophical naturalism, inference to the best explanation, and reflective equilibrium. From the consideration these methods of median philosophy and their inevitable reliance upon presuppositions, a new approach to philosophical methodology will emerge.

Yet before proceeding to examine these methods, there is one

---

[12]According to the conception of philosophy outlined here, philosophy ends only after every other discipline ends. So long as other disciplines need to be reconciled together in the overall system of knowledge, philosophy will still have work to do, in addition to exploring any fields of knowledge not already bounded by an existing discipline.

troubling aspect of philosophy from the middle that needs to be addressed, namely the problematic metaphor of bootstrapping that appears associated with it.

Chapter 5

Bootstrapping

With neither the firm foundations of first philosophy nor the projected end state of last philosophy, it would seem that philosophy from the middle must pull itself up by its own bootstraps. The metaphor of bootstrapping here is a curious one. Colloquially it is used positively to signify rough self-reliance by improving oneself by means of one's own efforts. Yet interpreted more literally, the metaphor has the negative connotations of a manifestly absurd impossibility: "Except in fairy tales, all that happens if someone pulls hard at his own bootstraps is that they break" (Worrall, 1982, p. 127). D. H. Mellor offers a definition of bootstrapping that makes its negative connotations explicit: "using two otherwise unsupported hypotheses to provide specious support for each other" (Mellor, 2005, p. 58).

Before proceeding to investigate a number of methods for philosophy from the middle, I will review several instances of the bootstrapping metaphor in philosophy, some of which embody bootstrapping in a positive way, some in a negative way. By paying attention to the positive and negative applications of this metaphor, I hope to clarify some aspects of what philosophy from the middle seeks to attain, and thereby to avoid any negative connotations of an application of the bootstrapping metaphor to it.

1. Following the appearance of Thomas Kuhn's discussion of paradigms in the philosophy of science (Kuhn, 1996), a concern began to develop that his arguments implied that the notion of rationality itself was subject to conceptual paradigms and therefore that all rational argumentation was

embroiled in a kind of historicist relativism. If the standards for theory evaluation are relative to a paradigm, and rationality is embodied in certain standards that are recognized as rational standards, then it would appear that rationality itself should vary according to paradigm as well. What was once rational is no longer rational, and what is now rational may not be rational in the future.

In response, a number of philosophers have proposed that what might appear to be a case of the relativity of rationality is really a process of bootstrapping rationality (Agassi, 1974; Briskman, 1987; Nilsson, 2005). Rationality is neither given in its entirety from the beginning, nor is it relativized to historical paradigms. Rather, the notion of rationality emerges slowly in a process of refinement whereby later conceptions of rationality are better than earlier ones. For example, according to one conception of this bootstrapping process, one starts with some conception of rationality that embodies certain criteria for rationality, and that conception is replaced by successive conceptions with increasingly better criteria for rationality, where the later conception is judged according to the criteria for rationality given by the immediately preceding conception (Agassi, 1974, p. 414). In this way, an earlier conception provides the criteria for developing better later conceptions, and the overall theory of rationality consists of general goals that any conception of rationality must embody, though these goals are apparently too weak in themselves to constitute a definite conception of rationality.

So according to this account of rationality, the nature of rationality itself is bootstrapped from some initial conception of rationality, however flawed it may be, so that it may be used as a criterion of rationality for the development of a better successor conception of rationality.

2. The Liar paradox involves sentences such as "This sentence is false". If true, the sentence says that it is false. If false, then the sentence would appear to indicate that it is true after all. In response to the Liar paradox and other semantic paradoxes, a revision theory of truth has been proposed independently by Hans G. Herzberger (Herzberger, 1982b, 1982a) and Anil Gupta and Nuel Belnap (Belnap, 1982; Gupta, 1982;

Gupta & Belnap, 1993). The key idea is that the truth-values for a set of sentences are not determined immediately, but emerge from a process of revision. Initially the truth-values for all sentences are undetermined, and an arbitrary assignment or partial assignment of truth-values is made. Belnap characterizes this initial assignment as a "bootstrapper" (Belnap, 1982, p. 105). By means of these initial assignments, the truth-values for other sentences can be determined by a series of revision rules. Through a successive application of these revision rules, either a stable pattern of truth-values emerges for all sentences in the set regardless of the initial bootstrapping assignments, in which case it would seem that the resulting truth-values are established non-arbitrarily, or no stable pattern emerges either because the pattern of truth-values oscillates within the revision process without stabilizing, or because the pattern of truth-values that does ultimately stabilize out of the process is dependent upon the initial bootstrapping assignment.

Sentences featuring in the Liar paradox turn out to be unstable. As Gupta explains, they are equivocal:

> It is this, I suggest, that explains our attitude towards the problematic sentences that we cannot with any reason say that they are true or that they are not true. Either claim seems equally arbitrary and counter to what we intuit about truth. We feel that these sentences are problematic because we think that there must be something that is the extension of truth. But there is no such thing when vicious self-reference is present in the language. (Gupta, 1982, p. 48)

So according to the revision theory of truth, the truth values of a set of sentences are bootstrapped from some arbitrary initial assignment of truth values, on the basis of which a non-arbitrary pattern of truth values are determined by means of repeated applications of revision rules.

3. Clark Glymour has proposed a bootstrap account of confirmation in the philosophy of science (Glymour, 1980b),

adapting a strategy employed by Rudolph Carnap and Hans Reichenbach. A bootstrap account stands opposed to a hypothetico-deductive account of confirmation according to which one starts with the proposed theory, then deduces what evidence would need to appear if the theory were true. If the predicted evidence matches the available evidence, then the theory is confirmed. By contrast, a bootstrap account starts with the available evidence, then argues for the confirmation of a theory on the basis of that evidence. Yet whereas it might be thought that a theory must be confirmed using principles that are not contained within the theory in order to avoid potentially circular arguments, a bootstrap account holds that confirmation can be obtained on the basis of auxiliary hypotheses that are indeed part of the theory to be confirmed. So if a theory holds that lead can be transmuted into gold, for example, the transmutability of lead can be used as an auxiliary hypothesis in the argument from the available evidence to a confirmed theory.

Of course, not every argument from the evidence to a theory can count as confirmation, since some arguments may rely on additional unscientific principles, such as the perfection of some god or the infallibility of scripture. Accordingly, Glymour outlines various conditions under which a bootstrap argument would count as confirmation, including the consistency of the proposed theory with the hypotheses and the evidence, as well as the ability to compute all the quantities occurring in the hypotheses on the basis of the evidence, among others (Glymour, 1980b, pp. 130–131). Glymour later amends these conditions (Glymour, 1983) as well as extends these conditions to cover probabilistic theories (Glymour, 1980a). So according to this account of confirmation, the confirmation of a theory is bootstrapped from evidence that might be taken from the theory itself, so long as this pattern of confirmation meets certain criteria.[1]

---

[1] Interestingly, the notion of bootstrapping also appears at one point in the history of particle physics, though not on the basis of Glymour's later bootstrapping account of confirmation. As analyzed by Yehudah Freundlich, the bootstrapping hypothesis constitutes a distinct kind of explanation. According to this hypothesis, the existence of particles can be explained if they can serve the particular roles they are hypothesized to serve with regard to other particles. Therefore,

4. Although the term 'bootstrap' is not always used to discuss self-supporting arguments, the general pattern of bootstrapping seems readily apparent in the structure of such arguments. Perhaps the most notable example of such arguments is Max Black's defense of the use of induction to support the method of induction (Black, 1954, 1958). For example, Black considers an argument supporting the following inductive rule: "R_1: To argue from *All examined instances of A's have been B* to *All A's are B*" (Black, 1954, p. 196). The self-supporting argument he offers in support of this rule is as follows:

> All examined instances of the use of R_1 in arguments with true premises have been instances in which R_1 has been successful.
>
> *Hence:*
>
> All instances of the use of R_1 in arguments with true premises are instances in which R_1 is successful. (Black, 1954, p. 197)

Here it appears that the use of an inductive rule can bootstrap the justification for its own use. The problem is that there seems to be a kind of vicious circularity in this argument. Using a rule to justify itself tends to beg the question. However, Black argues that the charge of vicious circularity in this case is mistaken, since an argument that does beg the question would need to be deductively valid, but the self-supporting arguments for induction are only inductively valid, and therefore cannot beg the question (Black, 1954, pp. 199–200).[2]

So in a self-supporting argument, the justification for the use of a principle might be bootstrapped from an argument that uses the principle itself, so long as its use somehow avoids the charge of begging the question.

"Particles, in this conception, do not bootstrap themselves individually; the entire universe of hadrons bootstraps itself all at once" (Freundlich, 1980, p. 268). It appears that this bootstrapping hypothesis has gone out of favor in physics.

[2] See (Achinstein, 1962) for a critique of Black's argument.

5. Finally, Jonathan Vogel uses the term 'bootstrapping' as part of a critique of reliabilism in epistemology that has come to be known as the problem of easy knowledge.[3] Reliabilism holds that beliefs count as knowledge when they result from a reliable belief-forming process. The problem of easy knowledge is that if reliabilism is true, then some knowledge may be available too easily, in a way that seems to be illegitimate. Vogel uses the example of someone gaining beliefs about the reliability of a fuel gauge in a vehicle through the following argumentative stages, where F indicates that the fuel tank is full:

> (20) On this occasion, the gauge reads 'F' and F.
>
> (21) On this occasion, the gauge is reading accurately.
>
> (22) The gauge reads accurately all the time.
>
> (23) The gauge is reliable. (Vogel, 2000, pp. 613–614)

The problem as Vogel sees it is that

> ...for the reliabilist, knowledge of how much fuel is in the tank is knowledge of one empirical fact, and knowledge that the gauge is reliable is knowledge of another, independent empirical fact. One should not be able to transmute the first into the second, as boot-strapping would allow one to do. (Vogel, 2000, p. 621)

So according to this critique, reliabilist epistemology is problematic since empirical knowledge can be bootstrapped on the basis of other empirical knowledge and therefore comes too easily, whereas empirical knowledge by its very nature is something that must be gained by direct experience.

---

[3] Richard Fumerton makes essentially the same critique (Fumerton, 1995), but since Vogel explicitly uses the term 'bootstrapping', I will present his version. Interestingly, Vogel's own account has been accused of falling victim to a bootstrapping problem, as recounted and evaluated in (Brueckner, 2013).

Given these examples of bootstrapping, I offer the following points regarding the apparent bootstrapping nature of median philosophy:

First, some of these examples are concerned specifically with the confirmation of theories or rules, as in the bootstrap theory of scientific confirmation and self-supporting arguments for induction. Yet it seems to me that the image of bootstrapping as applied to philosophy from the middle would involve the generation of new theories in addition to the confirmation or at least evaluation of those theories. Just as Agassi and others argue that the notion of rationality gets bootstrapped, the specific methodologies employed in philosophy from the middle that generate philosophical theories could get bootstrapped, since the very notion of philosophy from the middle implies that those methodologies are not given in advance as in first philosophy. Certainly, once some philosophical theories are available, a further question arises concerning the confirmation or at least evaluation of those theories. Here a second instance of bootstrapping becomes apparent in philosophy from the middle, whereby the principles used in the process of evaluation should likewise be bootstrapped. If the results of the theory itself are employed in the evaluation of that theory, as in Glymour's account, then a third instance of bootstrapping might be identified. In short, it appears that just about everything about the enterprise of philosophy from the middle would be subject to bootstrapping. This might lead one to believe that philosophy from the middle is a hopeless enterprise; however, this attitude is premature since it would dismiss the enterprise even before it can be examined properly.

Second, many of the examples of bootstrapping involve an iterative process, as in the bootstrapping of rationality and the revision theory of truth. If a complete philosophical theory could be bootstrapped in one single operation, that theory might seem to be preferable to one that emerges from a protracted process, but this preferability appears to be grounded primarily in impatience, rather than in a demand for truth. Given that not only the generation of theories but the evaluation of those theories must be bootstrapped, according to median philosophy, it seems clear that philosophy from the middle must ultimately be embodied in an iterative process. New methodologies and new theories would be developed, and the critique of these new methods and theories would in turn generate new methods and theories that would be subject to the same process. Indeed, the long and contentious history of philosophy itself suggests that future iteration is inevitable in philosophy.

Third, some of the examples of bootstrapping considered above seem to rely on the self-application of principles, as in inductive arguments for induction and reliabilist judgments concerning reliability. However, it is not clear that philosophy from the middle must bootstrap itself specifically by means of self-application. Since the bootstrapping of philosophy in general concerns the generation of new theories and not merely the confirmation of theories, the process of bootstrapping a new theory into existence could not very well rely on the application of a theory that did not already exist. The notion of self-application appear to lie at the heart of what seems most objectionable about the metaphor of pulling oneself up by one's bootstraps, and this accounts for the negative aspects of self-supporting arguments and reliabilist epistemology as reviewed above. Perhaps, though, rather than relying on self-application according to the pattern of self-supporting arguments, philosophy from the middle proceeds more properly like the bootstrapping of rationality, unfolding new theories on the basis of standards established by previous theories, inadequate though those predecessors may be. In this way, some methodology might initially be adopted in median philosophy, and this methodology might generate certain philosophical theories. On the basis of those theories and the criteria for truth and justification that may be explicit or merely inherent in them, an improved methodology might be developed to meet those criteria better than the initial methodology. This new methodology would in turn generate further philosophical theories with criteria for truth and justification that get progressively refined, and the process continues. Yet I would not want to claim that this is the only way that new theories may be bootstrapped within philosophy. In fact, the method of perspectival reduction developed in this study adopts a distinctly different pattern of iterative process, as will be discussed later.

Last, whereas it appeared that the self-application of principles was a chief reason for the objectionable nature of certain bootstrapping arguments, since this self-application appeared to involve vicious circularity, perhaps it is more accurately the narrow scope of the self-application that is most objectionable in such arguments. Both the inductive argument for induction and the reliabilist argument for knowledge of reliability of a fuel gauge seemed particularly narrow. For example, in the latter argument, Vogel complains about the lack of "independent information at all about the reliability of the gauge — whether it is broken or likely to be broken, whether it is hooked up properly, and so on" (Vogel, 2000, p. 614). All that enters critically into the argument is the perceived reliability of the gauge, so the scope of reliability appears objectionably narrowed to mere perception of that alleged reliability without any independent confirmation that might broaden the scope.

Yet with regard to any adequate, comprehensive epistemological theory, some measure of self-application seems inevitable. Such a theory would need to include principles concerning the justification of theories in general, principles that should ultimately be employed in the argument for that epistemological theory precisely by virtue of its comprehensive nature. Any epistemological theory that did not exemplify its own principles could thereby be convicted of hypocrisy. If the kind of circularity inherent in this instance should count as a virtuous circle rather than a vicious one, perhaps it is primarily because of the broad scope of its application rather than the particularly narrow scope evident in the inductive support for induction. The problem at this point is that it is not immediately clear how a broad scope should be understood in this case. Against what factor should the scope be measured? What degree of breadth will be sufficient?

One way of measuring scope is against a range of alternatives, and sufficient breadth of scope in this case could be achieved by considering an exhaustive range of alternatives. Consider the following proposed methodological principle based upon such an exhaustive range of alternatives.

Those familiar with elementary formal logic will have encountered the technique of argument by cases. Briefly, this pattern of argument proceeds as follows:

> *A* or *not-A*
>
> Assume *A*
>
> From this assumption, deduce *B*
>
> Assume *not-A*

From this assumption, deduce B

Therefore, B

More generally, if from an exhaustive list of possible cases each alternate case entails the same conclusion, then the conclusion simply follows. In this case, the conclusion of an argument by cases appears to be bootstrapped from a disjunction, as B seems to be bootstrapped from the disjunction of A or *not-A* in the example.

Parmenides uses this form of argument in Plato's dialogue named after him: "If you want to be thoroughly exercised, you must not merely make the supposition that such and such a thing is and then consider the consequences; you must also take the supposition that the same thing *is not*" (Plato, 1961, p. 930, 135e–136a). Parmenides' conclusion in the dialogue shows the argument by cases form clearly: "It seems that, whether there is or is not a one, both that one and the others alike are and are not, and appear and do not appear to be, all manner of things in all manner of ways, with respect to themselves and to one another" (Plato, 1961, p. 956, 166b). The disjunction for this argument by cases is that either there is a one or there is not, and a single conclusion emerges from the assumption of either disjunct.

If argument by cases could be used as a general philosophical methodology, then it would appear to meet the needs for philosophy from the middle by bootstrapping particular conclusions that could in turn be used to deduce the rest of a philosophical theory. The logical validity of the technique of argument by cases, at least within classical logic, seems to make its use as a general methodology particularly tempting. In effect, this method might be understood to bootstrap the clear and distinct ideas needed for a first philosophy, while deduction would fill out the remainder of a last philosophy. Yet because the foundations of the resulting theory would be grounded in a process of bootstrapping, the method would fundamentally consist of a median philosophy.

Of course there are clear problems with this proposed general methodology. First, while argument by cases is valid in classical formal logic, it is not valid in every non-classical system of logic. For example, it fails in supervaluation theory (Williamson, 1994, p. 151). Perhaps this is a problem only if those non-classical logics are strictly applicable to the subject matter being investigated, but it is not certain at the beginning of a process of philosophy from the middle whether they would be applicable or not.

Second, perhaps the conclusions that emerge from this use of argument by cases may be well established thereby, but it is not clear that they could be foundational in the sense that any significant conclusions could be based upon them. They may turn out to be merely tautological or perhaps at such a high level of generality as to be useless for further deduction or possibly even to deduce too much. Consider Parmenides' conclusion as cited above. If he is correct and everything both is and is not, what could be deduced from this result? It would appear that just about anything could be deduced, which seems problematic, at least if one adopts classical formal logic. Indeed, this result would require significant interpretation to make proper sense of it, and it is not clear that any argument by cases could be used to derive a suitable interpretation.

Third and most importantly, the conclusion of an argument by cases does not emerge mystically from out of a disjunction, as in a kind of Hegelian dialectic. Rather, it is based upon additional premises or presuppositions not made explicit in the schematic example given above. It would seem that the disjunction acts mainly as a way to tease out the conclusions inherent in these additional premises. How to establish those premises then becomes an issue. If they could be established likewise through an argument by cases, then which premises would they in turn rely upon? If there would ultimately need to be some foundational premises to establish anything, then this method would appear ultimately to devolve into an instance of first philosophy. If on the other hand the premises and conclusions in every argument by cases were mutually supporting, the resulting coherentist system would ultimately devolve into an instance of last philosophy, since the totality of mutually supporting statements would need to be taken in advance in order to establish any one of them. In either case, the apparent applicability of the method of argument by cases to philosophy from the middle would be undermined.

Still, despite these problems, I find the general pattern of argument by cases to be especially suggestive and intriguing. What interests me most is not that the conclusions of such arguments are independent of any assumptions, but rather that the conclusions are reinforced by multiple assumptions, particularly by contrary assumptions. If there were a comparable method that were not so problematic, it would seem to be precisely the sort of thing needed to pursue philosophy from the middle. Relying upon a single set of assumptions would be risky, where those assumptions may be challenged or undermined. Relying upon multiple, different sets of assumptions taken alternately would seem to provide more secure grounds for establishing some conclusion.

As noted earlier, though, there are philosophical methodologies currently available that would qualify as median philosophy, some of which likewise seem to explore multiple assumptions. Before developing a new proposal as a general method for median philosophy, it is worth examining these methodologies already at hand.

Chapter 6

Naturalism

Given the description of philosophy from the middle given above, it appears that science is in much the same situation as contemporary philosophy. The substantive foundations of particular scientific theories are not perfectly secure, since scientific theories and models are continually being reappraised in light of new experimental evidence. Nor is it clear what the final complete system of scientific knowledge will be, since those models might eventually be abandoned in favor of a radically different explanatory model. Yet modern science progresses well enough according to its methodology without much further debate concerning what the methods of science should be.

According to many measures of success, science has been far more successful than philosophy, despite lacking firm doctrinal foundations and being unsure of its final state. Since science is so successful, it may be thought that the scientific method should provide a good model for philosophical methodology as well. The search for a proper philosophical methodology would seem to be a needless waste of time if there is already a viable candidate available that has proven its merit in another discipline. In short, perhaps scientific methodology should also be philosophical methodology.

This notion has gained prominence in at least one area of philosophy, namely epistemology, due in large part to the arguments of Willard Van Orman Quine in his paper "Epistemology Naturalized". The conclusions of this paper clearly argue for the replacement of the methodology of epistemology with scientific methodology, specifically the methodology of psychology: "Epistemology, or something like it, simply falls into place as a chapter of psychology and hence of natural science" (Quine, 1969, p. 82). This conception of the relation between science and at least one branch of philosophy tends to invert the relation outlined earlier in this study, where I suggested that science represents a chapter of philosophy by virtue of its specialization.[1]

Naturalism in general encompasses a wide array of positions that in some way hold natural entities and methods to take precedence over any others. Quine's naturalized epistemology appears to be a very strong version of naturalism according to which only the methods of natural science should count for anything in philosophy. However, Richard Foley has argued that this strong interpretation of Quine's naturalism with regard to epistemology is not accurate in light of Quine's other writings on naturalized epistemology, concluding that "Quine's practice as a naturalized epistemologist is not discernibly different from that of any other famous epistemologist in the history of the subject" (Foley, 1994, p. 259).

A weaker form of naturalized epistemology can certainly be identified according to which epistemology is continuous with natural science though not necessarily restricted to the methods of natural science. Indeed, the relation between science and philosophy outlined in this study represents one such weaker conception of naturalized epistemology, whereby the specialization of psychology from philosophy requires philosophy to reconcile the results of psychology with the results from other fields of study, including philosophical epistemology. Any incompatibilities that emerge as a result of such reconciliation would require a revision either of epistemology or of psychology or of both. However, this conception of the relation between science and philosophy still leaves the question of the proper methods of philosophy open for inquiry. So the key methodological question with regard to naturalized epistemology is whether the methods of natural science should properly replace the methods of philosophy, in accordance with a strong conception of naturalized epistemology.

---

[1] Quine suggests a "reciprocal containment, though containment in different senses: epistemology in natural science and natural science in epistemology" (Quine, 1969, p. 83). Yet with regard to methodological considerations, the sense in which natural science is contained in epistemology does not seem to count for much, since it is the methods of natural science that are primary.

Consequently, I will ignore Quine's other writings on naturalized epistemology that might present a more moderate view according to Foley and will focus instead on the article "Epistemology Naturalized", which does advocate the replacement of the methods of epistemology with those of natural science.[2]

Much of the debate surrounding Quine's doctrine of naturalized epistemology has centered on the question of whether the methods of natural science can properly account for the factor of normativity that seems essential to traditional epistemology.[3] I think this question is certainly important to the question of naturalism in epistemology, but it only forms a small part of my overall concern with the question of adopting the methods of natural science in philosophy in general. My concern is not merely whether scientific methods can address topics that currently fall within the recognized scope of philosophy, but also whether those methods can expand the scope of philosophy. I suggested earlier that philosophy serves a function beyond the study of traditional philosophical fields such as epistemology, metaphysics, and ethics, and beyond reconciling various fields of knowledge including the sciences. That further function is the exploration of regions of knowledge that are not subsumed under existing recognized disciplines, whether philosophical, scientific, or otherwise.

In what follows, I propose to examine the presuppositions of Quine's particular arguments for naturalized epistemology, since these arguments tend to generalize very well to reasons that one might think that philosophy should simply adopt scientific methods beyond epistemology. For reasons that will become clearer later in this study, I will not argue that these presuppositions are erroneous or flawed in some way, though my presentation may suggest that I am not entirely sympathetic with many or even most of these presuppositions. My intended argument here is not that philosophy should not adopt the methods of science, though my preferred characterization of the nature of philosophy would indeed appear to require such an argument, and though my presentation

---

[2] Interestingly, Husserl had already argued against basing epistemology upon natural science (Husserl, 1965, pp. 84–85). Husserl's methodological views will be examined later in Chapter 10.

[3] See for example, Hilary Kornblith's introduction to his anthology on naturalized epistemology (Kornblith, 1985) as well as Robert Almeder's sustained critique of various forms of naturalized epistemology (Almeder, 1998).

of these presuppositions is clearly laced with suspicions. Rather, my main argument is merely that certain presuppositions can be identified in Quine's proposals for naturalized epistemology that would seem likewise to support more general recommendations for philosophical naturalism.

Right at the beginning of his article, Quine makes a simple assertion that conceals a significant presupposition: "Epistemology is concerned with the foundations of science" (Quine, 1969, p. 69). As stated, this assertion may seem unproblematic; however, if the suggestion is that epistemology is only concerned with the foundations of science and nothing else, then the statement becomes highly problematic. Insofar as the rest of Quine's argument follows from this opening statement, the conclusion of Quine's argument would more properly seem to be that the part of epistemology that is concerned with the foundations of science should be naturalized, not necessarily that all of epistemology should be naturalized. However, if Quine's conclusion is that all of epistemology should be naturalized, it would appear that he thereby presupposes that all epistemology is concerned specifically with the foundations of scientific knowledge.

Indeed, the foundations of science do seem to form Quine's primary concern in his article. He notes that studies in the foundations of mathematics as one department of science divides into two varieties: conceptual and doctrinal. "The conceptual studies are concerned with meaning, the doctrinal with truth" (Quine, 1969, p. 69). Yet when he proceeds to use this observation with regard to mathematics to "illuminate the rest of epistemology somewhat by drawing parallels to this department" (Quine, 1969, p. 69), I become suspicious concerning the extent to which mathematics as a particularly abstract discipline is properly analogous to more concrete sciences such as biology or psychology. Of course, insofar as the scientific method relies upon quantification, the relevance of the analogy with mathematics may seem less dubious. However, if there is any non-scientific knowledge, then the analogy with mathematics as a means toward illuminating the whole of epistemology becomes less secure. Perhaps it would be more charitable to interpret Quine's arguments as applying only to knowledge that is specifically scientific, rather than attributing to him the presupposition that all knowledge is scientific. However, as written, Quine's article makes little allowance for the possibility of non-scientific knowledge and therefore appears to presuppose that the only worthy goal of epistemology is scientific knowledge.

Even if the scope of epistemology is restricted to scientific knowledge, there is the question concerning what epistemology seeks with regard to scientific knowledge. With regard to doctrinal rather than conceptual studies, as distinguished earlier, Quine notes two ideals related to the definitions of concepts and the proof of laws: "Ideally the definitions would generate all the concepts from clear and distinct ideas, and the proofs would generate all the theorems from self-evident truths" (Quine, 1969, p. 70). These are clearly ideals that are associated with Cartesian first philosophy. After noting the failures of Hume and Carnap to achieve reductions or reconstructions that meet these ideals, Quine begins to argue for the primacy of psychology in epistemological concerns as a means to overcome the failures of first philosophy.

At this part in his argument, there are two conditional statements that indicate a further presupposition underlying Quine's argument: "If the epistemologist's goal is validation of the grounds of empirical science, he defeats his purpose by using psychology or other empirical science in the validation.... If we are out simply to understand the link between observation and science, we are well advised to use any available information...." (Quine, 1969, pp. 75–76). Quine's concern here is for the apparent circularity of using a branch of science in order to investigate the foundations of science, but my interest is the conditional presentation of the goals of epistemology that Quine presents here. If the goal is to validate science, then naturalized epistemology fails, but if the goal of epistemology is altered, and altered importantly in such a way as to accord with naturalism, then of course naturalizing epistemology would make sense. What is questionable here is that Quine appears to be restricting the goals of epistemology to suit his conclusions.

Of course, this restriction is precisely part of Quine's argument here: that the goals of first philosophy cannot succeed and therefore should be abandoned. However, Quine does not provide much strict argument for his proposed solution, merely rhetoric: "Why not settle for psychology?" (Quine, 1969, p. 75). "However, such scruples against circularity have little point once we have stopped dreaming of deducing science from observations" (Quine, 1969, p. 76). What Quine appears to rely on here is a kind of quitter's argument based on the failures of Hume and Carnap with regard to first philosophy. They failed; no one else has succeeded; so it seems proper to quit the endeavor entirely. Yet more importantly, the operative presupposition that underlies Quine's resignation here is that there are no other worthy goals in epistemology besides either a reductionist first philosophy or a naturalist link between observation and theory. His argument thus seems to be based upon a failure of imagination to identify any other worthy epistemological goals, leading to a presupposition regarding the possible goals of epistemology. This presupposition is clearly limited to the two kinds of methodologies that Quine explicitly considers. Besides first philosophy and naturalism, Quine does not consider any other alternative methodologies. Indeed, one might be inclined to settle for psychology if there are only two available goals and only two available methodologies, where one goal and its corresponding method are hopeless. If there are other goals and other methodologies, ones not considered by Quine, then the argument seems to rely essentially upon a presupposition embodying a failure of imagination.

To generalize, I think there are two complementary presuppositions underlying Quine's argument: (1) that the scope of epistemology is restricted in some important way, and (2) that there are no viable methodological alternatives beyond first philosophy and naturalism. These kinds of presuppositions might likewise underlie an argument for the adoption of scientific methods in all of philosophy. If the scope of philosophy is restricted in a way to coincide with the scope of science, and if there are no other methodological alternatives, then the proposal to use of scientific methodology in philosophy might seem to be compelling.

Yet the adoption of scientific methodology in philosophy more broadly would also appear to require the adoption and endorsement of the presuppositions of that scientific methodology as well. One notable presupposition embodied in scientific method is that results must be confirmed by repeating experiments. This presupposition ensures objectivity throughout scientific discourse, but it also places restrictions on what can be investigated using this method. Specifically, the method would seem to be useless in investigating the question of whether everything is causally connected or whether there are causal gaps. It is not clear what kind of experiment could possibly be devised to provide evidence to decide this question. Suppose that some extremely clever experiment could be devised to reveal a causal anomaly. Scientific methods require that those results should be confirmed by repeating the experiment. Yet if a causal anomaly were discovered, then by definition those results could not be confirmed in another instance, since that prior instance was anomalous. If circumstances could be arranged such that the alleged causal anomaly could be confirmed, then that the alleged anomaly would appear to be causally connected to those circumstances in some way and therefore would not be a causal anomaly after all. The presuppositions of the methods of science seem to preclude the investigation of such questions directly. Therefore, if causal gaps are acknowledged within science, it would have to be on the basis of broad theoretical interpretation, such as in quantum mechanics, not by some direct critical experiment, as demanded by scientific methodology. Since causality is a fundamental problem of philosophy, it is not clear whether the adoption of scientific method in philosophy would permit any significant investigation on the question of causal anomalies, rather than merely presupposing that there are no causal anomalies.[4]

Another presupposition of scientific methodology concerns the quantification of data, as discussed by E. A. Burtt (Burtt, 1925, pp. 56ff). Whereas older natural philosophy, such as that of Aristotle, tended to argue on the basis of heat, cold, and other qualitative factors, modern science tends to reject qualitative factors in favor of quantifiable data. Qualitative factors are admissible only insofar as they can be quantified, for example, in a statistical survey of subjects who report water of a certain temperature to be warm or cold to the touch. Philosophy, by contrast, rarely concerns itself with the quantification of evidence used in philosophical arguments.

Yet there is a more recent incarnation of methodological naturalism called "experimental philosophy" that is vitally concerned with quantification of philosophical evidence. According to proponents of this movement, "Experimental philosophers proceed by

---

[4]Many other topics in metaphysics would be similarly affected. "Scientists inevitably make metaphysical assumptions, whether explicitly or implicitly, in proposing and testing their theories — assumptions which go beyond anything that science itself can legitimate" (Lowe, 1998, p. 5). See also Collingwood's conception of metaphysics as the absolute presuppositions of natural science, discussed in Chapter 9.

conducting experimental investigations of the psychological processes underlying people's intuitions about central philosophical issues" (Knobe & Nichols, 2008, p. 3). Where some philosophers may bluntly assert that our intuitions about some issue are one way or another, without providing much justification for such assertions beyond a report of their own intuitions, experimental philosophy seeks to evaluate claims concerning intuitions, primarily by conducting surveys.[5]

The pioneering work in experimental philosophy is the study conducted by Jonathan M. Weinberg, Shaun Nichols, and Stephen Stich concerning epistemic intuitions (Weinberg, Nichols, & Stich, 2001). Following experimental research by Richard Nisbett concerning differences in cognitive processes between Western and East Asian subjects, Weinberg, Nichols and Stich ran surveys to test for differences in epistemic intuitions in a number of well-known philosophical thought experiments, such as Keith Lehrer's Truetemp case, Gettier cases, and Dretske's case of zebras vs. painted mules in a zoo. In each case, the surveys suggest that there are statistically significant differences in epistemic intuitions across cultural groups in the same way that Nisbett's studies indicate, thus challenging the presumed universality of epistemic intuitions as is commonly presented in various epistemological arguments.

This kind of methodological naturalism is fairly consonant with the preferred conception of philosophy articulated in this study. If philosophy needs to incorporate and reconcile the results of psychology with philosophy and other disciplines, then the use of psychological methods within philosophy would not appear to present any special problems. I think that philosophy in general benefits when it has more evidence not less, and where psychology and other sciences have not provided investigations that would provide the kind of evidence that philosophy needs, experimental philosophers are clearly willing to conduct those investigations themselves. Furthermore, insofar as experimental philosophy seeks to challenge unsubstantiated claims concerning shared intuitions, this approach to philosophy seems quite refreshing.

---

[5]However, this reliance on surveys in the early history of experimental philosophy is changing, as reported in (Sytsma, 2025, p. 189), most notably in an empirical investigation of the ethics of ethicists regarding library books in (Schwitzgebel, 2009).

The way in which some philosophers rely on various intuitions appears to be based on a sloppy kind of induction of the form: "I and my philosophical colleagues have the following intuitions, therefore...". Any further investigations that bring such dubious pronouncements into question would certainly be welcome.

Yet experimental philosophy has certain presuppositions, including many of the presuppositions noted with regard to Quine's naturalized epistemology, as well as a few that are distinct to its particular approach. Specifically, where it focuses on intuitions, the value of experimental philosophy would correlate directly with the value of such intuitions in philosophy. If certain conceptual analysts are correct, then it would seem that intuitions, particularly shared intuitions in a group of language users, are central to the very nature of philosophy. If they are wrong, though, perhaps the fascination with intuitions is deeply misplaced and represents a temporary fashion within philosophy that will ultimately be discredited or at least be emphasized less. In the latter case, the value of empirically testing intuitions will be correspondingly low. By predominantly focusing their experimental researches on the reporting of intuitions, experimental philosophers appear to be presupposing that intuitions do indeed have a central value to philosophy.[6]

Note also that while experimental philosophy embraces a method for conducting its experiments by explicitly adopting the methods of psychology and perhaps other sciences, it does not clearly specify any method for incorporating the results of those experiments into philosophy. Whereas Quine's naturalized epistemology claims that there is nothing more to epistemology other than what empirical psychology could establish, some experimental philosophers do not make such a strong claim, but propose only "to add another tool to the philosopher's toolbox" (Knobe & Nichols, 2008, p. 10). Of course, since the aim of this study is to investigate the methodology by which philosophy in general should be pursued, the claim of experimental philosophy to provide one tool among many without specifying how the various tools should work together still leaves the question of general philosophical methodology unsolved. As one tool among many, experimental philosophy in itself can only provide an inadequate or incomplete

---

[6]See Chapter 15 for further reflections on intuitions.

picture of philosophical methodology, which of course does not indicate that the tool of experimental philosophy is completely useless.

For my part, what I find most troubling about experimental philosophy is that the efforts to date seem like fairly amateur endeavors. Within the published results of this movement,[7] there are certainly numerous tables and graphs of results, with Fisher exact tests and other mathematical means to determine statistical significance. It seems perfectly scientific, but with regard to the design of the experiments and the significance of the experiments themselves, I have a few doubts.

For example, it is not clear whether sufficient controls have been built into these experiments, particularly when the study subjects are students, especially philosophy students. Giving a student a case study and having the student choose one of several options seems suspiciously like taking a test, and I think it should be questioned whether the nature of the experiment in such cases may affect the results. Are the students always accurately reporting their own intuitions, or are they giving the answers they thought were expected of them, as in a graded test? This question itself demands experimental investigation. Note that it is not always adequate simply to inform the subjects in advance that they should be perfectly honest and that their answers will be anonymous. The very nature of the experimental situation may affect the reported intuitions. The question here is what psychologists call experimental realism: "If an experiment has an impact on the participants, forces them to take the matter seriously, and involves them in the procedures" (Aronson, 2004, p. 339), then it demonstrates experimental realism. I think this question is especially important with regard to students, some of whom may intentionally try to outthink the aims of the experiment and seek to subvert those aims. I myself have been such a subversive student at times, and it is not clear whether the design of the experiments in question has built in sufficient controls to account for mischievous students such as I have been.

Beyond the questions specifically surrounding the use of students in these survey experiments, there is a broader question concerning the nature of the resulting data in the form of first per-

---

[7] For example, in the collection (Knobe & Nichols, 2008).

son reports of intuitions. Are intuitions always accurately gauged merely by asking about them? Psychologists are often obliged to design experiments such that the true aim of the study is hidden from subjects in order to obtain the kind of experimental realism that would provide accurate experimental data. So a subject might be recruited under the guise of some cover story, and the subject may actually participate in some experimental setup in accordance with that cover story, but the experiment may have been designed such that the true investigation concerns some aspect of the study that is inherent in the design but not made explicit to the subject. Thus psychologists are often obliged to resort to deception in order to get accurate experimental results (Aronson, 2004, pp. 340–342). For example, in the notorious experiment performed by Stanley Milgram in which subjects apparently administered increasingly painful electrical shocks to other subjects, the subjects were ostensibly recruited for a study on learning and memory, but the true study concerned obedience to authority (Milgram, 1963). In order to obtain a subject's true intuitions, therefore, it may be necessary to employ a measure of deception in the design of the experiment, rather than simply to ask the subject to report intuitions.[8]

So perhaps this question concerning the design of experiments merely reveals another presupposition underlying experimental philosophy, namely that intuitions are what people report them to be. According to this presupposition, if you ask a subject whether a given thought experiment embodies an instance of knowledge or not, the subject's response is the subject's true intuition. Yet contrary to this presupposition, it may be that a subject's true intuitions lie concealed in some way from such first person reports. Perhaps true intuitions are only made manifest after a process of Socratic dialectic whereby those intuitions are drawn out and evaluated by a series of questions and challenges.[9] One could indeed use experimental methods to test people's intuitions concerning the nature of intuitions. If they support the presuppositions of ex-

---

[8] For similar concerns, see (Woolfolk, 2013).

[9] Of course it might claimed that in the Socratic method, the subject's true intuitions were indeed the initial response, but that the dialectic method merely tests those intuitions, rather than reveals true intuitions. Yet the difference in interpretations available here is precisely my concern, not the nature of true intuitions.

perimental philosophy, then perhaps the practice of experimental philosophy would at least be consistent in this respect. If they run counter to those presuppositions, then it is not clear how proponents of experimental philosophy would properly respond.

Leaving aside the identification of presuppositions in philosophical naturalism in general and in experimental philosophy in particular, I will comment briefly on the relation between experimental philosophy and the conception of philosophy outlined earlier in this study. Certainly the concerns I just outlined about the design of experiments as employed in experimental philosophy, even if substantiated, do not argue against the validity of experimental philosophy. They would appear merely to argue for better experimental philosophy. Whatever deficiencies existing experiments may have, these could indeed be remedied if experimental philosophers would receive better training in psychological experimental methods. With such training, the apparently amateur aspect of these experiments could be reduced or eliminated, and experimental philosophy could be established on a more rigorous basis. Of course, better training in psychological methods would tend to make one a better psychologist, not a better philosopher. So it seems to me that the practice of experimental philosophy would be more proper to psychology than to philosophy, on precisely methodological grounds.

Jesse J. Prinz argues against such methodological purism, arguing that experimental philosophy does not collapse into psychology but remains a part of philosophy. Prinz distinguishes between empirical philosophers who "make use of empirical results that have been acquired by professional scientists", and experimental philosophers who "conduct their own psychological experiments" (Prinz, 2008, p. 196), while noting that "the experiments that philosophers perform could be performed by behavioral scientists" (Prinz, 2008, p. 197). The question then is what is the difference between experimental philosophers and psychologists. Prinz offers two differences. First, "experimental philosophers tend to have a theoretical orientation. Even when writing up results, they tend to dedicate more space to theoretical reflection than they do to reporting research methods and results" (Prinz, 2008, pp. 205–206). Second, "experimental philosophers tend to focus on questions about specific lay concepts rather than general questions about underlying psychological processes" (Prinz, 2008, p. 206). He continues to suggest that these differences can even be tested by survey methods by "asking people to sort publications into these three categories" (Prinz, 2008, p. 206), namely empirical philosophy, experimental philosophy, and experimental psychology.

I find Prinz's arguments unpersuasive. The differences he notes are on the basis of tendencies, so the differences between experimental philosophers and psychologists could merely represent the current state of the practice of psychology, not a fundamental difference between experimental philosophers and psychologists. The arguments that Prinz offers for the distinctness of experimental philosophy from both empirical philosophy and experimental psychology could just as well argue for the need for a new branch of psychology rather than a new technique in philosophy, particularly if I am right that experimental philosophers need better training in psychological methods to incorporate better controls into the design of their experiments.[10]

Against the experimental philosophers, then, I would suggest that disciplines are best distinguished by methodologies. My argument for this kind of methodological purism concerns the unity of practice within a discipline. In order to evaluate the data and results within a given discipline, it should not require special training in the distinctive methods of some other discipline. So it should not require special training in psychology to evaluate the findings of amateur psychologists working in philosophy. Nor should philosophers properly build conclusions on the basis of experiments whose design has not been scrutinized by those competent to evaluate them. Let those interested in experimental philosophy get sufficient training to become proper psychologists to explore the kinds of questions that interest them. Let those results be incorporated into the best psychology theories before being incorporated prematurely into philosophy. In the end, such results should be incorporated into philosophy, according to the conception of philosophy outlined earlier in this study. I would simply want to have the benefit of the scientific insight of the best psychologists on these projects before philosophers begin working with them.

---

[10]Williamson claims of the efforts of some experimental philosophers that "such experiments have been redone many times, more carefully, with more involvement of fully trained psychologists, and the picture is now very different" (Williamson, 2020, p. 56). However, he does not provide a specific reference for this claim.

My suspicions concerning naturalized epistemology and experimental philosophy are certainly not decisive arguments against them. Rather, these suspicions merely reveal certain presuppositions concerning the adoption of naturalistic methods in philosophy, and it is these presuppositions that I have mainly aimed at identifying here. Other methods that embody median philosophy likewise have certain presuppositions. The next chapter explores the presuppositions of inference to the best explanation.

Chapter 7

Inference to the Best Explanation

Charles Sanders Peirce claims to have identified a third mode of inference, distinct from deduction and induction, initially calling this third mode "hypothesis" before settling upon the term "abduction". Although Peirce does not claim credit for discovering abduction, and cites some form of this mode in the works of Aristotle and Auguste Comte, Peirce discusses this mode of inference in a more systematic way than any earlier writer.[1]

In an early exposition, Peirce gives examples of the three modes of inference to demonstrate the contrast between these modes:

> DEDUCTION
> *Rule.*—All the beans from this bag are white.
> *Case.*—These beans are from this bag.
> ∴ *Result.*—These beans are white.
>
> INDUCTION *Case.*—These beans are from this bag.
> *Result.*—These beans are white.
> ∴ Rule.—All the beans from this bag are white.
>
> HYPOTHESIS
> *Rule.*—All the beans from this bag are white.
> *Result.*—These beans are white.
> ∴ Case.—These beans are from this bag. (Peirce, 1998a, p. 188)

---
[1] See (Anderson, 1986) for an account of the way that Peirce's conception of abduction developed.

As Peirce continues to describe the nature of hypothesis or abduction,

> Hypothesis is where we find some very curious circumstance, which would be explained by the supposition that it was a case of a certain general rule, and thereupon adopt that supposition. Or, where we find that in certain respects two objects have a strong resemblance, and infer that they resemble one another strongly in other respects.
>
> I once landed in a seaport in a Turkish province; and, as I was walking up to the house which I was to visit, I met a man upon horseback, surrounded by four horsemen holding a canopy over his head. As the governor of the province was the only personage I could think of who would be so greatly honored, I inferred that this was he. This was an hypothesis. (Peirce, 1998a, p. 189)

In a later exposition, he describes abduction as follows: "Abduction consists in studying the facts and devising a theory to explain them. Its only justification is that if we are ever to understand things at all, it must be in that way" (Peirce, 1998b, p. 205). He further explains the contrast between abduction on the one hand and induction and deduction on the other:

> Abduction is the process of forming an explanatory hypothesis. It is the only logical operation which introduces any new idea; for induction does nothing but determine a value and deduction merely evolves the necessary consequences of a pure hypothesis.
>
> Deduction proves that something must be, Induction shows that something *actually is* operative, Abduction merely suggests that something *may be*. (Peirce, 1998b, p. 216)

Finally, Peirce elaborates on the general form of an inductive inference:

> The surprising fact, *C*, is observed;
> But if *A* were true, *C* would be a matter of course.

> Hence, there is reason to suspect that *A* is true. (Peirce, 1998b, p. 231)

Clearly, abduction for Peirce is an inference to an explanation. However, it has become common to equate abduction with what has been called "inference to the best explanation". I think this identification is a mistake.[2] In the exposition of abduction cited above, Peirce does not speak of the results of abduction as best explanations. Since he claims that "Abduction merely suggests that something may be" (Peirce, 1998b, p. 216), it would seem that abduction represents inference only to one possible explanation, not to a best explanation. Indeed, from the schematic forms of abduction that Peirce presents, any conclusion that the results of abduction represent a best explanation would be completely unfounded. Peirce notes that abduction is a weak form of inference (Peirce, 1998a, p. 189), and claims that abduction produces "a prediction which can be tested by induction" (Peirce, 1998b, p. 216). Yet if abduction were an inference to best explanation, such inductive testing would be unnecessary, since the best explanation was already inferred. If further testing were required, as Peirce claims, then it would appear that abduction is not yet an inference to a best explanation.

Perhaps it is the following statement from Peirce that leads some to equate abduction and inference to the best explanation: "Think of what trillions of trillions of hypotheses might be made of which one only is true; and yet after two or three or at the very most a dozen guesses, the physicist hits pretty nearly on the correct hypothesis. By chance he would not have been likely to do so in the whole time that has elapsed since the earth was solidified" (Peirce, 1998b, p. 217). It may seem that by hitting nearly on the correct hypothesis, the physicist in question was inferring to the best hypothesis or explanation. However, upon closer analysis this passage does not very well support the interpretation of abduction as resulting in the best hypothesis. The physicist of whom Peirce speaks makes up to a dozen guesses, each of which would seem to be the result of an abductive inference. Peirce's point here is to establish abduction as a genuine mode of inference different from merely selecting a hypothesis at random or from a complete

---

[2] Jaakko Hintikka also disagrees with this conflation (Hintikka, 1998).

set of logical possibilities. As Peirce claims shortly after this passage, the use of abduction appears to rely on a faculty of insight (Peirce, 1998b, pp. 217–218), whereby an extremely small percentage of the trillions of possible hypotheses are recognized as likely explanations. The means by which Peirce's physicist establishes one of a dozen or so likely explanations to be the best explanation would require more than just abduction, which can only provide potential explanations, not the best one.

Consequently, it seems to me that inference to the best explanation should be considered as a composite mode of inference, employing potentially all three modes of inference that Peirce describes. The surprising fact that occasions an abductive inference might be a surprising individual observation, such as that some particular raven is black, but it might also be a surprising result of an inductive inference, such as that all ravens are black. If someone had only recently discovered the existence of ravens, the fact that all of them appear to be black might indeed be a surprising fact. In the same way, perhaps the result of a deductive inference might be surprising, even though the logical grounds of the result of the inference was fully contained within the premises. Sometimes certain consequences can be surprising even if the basis for those consequences is well known. So both induction and deduction might provide the occasion for an abductive inference. Once one or more abductive hypotheses are made available, further inference is required to establish a hypothesis as a best explanation. As already noted, Peirce claims that an abductive hypothesis can be tested by induction, but there appears to be a role for deduction as well in the establishment of a best hypothesis, particularly with regard to what criteria are used to determine the best hypothesis. For example, if simplicity were the pre-eminent criterion for claiming one hypothesis to be the best, the inference that applies that criterion would appear to be a deductive one.

Though Peirce did not explicitly discuss best explanations, his contemporary Alfred Sidgwick did, in describing the method of disproof by exceptions.[3] "The 'best explanation,' or 'proved theory,' is that which remains over as a residue when all possible holes have been picked in the crude or sweeping assertion first put for-

---

[3] I became aware of Sidgwick's work on best explanation from the reference given in (Walton, 2004, pp. 22–23). I am not sure Sidgwick is the first to discuss best explanation explicitly, but his is the earliest work of which I am aware.

ward as a guess" (A. Sidgwick, 1884, p. 250). Here Sidgwick seems to presume that there will be one and only one explanation that does not have any exceptions, and later he clarifies his point:

> By the best explanation is meant, however, not only any law from which all the facts observed are deducible, — for we may often frame many different hypotheses which, while explaining all the facts already in view, is narrowed, limited, hedged, or qualified, sufficiently to guard in the best possible way against *undiscovered exceptions* also. The wider the law the greater the danger, until precautions are taken: and it is in the strength of these precautions that the value of any Theory lies. It is a merely negative condition, or absolute *sine quâ non*, that a Theory shall at least explain the facts already in view: failing this, it is condemned, or seen to need qualification, on the threshold. But beyond and above the preliminary condition that no known fact as yet contradicts the theory, we need also the assurance, in some shape or other, that *if there were* exceptions (or contradictory instances) their existence would already have been discovered or inferrible. (A. Sidgwick, 1884, pp. 271–272)

The best explanation for Sidgwick is thus the one that accounts not only for existing observations but for future ones as well. Though recognizing that "Disproof is easier than Proof" (A. Sidgwick, 1884, p. 275), he explains how a best explanation can be established. "The important point is always, to show that all other possible theories are weighed in the balance and found wanting: that is to say, that all precautions have been taken against the crudest kind of unchecked generalization which the least trained mind possesses ever in greatest abundance" (A. Sidgwick, 1884, pp. 275–276). If it should seem an impossible task to identify every possible alternative theory or explanation before judging that an explanation is the best one, Sidgwick is kind enough to summarize the possible alternatives in an appendix. This list of alternative possibilities is generated on an *a priori* basis by considering the logical possibilities between events, for example, either one event precedes another, or both are co-existent, either one event is the cause of another or it is accidental, and so forth (A. Sidgwick, 1884, pp. 333–339).

Of course, even if Sidgwick is correct in his characterization of best explanation, it would still appear to be impossible to know that any given explanation is the best one. At the time the explanation is formulated or evaluated only known exceptions are available. Unforeseen exceptions are by definition not anticipated and therefore unknown. So perhaps a given explanation may be sufficiently well formulated to guard against both known and unforeseen exceptions, yet until the proposed explanation has been tested against all such exceptions, including the unforeseen ones, the status of the explanation as a best one would remain unconfirmed, and until some projected ideal end of inquiry, it would seem that such confirmation could not be completed. Taking all alternative possibilities into account may indeed be an intellectually responsible method in formulating an explanation, but the demand for an explanation to account not only for existing exceptions but also for unforeseen ones would appear to result in a kind of skepticism whereby a best explanation cannot be known.

Since the early work by Peirce and Sidgwick, inference to the best explanation has been recognized as an important aspect of the scientific method as well as other forms of rational inquiry, so considerable effort has been taken to analyze this kind of inference more rigorously. In the process, a number of issues and items of controversy have arisen with regard to inference to the best explanation. One of which is precisely what kind of explanation should be recognized. The nature of explanation itself is a controversial issue with a multitude of proposed theories of explanation available.[4] Given these alternative theories of explanation, should an inference to the best explanation involve only causal explanations, for example, or should they rely on deductive-nomological explanations, or some other characterization of explanation? Perhaps inference to the best explanation should be employed only within a given explanatory scheme, for example as an inference to the best causal explanation. Or perhaps better still, inference to the best explanation should incorporate every explanation according to any account of explanation. However the controversy over the nature of explanation may be resolved, perhaps that controversy should

---

[4] See the discussion of explanation in Chapter 14.

not properly affect concerns over inference to best explanation. It may be that any potential explanation could be considered, so long as the best explanation of any kind wins out in the end.

Of course, this latter alternative would appear to put increased focus upon the criteria for what qualifies as the best explanation, and the nature of such criteria is itself a contentious issue. It seems easy enough to claim that one should always infer to the best explanation, but much more difficult to specify precisely how to select the best one. Paul Thagard has proposed three criteria for best explanation: "consilience, simplicity, and analogy" (Thagard, 1978, p. 79), where consilience is "a measure of *how much* a theory explains" (Thagard, 1978, p. 79), simplicity is a function of the size of the set of auxiliary hypotheses needed to provide an explanation (Thagard, 1978, p. 86), and analogy is a measure of familiarity within the explanation (Thagard, 1978, pp. 89–91). Peter Lipton distinguishes between criteria that establish the most probable explanation and those that establish explanatory power (Lipton, 2004, pp. 59–60), arguing that it is explanatory power that should most properly be employed in any inference to the best explanation.[5] Perhaps some set of criteria will ultimately be established as the operative ones employed in any inference to the best explanation, or perhaps there is a pragmatic aspect to the criteria whereby the use of inference to the best explanation can employ different criteria for the best explanation in different contexts. So perhaps the criteria used to argue for a best explanation in literary criticism need not be the same criteria used in scientific investigations. Still another alternative is that the specific criteria for best explanation get bootstrapped as science or other fields progress. According to this alternative, there may be some loose initial criteria applied in inferences to the best explanation, but on the basis of the explanations that are selected as the best ones, these criteria get refined over time to select increasingly better explanations. Therefore, inference to the best explanation might not simply be a single operation, but may be an iterative process that demonstrates a best explanation only at the end of the course of an inquiry.

---

[5]Lipton designates this distinction as one between 'likely' explanations and 'lovely' explanations. I think this designation is puerile and refuse to use it. In fact, I was reluctant even to mention the designation in a footnote, but since it has entered into the literature, I feel that I need to confirm that I am referring to Lipton's distinction even if I reject his terminology.

Related to this latter suggestion, there is a further concern over the scope of the explanations considered in an inference to the best explanation, namely whether the best explanation is the best of the available explanations at any given time or whether it is the absolute best of all possible explanations. From Sidgwick's descriptions of best explanation, it is clear that he intended it to be the absolute best explanation. Indeed, if the inference were only to the best available explanation, then the resulting inference may be useless if all available explanations are particularly dreadful.[6] Yet if inference to the best explanation is understood as an iterative process, even an inference to the best of a set of rotten explanations may contribute to progress toward a better explanation, if the best available rotten explanation encourages the development of better and less rotten explanations in the future.

Finally, there is a controversy whether inference to the best explanation represents a distinct mode of inference. Peirce of course claims that abduction, deduction, and induction are all irreducible to each other (Peirce, 1998b, p. 206). However, Gilbert Harman argues that enumerative induction is a special case of inference to the best explanation (Harman, 1965). To the contrary, Richard Fumerton argues that inference to the best explanation should be recognized simply as enumerative induction with certain premises suppressed (Fumerton, 1980). Yet if my prior suggestion is correct that inference to the best explanation is a composite inference employing instances of abduction, deduction, and induction, it would seem that both Harman and Fumerton are mistaken. Harman would appear to be mistaking the part for the whole, while Fumerton mistakes the whole for the part.

For the purposes of this study, though, it does not much matter whether inference to the best explanation is distinct from induction, nor does it matter how the other items of controversy get resolved. What does matter is that inference to the best explanation does qualify as a broad philosophical methodology that exemplifies what I have been calling median philosophy or philosophy from the middle. Inference to the best explanation does not require any philosophical foundations as with first philosophy, since it derives its potential candidate explanations from a process of ab-

---

[6]This observation forms the beginning of van Fraassen's criticism of inference to the best explanation (van Fraassen, 1989, pp. 142–143), as will be discussed later.

duction, not deduction or even induction. Consequently, it would seem that what ultimately counts as a best explanation could be initially pulled out of thin air or even dreamed out of a drunken stupor, so long as it can ultimately be demonstrated to provide a best explanation. Nor do the criteria for what counts as best explanation need to be considered as foundational either, given the suggestion that these criteria might be bootstrapped as part of the process of finding increasingly better explanations on the basis of increasingly better criteria. Furthermore, inference to the best explanation does not depend upon a projected end state, as with last philosophy, particularly if it is considered as an iterative process. Rather, the end state for some domain is not known until all best explanations have been established within that domain.

While naturalistic scientific methods do tend to employ inference to the best explanation, the two are not identical. Most importantly, whereas the scientific method relies heavily upon quantifiable measures and experimentation, there seems to be no such presumption in the use of inference to the best explanation. Consequently, inference to the best explanation might be employed broadly in the humanities, to argue for one interpretation of a poem over another, for example, if one interpretation explains better than the other the particular expressions and idioms the poet used, without any appeal to quantification. Besides the obvious difference in explicit methods, methodological naturalism and inference to the best explanation differ with regard to their presuppositions, which are important to this study.

Before exploring these presuppositions, I should point out a few objections to inference to the best explanation, which, if correct, would appear to preclude this pattern of inference from being considered as a viable philosophical methodology. Nicholas Rescher levies an entire battery of problems against inference to the best explanation:

1. The best explanation of one fact may not be the best explanation of another (Rescher, 2001, p. 133);

2. the method of inference to the best explanation may not work in all contexts (Rescher, 2001, p. 134);

3. the best explanation may still not be very probable (Rescher, 2001, p. 134);

4. there is an ambiguity between best available explanation and best possible explanation (Rescher, 2001, pp. 134–135), which I have already noted; and

5. the multiple criteria employed in selecting the best explanation are often in conflict or at least in tension with each other (Rescher, 2001, pp. 136–137).

Rescher suggests that best systematization should be substituted for best explanation: "A proposition that is part of our best available systematization of all the relevant facts we can determine is not thereby necessarily true, but it indeed is thereby qualified to count as our best available estimate of the truth" (Rescher, 2001, p. 138). While Rescher formulates these points as problems for the validity of inference to the best explanation, I would merely note that these problems could be reformulated more positively as presuppositions. Rescher clearly suggests that these presuppositions are not well founded and therefore problematic, but I prefer to leave them recognized as presuppositions without further evaluation, for reasons that will be come clear later.

Bas van Fraassen, on the other hand, argues that inference to the best explanation is not merely problematic, but incoherent. His argument is that if inference to the best explanation is interpreted in a probabilistic sense as employing an orthodox Bayesian rule for adjusting personal probabilities to establish the best explanation, someone knowing that I use such a rule could pose a wager against me in which I was guaranteed to lose. Though my application of the Bayesian rule suggests that the wager is a reasonable one to take, I am fated to lose the wager, and thus the employment of that rule is incoherent (van Fraassen, 1989, pp. 160–169). Without examining this argument in detail, my initial reaction is that if a Bayesian interpretation of inference to the best explanation is incoherent, then I should not charitably interpret inference to the best explanation that way. Of course, van Fraassen's incoherence argument is just a part of his broader argument against inference to the best explanation. The overall structure of his argument is that inference to the best explanation pretends to provide objectively warranted beliefs, but it can only provide the best of available hypotheses, which may not include any true ones (van Fraassen, 1989, pp. 142–143). Furthermore, he claims that there are three possible interpretations of inference to the best explanation that might overcome this initial objection, each of which fails:

1. that we have an evolutionary privilege in selecting hypotheses that are true (van Fraassen, 1989, pp. 143–144),

2. that we are forced to make a choice of best explanations, even if the truth is not among the alternatives considered (van Fraassen, 1989, pp. 144-145), and

3. the Bayesian interpretation that leads to incoherence.

Ultimately, van Fraassen argues for a non-Bayesian probabilistic epistemology, but argues that once this epistemology is adopted, inference to the best explanation becomes useless. Again, without exploring van Fraassen's specific arguments in greater detail, I think the force of those arguments against inference to the best explanation can likewise be preserved by reformulating them as presuppositions, which is how I prefer to understand them for the purposes of this study.

Now, however the controversies outlined earlier surrounding inference to the best explanation get resolved, these specific resolutions themselves may depend upon certain additional presuppositions. Yet there are a number of presuppositions that can be identified in the general structure of inference to the best explanation itself, regardless of these specific issues. Richard Fumerton points out a few of them. One obvious presupposition is that there is an explanation of the phenomenon in question at all (Fumerton, 1992, p. 162), which may be a natural presupposition to accept, but it is a presupposition nevertheless. Another is that the explanation accepted by inference to the best explanation is better not only than each alternative considered separately, but better than the disjunction of all remaining alternatives. "...I can cheerfully admit that [one alternative] is the most attractive explanation while admitting that the disjunction of propositions asserting alternative explanations is more likely to be true" (Fumerton, 1992, p. 164). A further presupposition concerns the criteria used to establish some explanation as the best one. Fumerton claims "that whatever criteria we select for evaluating explanations, it will be a contingent fact that explanations with those characteristics are more likely to be true" (Fumerton, 1992, p. 169). While he notes that this poses a problem for internalists about justification, since internalism requires independent justification for contingent facts, I think this concern can be formulated as a more general presupposition regardless of concerns about internalism. It seems that inference to the best explanation presupposes not only that the criteria for a best explanation have some connection to truth, but also that the explanatory nature of certain statements has a connection to truth. If there were reasons for accepting a statement independent of the explanatory nature of that statement, perhaps deductive or inductive reasons, then there would be no need to invoke inference to the best explanation to accept that statement as true. Inference to the best explanation presupposes that explanatory power is itself a critical aspect of true statements. Clearly explanatory power is not a sufficient criteria of truth, since many very powerful explanations can be devised for any given phenomenon that can nevertheless be demonstrated to be false. However, inference to the best explanation puts explanatory power in a methodologically prominent position.

Besides Fumerton's concerns, other presuppositions can be identified, for example, with regard to the role of abduction in inference to the best explanation. Peirce claims that abduction relies on a kind of insight (Peirce, 1998b, pp. 217, 227). While Peirce puts great faith in this power or faculty to hit "pretty nearly on the correct hypothesis" (Peirce, 1998b, p. 217), for those without this faith, it appears to be a mere presupposition that this faculty is capable of identifying at least one alternative hypothesis that turns out to be true, rather than merely generating a series of fantasies. Of course, one need not understand abduction as relying on a kind of intellectual faculty. Perhaps there is some means for generating alternative hypotheses that does not depend on any form of imagination. Inference to the best explanation can operate on any set of potential explanations, however they are generated. Yet there does seem to be a presupposition that there is some means available to generate a hypothesis that ultimately turns out to be true.

Further presuppositions depend on the scope of the alternative explanations, namely whether it is the best of the available explanations or the absolute best explanation. Consider first the case in which the scope is merely the best available explanations, which may not include an explanation that is true. Earlier I suggested that this limitation in scope need not be a problem for inference to the best explanation conceived as a broad methodology, insofar as the best of the available explanations may be part of an iterative process in which increasingly better explanations are generated on the basis of previously selected best explanation, possibly even using increasing better criteria for evaluation of explanation. The presupposition that appears operative here is that this iterative application of inference to the best explanation does in fact reach a limit yielding explanations that are true, rather than terminate in some merely pleasant fantasy. The presupposition is that the interim recognition of best available explanations enables better candidate explanations to be devised, rather than entrenching investigators in a dead end by lulling them into a false sense of security. After all, if one is in possession of what one considers to be a best explanation, even if it is only the best of the available explanations, why go looking for a better one?

Consider now the case in which the scope of an inference to the best explanation includes all possible explanations. Recall that this is the scope that Sidgwick required in order to guard against unforeseen exceptions. He even attempted to summarize all possible alternative forms that an explanation could take. While it may be tempting to ridicule Sidgwick's *a priori* attempt at comprehensiveness in his brief summary of alternatives for its presumptuousness, there is a sense in which such comprehensiveness can be achieved. First, consider any abductive explanation whatsoever, regardless of how crazy it may seem. A comprehensive set of alternatives may be generated merely by taking this explanation together with its negation. Inference to the best explanation should select the better of these two alternatives. If the negation proves to be the better explanation, though, the exercise may not appear to have been worthwhile, if, for example, it was merely demonstrated that a given phenomenon must be explained by something other than the actions of fairies or demons. Yet it would seem that this application of inference to the best explanation could likewise form part of an iterative process, as with the case in which the scope of alternatives was restricted to the available or known alternatives. If the negative alternative turns out to be the better explanation, then on this basis, a more precise positive explanation may be proposed than the previous negation, with the result that further iterations of this process would yield increasingly better explanations. The presupposition here appears to be that it is possible to evaluate a purely negative explanation in the same way that the positive explanation can be evaluated. The concern here is that in order to evaluate the negative alternative, that something other than fairies must explain a given phenomenon, for example, it is necessary to know precisely how something other than fairies is involved. If simplicity is one criteria for selecting the best explanation, for example, then a full explanatory theory would need to be devised in order to evaluate the relative simplicity of the alternatives, and it would seem necessary to rely upon more than the mere explanatory absence of fairies and demons in order to formulate such a theory. It appears that some more positive explanatory alternative would be required after all.

It might be objected in favor of this presupposition that a negative alternative need not be evaluated at all, so long as the positive alternative can be evaluated properly. If for example the positive explanatory alternative is subject to critical exceptions and counter-examples, as Sidgwick described, then the negative alternative must be correct by default, without the need for further evaluation. However, I think this objection is questionable. The role of simplicity in theory evaluation clearly requires a comparative evaluation of all of the explanatory candidates, not just one of them, so it would seem that at least some criteria for theory evaluation require that the negative alternative be evaluated alongside of the positive alternative. Furthermore, the negative alternative might be subject to exceptions and counter-examples just as the positive alternative had been. Consequently, the negative alternative might not be the best explanation if it embodies more exceptions than the positive alternative. It may be that the positive alternative could be saved by changing auxiliary hypotheses or by reformulating it by making further distinctions, so accepting the negative alternative on the basis of the recognition of some problems in the positive alternative may be premature and detrimental to the overall inquiry. In any case, I think that the ability to evaluate negative alternatives as explanations must stand as a presupposition in this sort of inference to a best explanation.

Thus, just as methodological naturalism has its presuppositions, so does inference to the best explanation. As will be shown in the next chapter, so does reflective equilibrium, the third of the contemporary methods of median philosophy that this study will investigate.

Chapter 8

Reflective Equilibrium

The idea of reflective equilibrium appears originally to have been articulated by Nelson Goodman, though he did not use the name. The issue for Goodman arises with regard to the problem of the justification of induction inherited from Hume, and Goodman proposes reflective equilibrium as a way to dissolve that problem:

> ...rules and particular inferences alike are justified by being brought into agreement with each other. *A rule is amended if it yields an inference we are unwilling to accept; an inference is rejected if it violates a rule we are unwilling to amend.* The process of justification is the delicate one of making mutual adjustments between rules and accepted inferences; and in the agreement achieved lies the only justification needed for either. (Goodman, 1983, p. 64)

Reflective equilibrium is therefore the balancing of particular judgments and general rules or principles, and consequently, the method seems to have been part of philosophical reflection from the beginning. In most Platonic dialogues, for example, Socrates evaluates the general definitions offered by his interlocutors on the basis of particular cases. Typically, the result is that the proposed definition needs to be amended or abandoned, but occasionally the judgment regarding the particular case gets adjusted, as when Theaetetus makes a distinction to preserve his definition of knowledge as perception with regard to the particular case of hearing an unknown language (Plato, 1961, p. 868, 163b–c).

While Goodman does not spend much time explicating the notion of reflective equilibrium further, John Rawls discusses the method in greater detail, and it is Rawls who gives the method the name 'reflective equilibrium'. Unlike Goodman, Rawls' concern is not induction, but the structure of a just society and the distribution of rights, responsibilities, and benefits of cooperation. Since Rawls argues within the social contract tradition of political philosophy, he is concerned to identify an initial situation in which something like a contract can be identified, and it is with regard to this initial situation that he employs the method that Goodman described:

> In searching for the most favored description of this situation we work from both ends. We begin by describing it so that it represents generally shared and preferably weak conditions. We then see if these conditions are strong enough to yield a significant set of principles. If not, we look for further premises equally reasonable. But if so, and these principles match our considered convictions of justice, then so far well and good. But presumably there will be discrepancies. In this case we have a choice. We can either modify the account of the initial situation or we can revise our existing judgments, for even the judgments we take provisionally as fixed points are liable to revision. By going back and forth, sometimes altering the conditions of the contractual circumstances, at others withdrawing our judgments and conforming them to principle, I assume that eventually we shall find a description of the initial situation that both expresses reasonable conditions and yields principles which match our considered judgments duly pruned and adjusted. This state of affairs I refer to as reflective equilibrium. It is an equilibrium because at last our principles and judgments coincide; and it is reflective since we know to what principles our judgments conform and the premises of their derivation. (Rawls, 1999, p. 18)

Rawls expands on Goodman's account in a number of ways. One is his explication of considered judgments, since not every judgment made about justice enters into Rawls' process of reflective equilibrium. Rather, only considered judgments

> ... enter as those judgments in which our moral capacities are most likely to be displayed without distortion. Thus in deciding which of our judgments to take into account, we may reasonably select some and exclude others. For example, we can discard those judgments made with hesitation, or in which we have little confidence. Similarly, those given when we are upset or frightened, or when we stand to gain one way or the other can be left aside. All these judgments are likely to be erroneous or to be influenced by an excessive attention to our own interest. Considered judgments are simply those rendered under conditions favorable to the exercise of the sense of justice, and therefore in circumstances where the more common excuses and explanation for making a mistake do not obtain. (Rawls, 1999, p. 42)

It thus may appear that the requirement to employ only considered judgments represents a further restriction on the practice of reflective equilibrium. However, the reasons Rawls presents for rejecting certain judgments in favor of more considered judgments might be understood simply to be part of the application of reflective equilibrium itself, since they are based upon epistemic principles underlying moral theory whereby moral judgments must be made under circumstances not prone to error or representative of excessive self-interest. These principles might be abandoned to allow such blatantly self-interested judgments to play a role in moral deliberation, but Rawls clearly prefers to preserve the rules and to abandon such judgments in order to reach reflective equilibrium. Consequently, I do not see the requirement to employ considered judgments as an additional constraint upon the practice of reflective equilibrium in general, but merely as an exercise of reflective equilibrium within Rawls' specific application in moral theory.

Likewise, Norman Daniels is concerned with the moral principles that enter into reflective equilibrium, and proposes what seems to be an additional constraint upon the method. His concern is "how we can be sure that the moral principles that systematize the considered moral judgments are not just 'accidental generalizations' of the 'moral facts,' analogous to accidental generalizations which we want to distinguish from real scientific laws" (Daniels, 1979, p. 259). His proposal is to require that the moral principles entering into reflective equilibrium have independent support beyond the mere equilibrium attained against particular judgments. Yet here again I tend to see this putative additional requirement as itself an application of reflective equilibrium whereby Daniels adopts a certain principle rejecting accidental generalizations as a fixed point and rejects what conflicts with that principle. However, what Daniels rejects is not a particular judgment that conflicts with a general principle, but a principle that conflicts with another principle, and this kind of equilibrium involves a further development of reflective equilibrium that Rawls makes over Goodman's account.

Rawls draws a scope distinction between narrow and wide reflective equilibrium, where the simple equilibrium between particular judgments and general principles that Goodman describes counts as narrow reflective equilibrium. In wide reflective equilibrium, on the other hand,

> we investigate what principles people would acknowledge and accept the consequences of when they have had an opportunity to consider other plausible conceptions and to assess their supporting grounds. Taking this process to the limit, one seeks the conception, or plurality of conceptions, that would survive the rational consideration of all feasible conceptions and all reasonable arguments for them. (Rawls, 1974, p. 8)

According to Rawls' account of wide reflective equilibrium, then, the method seeks not only equilibrium between judgments and principles, but a kind of equilibrium between competing conceptions. As he notes elsewhere, wide reflective equilibrium with regard to justice is "reached when someone has carefully considered alternative conceptions of justice and the force of various arguments for them" (Rawls, 2001, p. 31). Unfortunately, Rawls is not particularly clear how this comparative process is intended to work, but the end result of the process is what he calls an 'overlapping consensus' in which a certain minimal shared conception underlies the various competing accounts. It is not perfectly clear how the process of reflective equilibrium is supposed to yield an overlapping consensus, even by keeping alternative conceptions in mind. Within Rawls' particular account of justice, wide reflective equilibrium is manifest insofar as alternative conceptions of just distributions, such as utilititarianism and perfectionism, are presented as choices in the original situation (Rawls, 1999, p. 107). However, it is not clear how such wide reflective equilibrium by choice could be extended to other areas in which choice is not seen as the primary metaphor, unless Rawls is assuming that every philosophical problem can be solved by setting up something like an original situation with various veils of ignorance. So, for example, should the nature of truth be determined by setting up a situation in which rational deliberators choose a theory of truth?

One alternative for understanding wide reflective equilibrium might be that the result of an initial application of reflective equilibrium should be compared with other theories to see which one is the best. However, it would appear to be inference to the best explanation that is really the fundamental method employed in this case, since it would not seem to matter whether a proposed explanation were generated by reflective equilibrium or otherwise, so long as it was ultimately demonstrated to be the best explanation. So perhaps this alternative is not the best way to understand wide reflective equilibrium.

Perhaps Rawls does not intend wide reflective equilibrium to be a single integrated operation. Perhaps it is supposed to function as a multiple stage process: First, apply something like narrow reflective equilibrium to derive some conception of justice. Second, evaluate the extent to which that conception provides an overlapping consensus with alternative conceptions of justice. If it does not provide such consensus, repeat the process with a different equilibrium until an overlapping consensus is reached. Perhaps also the process could likewise proceed by first seeking a minimal overlapping consensus within existing conceptions of justice, then applying narrow reflective equilibrium on that minimal consensus to balance the resulting principles of justice with particular judgments. Since Rawls does not clarify how wide reflective equilibrium should work, it is uncertain whether any of these alternatives meet his conception.

Daniels analyzes the notion of wide reflective equilibrium as follows: "The method of wide reflective equilibrium is an attempt to produce coherence in an ordered triple of sets of beliefs held by a particular person, namely, (a) a set of considered moral judgments, (b) a set of moral principles, and (c) a set of relevant background theories" (Daniels, 1979, p. 258). The equilibrium between moral judgments and moral principles represents narrow reflective equilibrium, but wide reflective equilibrium according to this analysis requires the extension of this equilibrium to include background theories. Apparently Daniels considers the role of these background theories as the most important aspect of Rawls' concern with competing conceptions, but it is not clear that the notion of wide reflective equilibrium articulated by Daniels is the same notion that Rawls proposes. Different balances between judgments, principles and background theories might be attained, and there is no guarantee that any given result of this kind of equilibrium will produce the overlapping consensus between alternative conceptions that Rawls thinks is important. It seems that the results of Rawls' conception of wide reflective equilibrium might indeed yield a shared set of background theories that could represent an overlapping consensus among competing accounts of justice, since the process of wide reflective equilibrium would be conducted among these competing accounts and a state of equilibrium attained between them, whichever way that equilibrium might have been attained. However, if according to Daniels' conception of wide reflective equilibrium, background theories are simply balanced and adjusted against principles and judgments, paying no specific attention to the alternative conceptions that Rawls thought important, then there appears to be no reason to expect that an overlapping consensus will result from the process, particularly with regard to those alternative conceptions that explicitly reject the background theory that ultimately settles into equilibrium. Consequently, the notions of wide reflective equilibrium as articulated by Rawls and Daniels seem to be distinctly different.

Moreover, according to Daniels' conception of wide reflective equilibrium, I am not sure that there is a strict distinction to be made between wide and narrow reflective equilibrium. In any application of reflective equilibrium, some particular judgments are held as fixed points, and some general principles are held immune to revision. With regard to the issue of these principles that are held firm, I would ask why some principles are retained in the face of dissonant judgments while other principles are revised. If it is a question of brute stubbornness or mere personal taste, it may be wondered how reflective equilibrium can provide sufficient justification on such an irrational basis. Yet if the question of which principles to hold and which to revise were evaluated against a broad range of background theories, including meta-theoretical theories concerning such virtues of theories as simplicity and explanatory power, there would appear to be greater systematic grounds for thinking that the method of reflective equilibrium could provide justification. Perhaps this is how Goodman had conceived reflective equilibrium initially. However, this kind of equilibrium is precisely what Daniels calls wide reflective equilibrium. So it would seem either that narrow reflective equilibrium rests on distinctly irrational grounds, or that the distinction between narrow and wide reflective equilibrium is simply that wide reflective equilibrium makes explicit the grounds for holding or rejecting certain principles. Of course these considerations only apply to Daniels' conception of wide reflective equilibrium, not to Rawls'.

There appears to be another kind of scope distinction to be made with regard to reflective equilibrium, whether wide or narrow, a distinction that concerns the individual or group employment of the method. Rawls, for example, understands reflective equilibrium to be a process involving a single person (Rawls, 2001, p. 31), though he makes repeated mention of "our considered judgments" (Rawls, 1999, p. 18). This seems to result from his argumentative structure, in which he claims that it is necessary only to consider the moral deliberations of a single person under suitable conditions that would be the same for any one (Rawls, 1999, p. 120). Goodman, however, appear ambiguous on this point, though he uses the first person plural in his formulation: "A rule is amended if it yields an inference we are unwilling to accept; an inference is rejected if it violates a rule we are unwilling to amend" (Goodman, 1983, p. 64). Here the first person plural might refer either to a group or to any given individual within the group.

The importance of this scope distinction becomes manifest in a line of criticism leveled against reflective equilibrium by Stephen Stich and Richard Nisbett. They argue that reflective equilibrium is faulty because it appears to justify certain fallacies such as the gambler's fallacy (Stich & Nisbett, 1980, pp. 192–193). However, they assume that reflective equilibrium is applied by an individual person with regard to that person's judgments and principles. Later they consider ways to amend the notion of reflective equilibrium to avert such fallacious reasoning by supposing that it is only the judgments and principles of experts that matter in the application of reflective equilibrium. With regard to the passage from Goodman just cited, they claim "Unfortunately he never pauses to say who 'we' are. Now on the most charitable reading, Goodman's 'we' is taken to refer only to himself and other authorities on inductive inference" (Stich & Nisbett, 1980, p. 200). Unfortunately, they find this interpretation of Goodman's reflective equilibrium to be inadequate as well.

For my part, I fail to see the charity in their interpretation. If the interpretation of Goodman's articulation of reflective equilibrium as applying either to individuals or to a group of experts leads to a conception of reflective equilibrium that is faulty, then perhaps the interpretation of Goodman is mistaken. Stich and Nisbett note that Goodman leaves the scope of the application of reflective equilibrium ambiguous, but perhaps Goodman left the scope intentionally ambiguous. Perhaps he intended it to apply to whatever group is relevant in any given context. If the issue in question is the justification of induction to philosophers, then it is the judgments and principles of philosophers that are relevant. If the question is the nature of justice directed toward a liberal society, then it is the judgments and principles of members of that liberal society that are relevant. As it happens, this more pragmatic interpretation of Goodman yields a view that is nearly identical to the position that Stich and Nisbett ultimately advocate: "On our amended view, an attribution of justification to a rule of inference can be unpacked as a claim that the rule accords with the reflective inductive practice of the people the speaker takes to be appropriate" (Stich & Nisbett, 1980, p. 201). Furthermore, this interpretation seems consonant not only with the kind of relativism Goodman advocates later (Goodman, 1978), but also with Stich's own later arguments with regard to rationality (Stich, 1990).

Finally, a further question of scope concerns the degree to which either judgments or principles get revised in the process of reflective equilibrium. One way to bring judgments and principles into equilibrium would be to revise all of one's judgments to accord with one's principles. Another way would be to revise all principles to accord with one's judgments. The latter course may ultimately be implausible, since one may hold particular judgments that conflict with each other, thereby appearing to preclude the systematization of such judgments into general principles. Likewise, the former course may seem dubious since one may hold multiple principles that yield conflicting judgments. Yet if one were fortunate enough to start with a set of consistent judgments or principles, it would appear that reflective equilibrium could be attained not by both abandoning some judgments and revising some principles, but simply by revising all judgments contrary to one's principles, or by revising all principles contrary to one's judgments. However, neither of these alternatives seems properly to embody the spirit of reflective equilibrium, but seem to represent a kind of rationalism in one case or intuitionism in the other. Perhaps to qualify as reflective equilibrium, it would need to be stipulated that at least one particular judgment must be abandoned and at least one general principle must be revised. This would appear to be an odd requirement to make, but perhaps it is best understood not as an absolute requirement that reflective equilibrium always be employed in this way. Perhaps it is more properly understood in terms of a range of methodological procedures with intuitionism and rationalism at the extremes and reflective equilibrium between them. In this case, reflective equilibrium simply seems the more likely way that equilibrium between judgments and principles can be attained, given the possibility of conflicting particular judgments noted earlier.

Reflective equilibrium is typically understood as an account of justification for inferences, and insofar as it aims at justification, presents a strong candidate for a philosophical methodology. Since it starts with the judgments and principles held at any given time, without assigning any priority to any particular judgment and principle, it likewise seems a good model for philosophy from the middle. Although some judgments and principles may be held as fixed points that are not abandoned throughout the process, reflective equilibrium does not hold those fixed points to be foundational in the way that first philosophy holds some items of knowledge. Rather, such judgments or principles are ones that appear too obviously correct to be abandoned. It may simply be accidental that one has happened to hold such correct judgments or principles, rather than it being necessary to hold them in order to support an entire edifice of knowledge. Likewise, reflective equilibrium does not identify the end state of the process at the outset, as in last philosophy. Rather, the end state appears only when equilibrium is reached.

While the method of reflective equilibrium seems to embody a kind of coherentism, some have argued that it is compatible with at least some forms of foundationalism (DePaul, 1986; Ebertz, 1993), in which case its status as a philosophy from the middle may appear to be threatened. Yet the compatibility of reflective equilibrium with foundationalism as an account of justification does not mean that it counts as a foundationalist methodology. Indeed, the end result of reflective equilibrium may yield a theory that is foundationalist in nature, but the process of reflective equilibrium by which that theory is established is not thereby a form of first philosophy, since the structure of the process is distinctly different from the kind of process involved in first philosophy as practiced by Descartes, for example.

Reflective equilibrium has been subjected to a series of additional criticisms, but rather than rehearsing and evaluating such criticisms here, I will simply outline the presuppositions that are apparent within the method, whether those presuppositions can ultimately be supported or not. The structure of reflective equilibrium groups these presuppositions into three categories: those concerned with particular judgments, those concerned with general principles and background theories, and those concerned with the interaction between judgments and principles.

Particular judgments are sometimes called intuitions, and the epistemic status of such intuitions is the subject of some controversy. Accordingly, there is some presupposition on the part of reflective equilibrium concerning the value of intuitions. This presupposition of value is not absolute, since of course some of these intuitions will be abandoned in the process of reflective equilibrium. Yet some are held as fixed points, immune to revision. As noted earlier, there may be some question concerning precisely why some intuitions become fixed points in the process, while others are rejected. If fixed points are grounded in stubbornness or some other irrational or emotive factor, it may be wondered how the results of such a process could provide justification. At the very least, reflective equilibrium presupposes that there is some valid reason for holding certain intuitions fixed, whether due to metatheoretical concerns such as simplicity and explanatory value or to some other reason.

Intuitions are balanced against general principles in reflective equilibrium, but they should likewise be balanced against other intuitions that may conflict. So it would seem that part of the reason that some intuitions are abandoned is that one's totality of intuitions may form an inconsistent set. Yet Joseph Raz points out that putatively conflicting intuitions may be contextual in nature, whereby certain intuitions are appropriate on some occasions while other conflicting intuitions are appropriate on quite different occasions (Raz, 1982, p. 321). The intuitions conflict only when those occasional constraints are ignored. So it would appear likewise that reflective equilibrium presupposes that the process of balancing intuitions against general principles sufficiently accounts for the occasions on which intuitions manifest themselves, where those occasions may support conflicting intuitions, as with Rawls' insistence on considered judgments, as discussed above.

With regard to those general principles, there is likewise a presupposition in reflective equilibrium that those principles should serve a strong role within the resultant account of some topic of inquiry. This presupposition may seem uncontroversial, since after all, it would appear that the major result of any philosophical inquiry should precisely be a set of general principles or doctrines. However, this line of thought merely focuses the key presupposition more clearly, namely that the topic of inquiry is one in which general principles are appropriate. Perhaps morality is a topic wherein there are no general principles concerning right or wrong, whether because judgments of right or wrong are governed by emotions or because of some other reason.[1] In such a case, the imposition of general principles on judgments would appear to be a distortion of the topic in question. If indeed such general principles are inappropriate with regard to any given topic of inquiry, it is not clear that the process of reflective equilibrium could determine whether that were so, given the role of general principles in the process of achieving an equilibrium. Even if wide reflective equilibrium in Rawls' sense were employed, whereby competing ac-

---

[1] See for example (Schroeter, 2004) on the question of anti-theory with regard to reflective equilibrium.

counts of the topic were considered within the process, and indeed if at least one of the competing accounts were one that claimed that general principles were inappropriate, it is not clear that the process of wide reflective equilibrium could result in an account in which general principles were held to be inappropriate. The result of wide reflective equilibrium for Rawls is an overlapping consensus among alternative accounts, but it is not clear what sort of overlapping consensus could be found among accounts that demand general principles and those that reject them. The presupposition operative here is either that wide reflective equilibrium will somehow result in an account without general principles where appropriate, or that there are no topics in which general principles are inappropriate.

With regard to the interaction between particular judgments and general principles, a number of presuppositions can likewise be identified. One concerns the proper convergence on a correct account through the process of reflective equilibrium. The process of balancing judgments against principles does not clearly guarantee that there will be a unique equilibrium point achieved by the process. Rather, there would appear to be many ways to reach equilibrium depending upon which intuitions or principles are held as fixed points. If different intuitions or principles are held fixed, a quite different equilibrium would seem to result. This appears to be precisely the point of Rawls' insistence on wide reflective equilibrium in which an overlapping consensus among alternative accounts is sought. As suggested earlier, such an overlapping consensus might be seen as an additional constraint upon the process of balancing intuitions against principles. Although narrow reflective equilibrium may not converge on a single correct account, given the possibility of holding different intuitions as fixed points, the demand for an overlapping consensus seems to restrict the range of results from narrow equilibrium to those that can provide such a consensus. Yet here again, there would appear to be a presupposition that wide reflective equilibrium will properly converge on a single correct overlapping consensus. Perhaps several different patterns of consensus can be identified that overlap alternative accounts in different ways. So the presupposition is that something in the process of reflective equilibrium, whether narrow or wide, can properly converge on the correct account, however that may be.

Yet with regard to Rawl's particular use of wide reflective equilibrium, this presupposition does not seem to be active. Indeed, Rawls acknowledges that a plurality of conceptions might emerge from wide reflective equilibrium (Rawls, 1974, p. 8), and for his purposes, it would appear that such a plurality is not problematic. If the aim is to identify a just distribution of resources in a society, then it would not seem to matter whether there were multiple conceptions of justice that might achieve a just distribution, since it is necessary only to find one such conception, and any conception that formed an overlapping consensus would suffice. Of course, for applications of reflective equilibrium that might not tolerate such a plurality of results, the use of reflective equilibrium would indeed presuppose that the application could provide convergence on a single correct account.

A related presupposition concerns relativistic topics. While narrow reflective equilibrium appears capable of producing a plurality of different accounts, it is not clear that relativistic topics can properly be identified using that method. Narrow reflective equilibrium ends when a single equilibrium point is reached. It does not demand that there be any attempt to identify different equilibrium points to test whether the topic in question is pluralistic in nature, nor does it clearly have resources to identify any possible relativizing factors, such as cultures or conceptual schemes. Nor does wide reflective equilibrium seem to help here, precisely because of Rawls' demand for an overlapping consensus to result from the consideration of alternative accounts. Insofar as an overlapping consensus can properly be identified, it would appear that the topic in question is not relativistic in nature, since there would then be agreement among the various perspectives.[2] Yet since Rawls is not explicit on how to identify an overlapping consensus, it is not even clear that the assertion of any given overlapping consensus properly demonstrates that the topic is not relativistic, since the putative consensus may simply be imposed on the various perspectives from outside, rather than representing a genuine consensus affirmed from within each perspective. Furthermore, the mere failure to identify an overlapping consensus does not thereby establish that the topic in question is actually relativistic. The failure in question may simply represent a failure of

---

[2] See the analysis of relativism in (Ressler, 2013).

insight or imagination to see an overlapping consensus that does in fact obtain. Moreover, a failure to identify an overlapping consensus would demonstrate at most that the topic in question is pluralistic in nature. The demonstration of relativism would require the identification of certain relativizing factors, and it is not clear how the process of wide reflective equilibrium would properly identify these. So there appears to be a presupposition either that something in the process of reflective equilibrium could identify relativistic topics where appropriate or that there are no relativistic topics.

Finally, there is a question concerning extraneous intuitions and principles. Certainly some intuitions and principles get abandoned or revised in the process of reflective equilibrium, so at least some extraneous intuitions or principles will be discarded, apparently properly so. Yet there is the possibility that some extraneous intuitions and principles together could achieve a point of equilibrium, whereby the process would retain them. As a particularly pointed example, many people have intuitions concerning gods, and many traditions have a series of principles concerning such gods. The application of reflective equilibrium in theology could thereby achieve some equilibrium between these intuitions and principles to justify some account of certain gods. Yet if it happens that there are no gods at all, both the intuitions and principles would be extraneous and would therefore need to be rejected rather than justified by reflective equilibrium, if indeed truth regarding gods is a concern. Here again, this issue would seem primarily to concern narrow reflective equilibrium, while it might be thought that some conception of wide reflective equilibrium would properly exclude all extraneous intuitions and principles. For example, under Daniels' conception of wide reflective equilibrium, intuitions and principles are brought into equilibrium not only with each other, but with a set of background theories, so it would appear that the role of such background theories might include the elimination of extraneous intuitions and principles. However, this elimination would depend upon the specific background theories, so if those theories themselves had extraneous theological aspects, they would not serve to eliminate any extraneous gods. Likewise, under Rawls' conception of wide reflective equilibrium, it might be thought that the very nature of an overlapping consensus would serve to identify elements of alternative conceptions that ultimately are treated as extraneous, whereby those extraneous elements are forced out of the equilibrium by the pressures of alternative conceptions that strongly reject them. Yet this identification of extraneous material by means of an overlapping consensus depends upon the specific alternative conceptions considered. If every available alternative conception were theological in nature, it would seem that the resulting overlapping consensus would be theological in nature as well. So there appears to be a presupposition either that something in the process of reflective equilibrium will ultimate weed out any extraneous judgments or principles, or that nothing is extraneous that results from reflective equilibrium.

These are the presuppositions that I can identify with regard to reflective equilibrium. I shall not continue merely to note presuppositions of various methods of philosophy in the middle, since the repetition of such an exercise is not particularly productive. Some further analysis is required regarding the way in which these presuppositions affect the validity of a philosophical methodology, and such an analysis requires an understanding of the nature of presuppositions in general.

Chapter 9

Presuppositions

The three prior chapters have reviewed three varieties of philosophy from the middle: naturalism, inference to the best explanation, and reflective equilibrium. There are likely other varieties that might be identified, but these examples will suffice for the purposes of this study. For the most part, I have chosen not to critique any of these methods as being inadequate by demonstrating their faults, but rather have merely identified a number of presuppositions apparently made by these methods. In each case, perhaps other presuppositions could be identified, but again for the purposes of this study, the ones already identified will suffice.

It may be thought that this casual identification of presuppositions rather than an intensive critique would count as a failing of my approach here, since surely a work on methodology should properly evaluate the feasibility or unfeasibility of existing methods, either arguing for the adoption of one or more of those methods or proposing a superior method if all existing methods are faulty. That would seem to be the main point of a study of methodology, namely to determine which methods to follow within a given field of study. As I intend to show later, this kind of critique would not be feasible given the specific nature of the methodological proposals I will ultimately make in this study.

Yet regardless of these dubious promises at this point, the mere articulation of presuppositions may appear hardly to advance this study much at all. Even granted that the methods discussed have the presuppositions that I have identified, some of them may be true and some may be false. If all of the presuppositions of a method prove to be true, then it would seem that the method in question would be vindicated and should therefore be adopted. So it appears that the question of truth with regard to the presuppositions identified within the three methods should properly be evaluated. However, this line of argument seems to presuppose that presuppositions are capable of being either true or false. Perhaps this presupposition does not hold, or perhaps it itself is incapable of being true or false. So even if I were intending to evaluate the presuppositions identified in the prior three chapters, what is needed is an investigation into the nature of presuppositions themselves.

It is common to distinguish presuppositions from assumptions, whereby assumptions are suppositions that are adopted consciously or explicitly. Such assumptions are common in indirect proofs to demonstrate that the assumption in question leads to a contradiction, thereby proving the negation of the assumption. An assumption might also be made in order to grant less controversial aspects of a theory or position in order to concentrate on more critical aspects. Further, an assumption might likewise be made at the beginning of a study in order to establish a common groundwork on which the study can proceed.

While the distinction between presuppositions and assumptions is an important one with regard to language and logic, for the purposes of this study, the distinction will not much matter. Initially a methodology might be formulated on explicit assumptions as a kind of experiment. I might assume something to be the case in order to see what might be discovered if that assumption held. Later, if the methodology becomes entrenched, these assumptions may no longer be held explicitly by practitioners, but would form the background of a common practice. The difference between these stages of a methodology would appear to be the level of commitment to the assumptions. In the early stages in which the assumptions are held explicitly, the level of commitment would seem to be fairly low, precisely because those assumptions are held explicitly as suppositions that ultimately might not hold. In later stages, the assumptions might recede into the background as presuppositions, representing a higher level of confidence precisely because those presuppositions are taken for granted without further question, given the success of the methodology. Likewise, a shift between assumptions and presuppositions might occur in the opposite direction, whereby elements that are merely presupposed in an initial formulation of a methodology may become explicit after further analysis, whether that analysis identifies them merely as assumptions that must be held by the methodology or whether it seeks to vindicate the presuppositions precisely by means of the good results achieved by the methodology.[1]

In general, a presupposition is something taken for granted. In studies of language, the analysis of presuppositions has centered around two main kinds of accounts: semantic and pragmatic. Semantic accounts tend to consider presupposition as a relation between two or more statements and focus on reference and truth conditions. Pragmatic accounts tend to consider presupposition as a relation between statements and broader contexts of utterance and focus on the backgrounds of shared beliefs.

Much of the semantic account derives from Peter Strawson's critique of Bertrand Russell's theory of descriptions. One of Russell's concerns was to account for phrases that do not seem to denote anything, such as "the present king of France" (Russell, 1905). Russell held that statements including such phrases express a number of subsidiary claims such as that France currently has one and only one king. Since such a claim is manifestly false, any statement including the phrase "the present king of France" is likewise false on Russell's account. Strawson, by contrast, denied that such statements expressed the claim that France has a king, but held that those statements merely presupposed this claim. As a presupposition, the claim provides the grounds for the statement to be true or false. Since France does not presently have a king, the statement "The present king of France is bald" is neither true nor false (Strawson, 1950).

Where the semantic account holds the presupposition relation to be something occurring between statements, the pragmatic account holds that it is persons not statements who make presuppositions. The pragmatic account derives from the work of Robert Stalnaker, who describes his conception of presupposition as follows: "A person's presuppositions are the propositions whose truth he takes for granted, often unconsciously, in a conversation, an

---

[1] As for example in Richard Boyd's defense of scientific realism based on the "instrumental reliability of scientific methodology" (Boyd, 1983, p. 64).

inquiry, or a deliberation" (Stalnaker, 1973, p. 447). Accordingly, the status of statements as particular kinds of speech acts becomes crucial in the pragmatic account, where presuppositions are governed by background beliefs and conversational implicature.

There appears to be no consensus among linguistic and philosophical theorists on the correct characterization of presuppositions, and hybrid theories incorporating elements of both the semantic and pragmatic accounts have followed the early work of Strawson and Stalnaker (Beaver, 1997, p. 941). Contemporary accounts tend to rely heavily on symbolic formulation and increasingly employ the mechanisms of possible worlds ontologies.

Fortunately, I do not think that it is necessary to explore these accounts any further here, since it is not clear that a purely linguistic account will help to clarify the kinds of presuppositions that I have identified with regard to various philosophical methods. Language enters into philosophical methodologies in at least two ways. First, the methodology is typically articulated in language to explain how the method is supposed to work. Second, the method almost always expresses its results in language, rather than in music or dance, for example. Yet the presuppositions that I have identified with regard to methods do not clearly represent presuppositions of any particular statement either in the articulation or the results of the methodologies. Consider the last presupposition I articulated with regard to reflective equilibrium relating to the question of extraneous intuitions and principles. It is not clear that there are any single sentences in Rawls' *A Theory of Justice* or indeed any of his writings that would presuppose this in the way that the semantic account of presuppositions holds. The pragmatic account of presuppositions seems more plausible in that it would appear more proper to understand that it is Rawls himself not any of the sentences he wrote that made the presuppositions that I had outlined with regard to his account of reflective equilibrium. Yet insofar as the pragmatic notion accounts for presuppositions within a conversational context, it is not clear how well it would apply to the writing of a book or to the thought processes involved in planning that book. Since a methodology might well be applied in thought without ever publishing the results or communicating them to anyone, it is not clear that the kind of pragmatism embodied in linguistic accounts of presupposition is applicable to the methodological presuppositions I have identified.

I therefore propose taking a more broadly pragmatic approach to understanding the presuppositions of methodologies. Rather than considering a methodology in terms of a set of statements or a conversational context, I think a methodology is best understood as a process or procedure that has certain aims, and the success of those aims is dependent upon the truth of certain claims that are the presuppositions of the method. If the presuppositions are false, then the success of the methodology is at least threatened, if not thwarted.

The aim of a methodology is not merely the communication of statements, but the identification of statements to be affirmed or denied. The primary aim tends to be the identification of truths and the rejection of falsehoods. Perhaps it might be claimed that a methodology might aim merely to advance a field of study not to seek truth. Yet I am not sure that anyone who propounds a philosophical methodology aims merely at the modest goal of advancing a field.[2] Indeed the advancement of a field might be seen as a secondary aim of a methodology. If the primary aims of the method fail, then at the very least the methodology may have been valuable in provoking a reaction that might yield a better methodology. However, I take it that anyone who expends the effort in developing a methodology aims toward truth rather than mere instrumental advancement. This at least was my assumption in identifying the presuppositions in the last few chapters, since those presuppositions tend to be centered on the issue of the ability of the methodologies in question to identify truths. If the aim of the methodology is the weaker goal of mere advancement, then there might be different presuppositions governing that goal.

Under this conception of methodological presuppositions, it does not seem important whether the suppositions are understood as being adopted consciously as explicit assumptions or whether they are merely taken for granted as presuppositions. The aims of a methodology are dependent upon those suppositions whether acknowledged explicitly or not. The only difference this question might make would be the extent to which there is any concern in establishing those presuppositions or not within the implementation of the methodology or in the argumentation for it.

---

[2] Perhaps Richard Rorty might fall into this category, as discussed earlier in the Preface. Yet it is not perfectly clear whether providing edification as Rorty recommends should count as advancing the field of philosophy.

Thus I return to the question that started this chapter, namely whether any or all of the presuppositions that I identified in the previous chapters are true or not. Unlike Strawson's semantic account, I can accept provisionally that the presuppositions of a given methodology could be true or false. If they are true, then it would appear that the aims of the methods could be achieved, and the methodology should be adopted. If they are false, then the method should be rejected. Therefore, it would seem to be vitally important to the study of methodology not only to identify the presuppositions of various methods, but to evaluate whether those presuppositions hold or not.

Suppose that I agree with this line of thought. How am I to evaluate the truth of those presuppositions? What method should I use? Should I use the same method that presupposes them or a different one? Suppose that I use the same method and the presuppositions come out true according to that method. How can I be sure that the results of this evaluation are not merely reiterating the presuppositions of the method? The method would be likely to validate the presuppositions precisely because they were presupposed in the method itself. In other words, the evaluation of the presupposition of a method according to that method would tend precisely to beg the question. Of course, if a method were to invalidate its own presuppositions, that result would seem to be significant in demonstrating the apparent incoherence of the method, if indeed such a demonstration were possible.[3] Yet if each method were to validate its own presuppositions, a kind of relativism based on self-supporting presuppositions would appear to result.

On the other hand, suppose that I use a different method to evaluate presuppositions. That different method will have its own presuppositions that need to evaluated as well by a further different method. There might be an infinite regress involved in this case. Yet the possibility of an infinite regress is not what interests me most in this case, but rather the possibility of a kind of mutual coherence. Suppose that the presuppositions of each method could be validated by some different method, whose presuppositions in turn were validated likewise by a different method. Suppose that thereby there is mutual support between a set of differ-

---

[3] Of course, I have articulated suspicions concerning incoherence arguments in Chapter 3 above, so merely apparent incoherence is not necessarily fatal.

ent methodologies. If each methodology yields exactly the same truths in every field of application, then there would appear to be no problem, as noted earlier with regard to the question of bootstrapping by means of argument by cases. In this case, it would seem that any of the mutually supporting methodologies involved would thereby be justified, yielding a methodological pluralism, whereby any of the methodologies could be employed, since they all yield the same results. More likely, though, each method would simply yield a different set of truths, in which another kind of relativism would result, whereby truths become relative to the methods that justify them, even if each method mutually supports and justifies the others.

This question of the proper evaluation of presuppositions represents a variant of the problem of the criterion that so troubled the ancient skeptics.[4] Either something is accepted with no independent support, in which case it may be wondered why it should be accepted at all, or something is accepted with independent support, in which case it may be wondered what justifies accepting that particular support, thereby leading to an infinite regress. There would appear to be two major attempts to solve the problem of the criterion, each challenging one horn of the skeptical dilemma.

First, foundationalism challenges the attribution of a problem to the case of something accepted with no independent support. If there are items of knowledge that can provide the foundations for the rest of knowledge, then the acceptance of these foundational item of knowledge would not need to rest on any further foundations or criteria, since they would be secure and indubitable. The acceptance of other items of knowledge would indeed require additional support, but the acceptance of these non-foundational items would rest on criteria that ultimately would be justified by an appeal to the foundational items of knowledge. So there would be no problem with items of knowledge accepted without additional support, so long as those items were properly foundational items for knowledge.

Second, coherentism challenges the attribution of an infinite regress in the case of something accepted with independent sup-

---

[4]See (Sextus Empiricus, 2000, pp. 43–44), (Sextus Empiricus, 2005, pp. 7–89), and (Hankinson, 1995, pp. 193ff).

port. Perhaps this independent support would likewise need additional support before it is accepted, but an infinite regress need not ensue as a result. Rather, what may emerge is a system of mutually supporting and coherent items of knowledge, as discussed earlier.[5] The justification for any single item of knowledge would be found in the totality of the other items of knowledge within this system. There would indeed be circularity in this pattern of justification, but coherentism denies that this circularity is vicious. Rather the very coherence of the system demonstrates that such circularity is virtuous. So there is no problem with items of knowledge accepted with additional support, and no need for an infinite regress, so long as the totality of items of knowledge forms a coherent system.

If either of the attempts were valid, then it would seem that the problem of the criterion would be solved, because the problems that the skeptics identified on one or other side of the dilemma would vanish. However, the problem of the criterion would appear to get reintroduced with regard to the question of applying either of these attempts in a particular case. How does one know whether any given item of knowledge is foundational or not? How does one know whether items of knowledge within a system cohere with each other? There would appear to be a need for some criterion in each case, and it is not clear whether appealing either to foundationalism or coherentism in this higher order question would suffice, since these appeals would likewise rest on particular instances of foundationalism or coherentism. The problem of the criterion tends to be reintroduced at each particular appeal either to foundationalism or coherentism, such that an infinite regress of appeals to criteria seems to follow. Additionally, the problem of the criterion tends to be reintroduced with regard to the question of the adoption of either of these approaches. Why should I think that foundationalism or coherentism is a valid approach? There would appear to be a need for some criterion to answer that question. If it is claimed that either the foundational nature of certain items of knowledge or that the coherence of a total system of knowledge justifies either foundationalism or coherentism, then this claim seems to rest on particular instances of foundationalism or coherentism, in which the question of the criterion arises yet again in a regress. Consequently, it is not clear that either of

---

[5]See Chapter 3.

these two approaches adequately solves the skeptical problem of the criterion.

Indeed, with regard to this study, a question comparable to the problem of the criterion was asked in the Introduction, namely: What methodology should be used in evaluating methodologies? The ancient problem of the criterion is intended by skeptics to have a paralyzing effect, leaving one unsure how to think about criteria and whether to use any. The question of the proper methodology for evaluating methodologies would likewise tend toward paralysis. It is for this reason that I have conducted this investigation into philosophical methodology not as an evaluation of existing methodologies, which tends to raise the problem of the criterion. Had I attempted to solve the question of what methodology to use in evaluating methodologies before beginning, this study might never have begun. Thus it seems to me that the question of philosophical methodology will need to be solved by investigating the relation between various methods and their presuppositions, not by evaluating and critiquing those presuppositions themselves. This approach certainly does not solve the problem of the criterion, but it at least puts the problem into the background long enough to get the investigation started.[6]

One account of the relation between methods and presuppositions is R. G. Collingwood's doctrine of absolute presuppositions. For Collingwood, all propositions are answers to questions, and all questions involve presuppositions. For example, he cites the question whether a man has stopped beating his wife, which clearly presupposes not only that the man has previously been beating his wife, but also that he has a wife (Collingwood, 1998, pp. 25–26).[7] Since questions pervade philosophical and scientific research, Collingwood focuses on the logic of question and answer and the role of presuppositions within that logic (Collingwood, 1998, pp. 29–43).

Within this logic of question and answer, presuppositions are

---

[6]See Nozick's comparable reflections on starting philosophy given the inevitability of making philosophical assumptions (Nozick, 1981, pp. 18–24). As will be seen in what follows, this study takes a different approach to pluralism and relativism than Nozick does.

[7]The form of the question has an earlier history, when Alexinus attempts to confound the notoriously elusive Menedemus by asking "if he had left off beating his father" (Diogenes Laertius, 1972, p. 267).

not all of the same kind. Collingwood distinguishes between relative and absolute presuppositions as follows: "By a relative presupposition I mean one which stands relatively to one question as its presupposition and relatively to another question as its answer" (Collingwood, 1998, p. 29). "An absolute presupposition is one which stands, relatively to all questions to which it is related, as a presupposition, never as an answer" (Collingwood, 1998, p. 31). Since all propositions are answers to questions, some presuppositions of questions can be understood to be propositions that are answers to other questions, and these questions themselves have presuppositions. Other presuppositions do not answer any questions, and therefore are not propositions at all (Collingwood, 1998, p. 32). Since they are not propositions, these absolute presuppositions are neither true nor false. Since they are not answers to questions, these absolute presuppositions cannot be questioned.

This doctrine of absolute presuppositions leads Collingwood to a historicist view of metaphysics. He understands the function of metaphysics to be the identification of the presuppositions of natural science and other inquiries (Collingwood, 1998, p. 47), and some of these presuppositions will be absolute ones. Yet Collingwood argues that these absolute presuppositions change over time, citing the differences in the absolute presuppositions of Newtonian and Einsteinian physics (Collingwood, 1998, pp. 49–57). Consequently, if absolute presuppositions can change from one era to the next, then it appears that metaphysics and its associated sciences will be relative to these changes in absolute presuppositions. These absolute presuppositions cannot be questioned, so there are no grounds for critiquing them, and all that metaphysics can properly do is to identify the particular absolute presuppositions active at particular periods of time, thus making metaphysics an essentially historical science.[8]

Insofar as a philosophical methodology tends to involve asking certain kinds of questions, the doctrine of absolute presuppositions thereby places the question of methodology itself firmly within a historicist framework for Collingwood. Some questions

---

[8] Feuerbach critiques J. F. Reiff's claim "Philosophy does not presuppose anything" (Feuerbach, 2012, p. 135). Perhaps it would be more accurate to say simply that the absolute presuppositions of philosophy belong to philosophy itself, not to some other discipline, given Collingwood's claim concerning the relationship between science and metaphysics.

are asked in certain methodologies that do not arise in other ones. Insofar as these questions involve absolute presuppositions, it would seem futile to critique these methodologies other than in a historical critique. All that can be done is to identify their presuppositions, as I have done with the methodologies in the previous chapters. However, this does not mean that I thereby endorse Collingwood's historicist relativism with regard to philosophical methodology, as I will make clear later.

Of course, Collingwood's own account likewise involves certain presuppositions, or rather assumptions, since Collingwood makes most of the important ones perfectly explicit. These include the claims that all propositions are answers to questions, that all questions have presuppositions, and even that there are absolute presuppositions (Collingwood, 1998, p. 40). If any of these assumptions fail, Collingwood's doctrine of absolute presuppositions seems threatened if not completely undermined. Yet Collingwood acknowledges the historicity of his own historicist account (Collingwood, 1998, p. 358). I do not thereby think that this demonstrates the incoherence of the doctrine of absolute presuppositions. However, if this doctrine is itself historically conditioned by certain absolute presuppositions that may change over time, then at at given time it appears that a philosopher interested in methodologies could only wonder what absolute presuppositions will become active next, what methodologies they will entail, and whether the doctrine of absolute presuppositions will survive according to those methodologies.

Yet Collingwood's account of the relation between methodology and presuppositions is not the only account, and a different approach that challenges the doctrine of absolute presuppositions will be explored in the next chapter.

Chapter 10

Phenomenology

Before Collingwood articulated his historicist or relativist account of absolute presuppositions, Edmund Husserl had already rejected it. In fact, in a barrage of arguments, Husserl rejects nearly every form of relativism, particularly psychologism, which holds that certain domains of knowledge, such as logic, are dependent upon the psychology of the knower. In opposition to the relativism inherent in psychologism and historicism and the skepticism he thought they entailed, Husserl seeks a return to the kind of absolute certainty provided by a first philosophy in the manner of Descartes.

Against psychologism with regard to logic, Husserl offers three arguments. First, psychological laws seem vague and inexact, whereas the laws of logic are exact and absolute. Since "only vague rules could be based on vague theoretical foundations" (Husserl, 2001a, p. 46), the laws of logic cannot be based upon psychology. Second, even if there were psychological laws that were sufficiently exact to provide the foundations for logic, psychological laws are derived from empirical generalizations, whereas the laws of logic are known *a priori* (Husserl, 2001a, pp. 47–48). Third, if the laws of logic were based upon psychology, then they should presuppose the existence of mental states in their content, whereas the laws of logic are purely formal and presuppose no matter of fact at all (Husserl, 2001a, pp. 51–54).

Against subjectivist relativism such as Protagorean relativism according to which man is the measure of all things, Husserl argues that such claims are clearly self-refuting since there is something universal in every assertion by the very nature of assertion. Since such relativists deny that there is something universal, and thereby make assertions in denying this, they objectively refute themselves (Husserl, 2001a, p. 78). Against anthropologism, which is a form of relativism according to which truth is dependent upon the constitution of humanity as a species, Husserl argues that such relativists not only fall into the same kind of problems as subjectivists given the nature of assertion, but they also encounter absurdities by basing relativism on the fact of the constitution of humanity. Since this fact is an objective one, other objective facts follow from it that ultimately undermine the relativistic thesis (Husserl, 2001a, pp. 78–81).[1]

Against historicism, Husserl argues that "historical reasons can produce only historical consequences" (Husserl, 1965, p. 126). Consequently, even if historical research shows that some philosophical field has been essentially influenced by historical factors, that in itself would only be a historical claim, not a philosophical one. This purely historical claim does not preclude objective and absolute philosophical results through a correction of the faulty historical influences. Some of these historical influences simply have led to errors, and the way to avoid such errors in the future is to focus on objective philosophical criticism, not history (Husserl, 1965, pp. 126–128).

Clearly Husserl here does not engage with the specific kind of historicism that Collingwood espouses. It is not the case that Collingwood argues from historical facts to a philosophical conclusion, in the way that Husserl criticizes. Rather, Collingwood argues from distinctly philosophical considerations to a historical conclusion. The role of absolute presuppositions is first established philosophically on the basis of the logic of question and answer, and Collingwood subsequently argues that if different theories are espoused at different historical periods, it must be because those periods relied upon different absolute presuppositions. So Husserl's criticism appears to miss the mark with regard to Collingwood's historicism, which is not surprising since Collingwood had not even developed his position at the time that Husserl was writing, let alone published it. Curiously enough, Hans-Georg Gadamer, writing in a later phenomenological tradition derived

---

[1] For my response to Husserl on relativism, see (Ressler, 2013, pp. 264–276).

from Husserl, ultimately affirms Collingwood's position and its inherent historicism (Gadamer, 1989, pp. 369–379).

Yet what is most important here is not any historical irony or anachronisms between Collingwood and Husserl, but the way in which Husserl proceeds given his criticisms of various forms of relativism, including historicism. If there is absolute objective truth, there is a problem concerning how to obtain it. Just as for Collingwood, the key for Husserl lies in understanding presuppositions. Yet whereas Collingwood tends to accept presuppositions and their apparently relativist consequences, Husserl attempts to transcend those presuppositions.

As part of his attack on psychologism, Husserl identifies a number of presuppositions or prejudices inherent in the psychologistic position, namely:

- that whatever regulates mental life must itself be mental in nature (Husserl, 2001a, p. 101),

- that the content of logic in the form of kinds of judgments is part of psychology (Husserl, 2001a, p. 108), and

- that judgments can only be true on the basis of inner evidence that consists of a certain mental feeling (Husserl, 2001a, p. 115).

In response to these presuppositions, Husserl claims, "One's delusion vanishes as soon as one abandons general argumentation and turns to the 'things themselves'" (Husserl, 2001a, p. 101). In this case, those things themselves are the judgments of logic as they are presented to the logician, and by paying attention to these judgments, Husserl thinks that the delusions grounded in the presuppositions of psychologism will disappear. What is of special interest here is his attempt to transcend the substantive presuppositions of a particular position by investigating the phenomenology of the subject matter.

Husserl develops this phenomenological insight into a definite phenomenological method. In order to focus attention specifically on the phenomenology of something, Husserl proposes to parenthesize or to bracket the question of whether what appears to the investigator actually exists or not (Husserl, 1982, pp. 58–61). By bracketing it rather than investigating or denying the existence of appearances, he claims that the question of the existence of appearances is still present in a sense, but it is simply not used in philosophical thinking. He calls this process of bracketing the *phenomenological epoché* (Husserl, 1982, p. 60), borrowing a term the ancient Greek skeptics used to express the suspension of belief. Yet what is suspended in Husserl's phenomenological *epoché* is not all belief, only beliefs concerning existence.

With the question of the existence of what appears thus bracketed, what comes to the forefront of the investigator's attention is the structure of appearances or what Husserl calls their *essences*. Thus when Macbeth hallucinates a bloody dagger in front of him and asks whether it is a bloody dagger he sees, he seems to be asking an existential question whether there is in fact a bloody dagger suspended in the air in front of him. However, there is a phenomenological aspect to whatever it is that appears in front of him, whether real or not. By bracketing the question whether what appears to him truly exists or is a hallucination, Macbeth could have focused on the phenomenological aspects of the pure appearance to investigate the nature of the object as such that appears to him, the qualitative aspects of the bloodiness of the object, and the spatial relations of being in front of one. These questions all concern the transcendental grounds for the possibility of any appearance to any consciousness.

Of course, not all phenomenologists following Husserl accept his phenomenological *epoché* or follow it precisely the same way that Husserl does. Yet it is Husserl's version of phenomenology that particularly interests me here, not only since it is the starting point for the later tradition of phenomenology, but more importantly because it seems that few other phenomenologists were as strongly concerned with presuppositions in the way that Husserl was. Indeed, Husserl claims that phenomenology requires "perfect freedom from presuppositions" (Husserl, 1982, p. 148).[2]

Husserl's phenomenological methodology does appear to provide a view "prior to all standpoints" (Husserl, 1982, p. 38), as he claims, where substantive positions in philosophy such as realism

---

[2]Yet Arthur Schopenhauer had earlier written, "Every method in philosophy which is ostensibly *without any assumption* is humbug; for we must always regard something as given in order to start therefrom" (Schopenhauer, 2000, p. 33).

and idealism will constitute such standpoints.[3] After all, whatever becomes a subject for philosophical investigation must start as an appearance, whether as a perceptual appearance through the senses or as a conceptual appearance of ideas directly to consciousness. Were there no such appearances, there would be no philosophy and no thought at all. Consequently, there would indeed be a need to investigate the structure of these pure appearances, and Husserl's methodology does seem to provide a foundational technique to enable such an investigation.

Other philosophical theories and methodologies appear to rely on a variety of presuppositions about the nature and value of what appears to consciousness. Rather than engage with such presuppositions on their own terms, Husserl seeks to investigate what underlies those presuppositions with regard to what makes it possible for anything to appear to consciousness in order for there to be presuppositions about them at all. It is fairly easy to see why Husserl thought he had achieved the kind of first philosophy that Descartes had envisioned.[4]

Yet despite Husserl's claims to have founded a presuppositionless science, certain presuppositions of his phenomenological method can in fact be identified. Ortega insists that "a presuppositionless science cannot be a science entirely without supposition or hypothesis" (Ortega y Gasset, 1975, p. 81). B. C. Postow argues that Husserl relies on the presupposition that the kind of reflection imposed by the phenomenological method accurately represents things in themselves as they truly are, rather than distorting them precisely by means of the phenomenological *epoché* (Postow, 1976). Perhaps this is so.

More interesting, though, is that Husserl seems explicitly to acknowledge one presupposition:

> For the sake of simplicity let us assume that it is a matter of "axioms," immediately evident judgments to which indeed all the other judgments in a mediate grounding lead back. Provided that, as presupposed

---

[3] Although Gadamer would later write, echoing Schopenhauer, "The standpoint that is beyond any standpoint, a standpoint from which we could conceive its true identity, is an illusion" (Gadamer, 1989, p. 376).

[4] Interestingly, Jean-Luc Marion argues that Husserl in fact has achieved a "last philosophy" (Marion, 1999), though his conception of a last philosophy is not the same as the conception I have used in this study.

> here, they judge in the above-stated manner about individual single particulars, such judgments need for their noetic grounding — i.e., in order to make them matters of insight — a certain seeing of essences which one could designate also (in a modified sense) as a seizing upon essences; and this seeing too, like the eidetic intuition which makes essences objects, is based on sighting but not on experiencing individual single particulars subsumed under the essences. (Husserl, 1982, p. 13)

As Paul Ricœur more concisely expresses it, "phenomenology presupposes that essences and a science of essences exist" (Ricœur, 1996, p. 63). No doubt phenomenologists and interpreters of Husserl have some explanation how phenomenology can still be a presuppositionless science given this presupposition acknowledged directly by Husserl. Perhaps Ricœur was merely careless in claiming that phenomenology presupposes the existence of essences, which appears to be precisely the kind of question that should be bracketed by the phenomenological *epoché*. Perhaps what seems to be an ontological presupposition is really only a phenomenological appearance of essences. Perhaps Husserl meant only that phenomenology was free of the presuppositions of existence claims in its application not in its methodology, which the phenomenological *epoché* effectively brackets.[5] Yet if this were the explanation, then phenomenology would still operate under the kind of presuppositions that have been the object of concern in this study, and therefore it would not constitute a clear refutation of the historicism of Collingwood, since the kinds of questions posed by phenomenology would have their own set of absolute presuppositions that would be historically conditioned. There would thus appear to be some relativity of philosophical truths to the presuppositions of the various methodologies employed, including phenomenology.

What concerns me most is the question of the propriety of phenomenological treatment to any given subject matter. Indeed if I am in fact interested in the phenomenological aspects of some-

---

[5] Thus Husserl writes, "This evident character will in any case give us a descriptive mark, free from presuppositions regarding metaphysical realities, which will enable us to sort out our various classes of perceptions" (Husserl, 2001b, p. 337).

thing, then Husserl's phenomenological method obviously seems most appropriate. However, if I am concerned not with phenomenology but precisely with the questions that are bracketed by the phenomenological method, namely metaphysical questions concerning what exists, then phenomenology would appear inherently incapable of answering such questions.

There is certainly considerable phenomenology involved in questions of existence, not only the phenomenology of the object about which the question of existence is raised, but also the phenomenology involved in any attribution of existence, namely the structure of an existential attribution. Yet if the specific existence of a particular object is my concern, phenomenology would seem to be useless, since its method of bracketing bars me from contemplating anything other than phenomena. If I were to reflect intently upon some thing in order to evaluate its existence, the phenomenological method forces me to see that thing in itself as mere phenomena, precisely because the technique of bracketing has precluded the question of existence.

Likewise, since Husserl claims that phenomenology is "a purely descriptive discipline" (Husserl, 1982, p. 136), it would appear that this kind of phenomenology would be useless in addressing specifically normative concerns except in a purely descriptive manner. Indeed, I could very easily investigate the phenomenology of normativity by focusing on the purely phenomenal structure of normative claims as presented to consciousness. Yet if my interest is in making and evaluating normative claims, phenomenology would appear to be distinctly unhelpful if it can only offer descriptive analysis of normativity merely as an appearance.

On first reading Husserl, I was disappointed to discover that questions of existence are never subsequently unbracketed such that the results of the bracketed analysis could be coordinated and reconciled with the unbracketed analysis. It seems to me that this operation would have provided a much stronger general methodology, one that might indeed have proved free of presuppositions. Yet the act of bracketing remains a permanent feature of Husserl's analysis. Despite his claims that "everything excluded phenomenologically in a certain change of sign still belongs within the boundaries of phenomenology" (Husserl, 1982, p. 332), it appears that they belong within phenomenology only in a certain limited sense, namely only as phenomena.[6] Thus if my concern is precisely with metaphysical questions of existence beyond mere appearance, Husserl's phenomenological approach seems mainly to change the subject.[7]

Instead of bracketing existential claims, I might bracket precisely the phenomenology of appearances. I might ignore the peculiarities of how something appears to me, even with regard to the necessary structure of appearances as Husserl sought to establish. I might rather attempt to focus on aspects of things in themselves independently of how they might appear to me. Since any direct investigation of a thing either in perception or in thought will simply thrust me back into the realm of phenomenology, I would therefore need to employ indirect methods of investigation, possibly through mechanical means directed toward quantitative measurements. Clearly, this is the kind of investigation that physical science aims to exemplify in its methods in order to achieve full objectivity. Yet what I have called the bracketing of phenomenology does not appear to be a permanent feature of science. Insofar as science still seeks to save appearances, this phenomenology should get unbracketed at some stage in scientific experience, whereby scientific theory either explains existing appearances or predicts what would appear under certain circumstances. Yet Husserl's phenomenological method does not have a comparable stage of unbracketing, only Husserl's assurances that whatever has been bracketed still remains importantly within the scope of phenomenology.

As it happens, Husserl acknowledges that a wide range of areas of study are excluded from phenomenological treatment: "the physical and psychophysical world, ... all the sorts of cultural formations, all works of the technical and fine arts, ... aesthetic and practical values of every form. Likewise, naturally, such actualities as state, custom, law, religion" (Husserl, 1982, p. 131). None of

---

[6]Ortega's criticisms of phenomenology flow in a similar direction, but with a different focus (Ortega y Gasset, 1971, pp. 280–281).

[7]Therefore Martin Heidegger takes a different approach to phenomenology in order to address specifically ontological concerns (Heidegger, 1962, p. 62). See (Ressler, 2024, p. 21) for similar disappointments regarding Heidegger's approach as with Husserl's. Notably, Heidegger and Gadamer following him are not as concerned with presuppositions or prejudices as is Husserl, even embracing prejudices to some degree.

these are amenable to phenomenological treatment. Arguably, this list would include some of the traditional subject matters of philosophy, particularly with regard to questions concerning values and existence. If these areas are excluded from phenomenology, then how could phenomenology provide a general method of philosophy? If not phenomenology, then what methodology should be used to investigate these areas?

This line of thought appears to represent a sharp criticism of Husserl, but I do not ultimately intend it to be so. It would indeed represent a criticism if Husserl had aimed to provide a general philosophical method according to the same broad conception of philosophy as I have espoused in this study. Yet his apparent failure to provide a general method according to my preferred conception of philosophy strongly suggests that he simply does not share my conception of philosophy.

I think that it is important to remember that at the time that Husserl wrote and thought, philosophy was under severe pressure from the physical sciences. Given the theoretical and practical successes of science, as well as the sense of its continual progress, philosophy seemed almost ridiculous in comparison. Not only was there no obvious progress in philosophy, but there was not even much agreement concerning its methods and aims. Indeed, this situation with regard philosophy and science has not much changed since Husserl's time. To understand Husserl properly, I think it is critical to consider his proposals in terms of this pressure from the sciences. Given the sad state of philosophy, it appears that Husserl thought that if philosophy is to become a "rigorous science" (Husserl, 1965) comparable in stature to the physical sciences, then it must adopt different methods. If this meant that certain traditional philosophical disciplines such as metaphysics and the normative disciplines must be abandoned, then so much the worse for those disciplines. I think this is the sense in which Husserl writes about "the conception of a phenomenological science destined to become philosophy" (Husserl, 1970, p. 28). The traditional conception of philosophy certainly will not obviously be realized by phenomenological methods, but perhaps those aspects of philosophy that are not amenable to phenomenological methods are the very same aspects that are responsible for the relative contemptibility of philosophy in comparison with science. In order to save philosophy as a discipline, philosophy must be conceived differently.

This is the presupposition about Husserlian phenomenology that strikes me most strongly, namely that philosophy cannot achieve its traditional aims and therefore that the scope of philosophy must be narrowed in order to make philosophy rigorous in its methods.[8] This is clearly a presupposition that I do not share. In this regard, I think there is room for definite criticism of Husserl, but only if it could be shown that philosophy can find the means to achieve its traditional aims using sufficiently rigorous methods. Obviously, I have not yet shown this in my presentation thus far.

Yet what I would affirm in Husserl's methodological researches is that he has demonstrated the way that philosophy can generate new disciplines of research. In Chapter 4, I suggested that the physical sciences and other disciplines can generate new fields by creating specializations within the scope of their parent disciplines, whereas it appears that only philosophy can generate completely new disciplines, precisely because it is not subject to the same methodological and constitutive constraints as the sciences. This is what Husserl has done admirably, and he seems perfectly conscious that this is what he was accomplishing: "But our purpose is to discover a new scientific domain, one that is to be gained by the method of parenthesizing which, therefore, must be a definitely restricted one" (Husserl, 1982, p. 60). Husserl clearly thought that all philosophy must become phenomenological, but in the end he appears merely to have founded a new branch of philosophy. While it initially had a clear methodology in Husserl's phenomenological *epoché*, unfortunately the methods of this new branch in the time since Husserl have become much less clear.

Thus the question of a general method of philosophy would seem to remain unanswered, so long as the question of the presuppositions of various methods remains open. Both Collingwood and Husserl had answers to this question concerning presuppositions, but these answers are distinctly different, and each answer likewise depends upon certain presuppositions. Rather than transcending the methodological question with regard to presuppositions, Husserl's phenomenological method appears simply to have fallen back into this same question. On the other hand, by

---

[8]Note the close parallel with Quine's arguments for naturalized epistemology reviewed in Chapter 6.

acknowledging the historicity of his own response to presuppositions, Collingwood allows that his own account will be followed by a different response with different presuppositions. Consequently, I propose to approach the question of presuppositions from a different perspective, namely precisely from the perspective to which this question appears to lead. If all philosophical theories seem relative to the presuppositions of various methods, then this relativism would tend to lead to an attitude of skepticism with regard to philosophy in general. Yet rather than embodying an attitude of despair, I think this skepticism can in fact represent a stronger, more constructive attitude toward the practice of philosophy. So I propose to start from skepticism to see what can emerge from that perspective.

Chapter 11

Skepticism

Thus far, I have examined a number of methodologies exemplifying philosophy from the middle and have identified a number of presuppositions of each of them. However, I have refrained from adopting the usual philosophical approach in evaluating and critiquing each of those presuppositions in order to determine whether and to what extent the methodology in question is valid. Accordingly, I seem to have fallen into a form of skepticism associated with the ancient problem of the criterion. It would appear that the validity of the methodologies in question depends upon the validity of their presuppositions, whereas the validity of those presuppositions depends upon the methodology used to evaluate them. The result would seem to be that no philosophical methodology could ever properly be affirmed. Many would consider this kind of skepticism to be unacceptable, as indeed many consider any form of skepticism to be unacceptable. I, however, have considerable sympathy with skepticism.

Yet my sympathy does not extend to the kind of skepticism typically discussed in contemporary epistemology, which for the most part is a position conjured up by its opponents specifically in order to refute it. This form of skepticism deploys skeptical hypotheses in order to demonstrate that there is no knowledge at all. Consider any given item of putative knowledge, such as that I have hands. I can invoke Descartes' thought experiment and imagine that there is an evil demon that has the power to deceive me about nearly anything, including about whether I have hands or not. Yet I do not have conclusive evidence concerning whether there exists such a demon or not, so I do not know that there is no evil demon deceiving me. Consequently, the following argument appears to hold:

> *Premise*: I do not know that there is not an evil demon with the power of deception.
>
> *Premise*: If I do not know that there is not an evil demon with the power of deception, then I do not know that I have hands.
>
> *Conclusion*: I do not know that I have hands.

Notoriously, Descartes argues that there is one thing that such a demon cannot deceive me about, namely that I exist. Perhaps this is so. Yet despite the way in which this skeptical argument has exercised modern philosophy from Descartes onward, it does not represent a kind of skepticism that elicits much sympathy, indeed not from me. Perhaps the lack of sympathy derives precisely from the artificiality of the argument. Descartes and his epistemological successors expended considerable cleverness on devising the evil demon notion and other skeptical hypotheses, and it may be that this excess of cleverness is precisely what diminishes its credibility.[1]

The kind of skepticism that interests me most is represented by the ancient skeptical tradition that derives from Socrates, who claimed to know nothing. Of particular interest is the form of skepticism associated with Pyrrho, who is said to have been influenced by the sages he met while accompanying Alexander into India. As opposed to the skepticism discussed in contemporary epistemology, this form of skepticism was a living tradition, with many generations of adherents.

Modern thinking associates skepticism importantly with doubt. Accordingly, I am skeptical about something because I have some reason to doubt it, perhaps because of a skeptical hypothesis such as that of an evil demon. Although this association with doubt seems perfectly consistent with modern ordinary usage of the word 'skeptical', it does not adequately represent the ancient

---

[1]Although Descartes may have been inspired by a historical instance in devising his evil demon hypothesis, an instance recounted by Aldous Huxley in (Huxley, 1952).

skeptical tradition, much like the modern usage of the word 'cynical' poorly represents the ancient tradition of Cynicism.

In the accounts of ancient skepticism, particularly in the Pyrrhonist tradition documented by Sextus Empiricus, it is not doubt that induces skepticism, but equipollence of contrary evidence (Sextus Empiricus, 2000, p. 4). Suppose I see a tower in the distance that appears round at one time but square at another (Sextus Empiricus, 2000, p. 31). The skeptics would say that the tower seems no more round than square. In other words, the evidence for the tower being round and the evidence for it being square are equally strong, hence equipollent. Of course, many of the examples that Sextus offers seem dubious, since there should be clear ways to tell whether a tower is really round or square, for example. Yet my aim here is simply to argue that the notion of doubt is not the operative force behind ancient skepticism, rather than to justify Sextus' examples.[2]

Still, the equipollence of contrary evidence might be taken as a reason to doubt. I might doubt that the tower is really round because it appears square under certain conditions, and I might likewise doubt that it is square because it seems round under other conditions. Doubt could possibly have been the skeptics' response to equipollence, but it is not the response they actually adopted, at least according to Sextus. Rather than doubting the apparent consequences of each contrary piece of evidence, the skeptics instead suspend judgment, which Sextus defines as "a standstill of the intellect, owing to which we neither reject nor posit anything" (Sextus Empiricus, 2000, p. 5), using the term *epoché* that Husserl would later appropriate for his phenomenological technique. The suspension of judgment might seem just the same as doubt, but where doubt suggests the rejection of the object of doubt, or at least a negative attitude toward it, suspension of judgment aims at neither rejection nor acceptance, neither a negative nor a positive attitude.

Skepticism commonly appears to imply a kind of practical paralysis, as suggested by the characterization of the suspension of judgment as a standstill. If I doubt something to be true, and furthermore take a general position of skepticism according to which

---

[2]Yet Sextus does on occasion refer to doubt or perplexity, as in (Sextus Empiricus, 1936, p. 219).

everything will be subject to such doubt, then what grounds will I have for doing anything? If I doubt that food is nourishing, then why should I eat? If I doubt that there is a hole in the ground in front of me, then why should I walk around it? If I doubt that anything good will happen to me today, then why should I even get out of bed? So when Sextus claims that skeptics can follow appearances even if they do not hold beliefs, this claim may seem patently absurd. To follow an appearance that I doubt to be true seems blatantly irrational.

Yet this line of reasoning simply demonstrates that it is inappropriate to characterize ancient skepticism in terms of doubt. The suspension of judgment leaves all appearances in a neutral condition, and in that condition, those appearances may be employed or dropped as needed. If the tower appears round in some conditions, I can act with regard to the tower in accordance with that appearance as though it were round. If the tower appears square in other conditions, I can act in accordance with that appearance, as appropriate. Again, even if the particular example of the tower seems dubious, this interpretation of skepticism without invoking doubt still allows for practical action given a neutral attitude according to which appearances can be utilized or ignored as appropriate. If contrary appearances are equipollent, then they have equal claim to acceptance, so I am rationally free to adopt any of them as circumstances demand, rather than being rationally required to reject them all, as would be required under a condition of doubt.

The word 'skepticism' derives from the Greek word for inquiring, and Sextus clearly characterizes skepticism in terms of its investigative character (Sextus Empiricus, 2000, p. 3). If skepticism is understood in terms of doubt, this claim seems absurd. If I always end up doubting everything, then what is the point in investigating anything? My response again is simply that this provides another demonstration of the inappropriateness of interpreting skepticism in terms of doubt. However, even if doubt is not invoked, there is a difficulty with the supposed investigative character of skepticism, again deriving from Sextus' definition of the suspension of judgment in terms of a standstill of the intellect. It seems difficult to understand how skeptics can be essentially investigative in nature if their intellects are continually brought to a standstill.

There is a notorious story told of the skeptic Carneades, who went to Rome to discourse on justice over several days (Hankinson, 1995, p. 95). On the first day, he spoke in defense of the conventional conception of justice, and the Romans were delighted. On the second day, he refuted all of the arguments he gave on the previous day, with apparently equal persuasiveness. The Romans were understandably scandalized.

Note that Carneades' intellect does not appear to be paralyzed in this case, if he is able to produce two different, though contrary arguments. Although Carneades did not belong to the same school of Pyrrhonist skepticism as Sextus, I think that this story illustrates the way in which skeptics can truly be characterized as inquirers. The suspension of judgment still allows for the recognition of appearances, even for intellectual appearances besides perceptual appearances. Consequently, the intellect is still free to use those intellectual appearances when appropriate. Thus Carneades was able to form coherent arguments based on the conventional appearances of justice on one day, and to produce equally coherent arguments based on contrary appearances on the next. The suspension of judgment merely prevents the dogmatic adherence to one set of appearances in spite of contrary appearances. Within that suspension, Carneades was free to investigate those appearances and their consequences.

A contrast of this story with the treatment of the topic of justice by John Rawls as described earlier seems instructive. In applying the method of reflective equilibrium, Rawls needs to sort out which intuitions to retain and which to reject in order to bring them into equilibrium with particular judgments. Carneades was not obliged either to reject or to affirm any intuitions or other appearances with regard to justice. In fact, as a skeptic he would have been able to recognize equally strong though contrary intuitions, perhaps occurring simultaneously. He could keep all such intuitions in suspense and continue to investigate them without having to decide among them, whereas Rawls ultimately needs to choose between conflicting intuitions in order to bring them into a systematic balance with particular judgments, concerning which he likewise needs to make a choice of which to affirm and which to reject.

This is the aspect of skepticism that most strongly elicits my sympathy. The ability to keep contrary appearances, judgments, and even theories in suspense represents a distinct kind of intellectual strength, by allowing the investigator to preserve a form of objectivity with regard to the object of the investigation.³ Such contrary judgments might represent different absolute presuppositions in Collingwood's sense that would condition the adoption of particular overall theories, but by keeping them in suspense, the skeptic is able to investigate them all at will without falling into a form of historicism with regard to any one of them.

Yet this intellectual strength clearly has some potentially negative consequences. If everything is maintained in suspense, although I may be able to investigate everything perfectly objectively, there does not appear to be any end to such investigation, nor even does there seem to be any sense of progress. Perhaps I can pursue the consequences of appearances to increasingly greater degrees of completeness and precision, but I would also pursue the consequences of contrary equipollent appearances. Rather than waiting for the passage of time to shift absolute presuppositions in the kind of historicism that Collingwood espoused, this kind of skepticism would appear to accelerate the process by collapsing all possible historicisms into the present. In this case, skepticism and the kind of relativism inherent in historicism seem to coalesce, and if there is no clear end to such inquiries, one might begin to wonder whether there really are any facts of the matter at all, thus apparently collapsing further into a form of anti-realism.

Ultimately, one might wonder why should anyone do philosophy at all, if this is the best that can be done. Perhaps some may think that Husserl was right that philosophy needs to become something quite different, not only to become rigorous, but to remain a respectable endeavor at all. Yet I think it would be premature to adopt a quitter's attitude at this point. The apparent relativism with regard to the presuppositions of philosophical methodologies and the skepticism it seems to entail certainly pose serious problems for philosophers, but these problems do not represent sufficient reason to quit the endeavor. Instead, I think that these problems represent an opportunity for philosophy to expand and to become stronger.⁴ The key to this opportunity lies within

---

³In accordance with Nietzsche's conception of objectivity (Nietzsche, 1994, p. 92).

⁴Compare: "For this relativism and scepticism compel self-criticism and self-control and lead to a new conception of objectivity" (Mannheim, 1960, p. 42). "Scepticism, uncertainty — the position to which reason, by practising its anal-

the nature of relativism itself.

---

ysis upon itself, upon its own validity, at last arrives — is the foundation upon which the heart's despair must build up its hope" (Unamuno, 1921, p. 106).

Chapter 12

Relativism

Any philosophical methodology will have certain presuppositions. Consequently, any philosophical position or theory will ultimately be relative to the presuppositions of the method from which the theory has been developed. This situation may undermine confidence in philosophy itself if the results of philosophy ultimately reflect a subjective choice in methods, rather than representing an objective account of its subject matter. Yet instead of a lapse into skepticism at this point, what is needed is a different approach to see a way forward through this apparent impasse.

Rather than seeking to avoid such relativity as Husserl had attempted through his phenomenological analysis, I suggest that the apparent relativity of philosophical theory to presuppositions be accepted, not thereby simply to affirm some ultimate form of relativism or historicism with regard to philosophy as Collingwood has argued through his notion of absolute presuppositions, but rather to use the apparent relativism as a methodological expedient. The structure of the apparent relativism in question will rely on certain features in order to support a claim of relativism. If those features can be denied, then the apparent relativism will ultimately only be apparent, and in the process, the effort to understand how an instance of apparent relativity can be reduced to some non-relativistic form should yield a better understanding of the philosophical issue in question than what would have been achieved if the apparent relativity is simply denied. I will call this process *perspectival reduction*, since the proposed method recognizes multiple perspectives on a philosophical issue represented by the presuppositions of alternative theories and methodologies, but the proposal seeks to reduce those collective perspectives to a non-relativistic form on the basis of their initial apparent relativity.[1]

I consider this proposal to represent a fundamentally skeptical approach to philosophy, in accordance with the spirit of the ancient skeptics, though not with their specific aims and techniques. I do not know whether any of the presuppositions of the various philosophical theories or methodologies are valid or not. Nor do I know which methodologies to use in order properly to evaluate those presuppositions. It appears that those philosophical theories are relative to their underlying presuppositions, but I do not know that they are in fact relative. The proposal merely seeks to use the appearance of relativity to investigate the matter further. The basic idea in this case is the principle that the structure of the problem should contain the clue to its solution. If the problem is that philosophical theories seem relative to the presuppositions of the methodologies that produced them, then the structure of that relativity should provide the way to resolve the apparent relativity, if indeed the relativity is merely apparent.

However, the success of the proposal requires a clear understanding of the nature of relativism in order to use that apparent relativity as a basis for a perspectival reduction. It is for this reason that I completed a prior study of the nature and logic of relativism (Ressler, 2013). In that study, I developed the hypothesis that relativism was essentially a structural phenomenon governed by three theses: (1) the formal requirements for relativity, (2) the thesis of objective equity, and (3) the thesis of incommensurability.

The formal requirements for relativity outline the structural conditions in order to support a claim in the form of 'x is relative to y', where x represents some topic, such as ethics, and y represents some set of relativizing factors, such as cultures. These requirements include the demand that there be multiple different theories on the topic in question, since perfect agreement on the topic

---

[1] The notion of reduction I invoke here does not entirely accord with issues of inter-theoretical reduction and reductionism as discussed in the philosophy of science. Reduction in general indicates that something becomes smaller or simpler in some sense. If a putatively relativistic system can be reduced to a non-relativistic system, then the system becomes smaller in the sense that the resulting system does not need the mechanism of relativity.

would not indicate an instance of relativity. Likewise, there must be more than one element in the set of relativizing factors, since if there were only one culture, for example, it would be inappropriate to claim that something was relative to that single culture. These and other conditions support the mere appearance of relativity.

The thesis of objective equity encompasses the common claim that in a case of relativity one perspective is as good as another, though it seeks to be more precise in the sense in which a perspective is considered good. Ultimately, the thesis of objective equity relies on the question of shared standards for theory appraisal among the rival perspectives. If there are no shared standards, then a kind of equity would be established among perspectives insofar as there are no means for evaluating which perspective's theory is correct without prejudicing the evaluation in favor of the standards of certain perspectives to the detriment of others. However, even if there are shared standards among perspectives, there may still be a kind of equity established among those perspectives if each perspective's theory evaluates equally well according to those shared standards.

The thesis of incommensurability determines how radical the relativity in question is, whether a deep form of relativism or a shallower sort of contextualism. Whereas prior discussions of incommensurability have focused on the question of meaning and translation, I claim that the kind of incommensurability required by relativism depends rather on a structural transformation, best exemplified by the Lorentz transformations in the special theory of relativity. The question is whether there is a rule that can transform one perspective's theory into the theory of another perspective without residue. If such a transformation is possible, then the theories are commensurable, and incommensurable if not. Accordingly, from a structural standpoint, two theories might be incommensurable even if the meanings of their terms are the same, and might be commensurable even if the meanings of their terms differ.

These three theses are discussed in much greater detail in the book on relativism. What is important here is the way that these theses can provide the methodological structure for perspectival reduction. If any of the theses can be denied, then what was apparently an instance of relativism ultimately reduces to something else. Which of the theses is denied and how that thesis is denied will determine the resulting form of the reduction. So the method proposed here with regard to the apparent relativity of philosophical theory to presuppositions requires first the articulation of the rival theories and the identification of their presuppositions. Next, this apparent relativistic structure will need to be evaluated with regard to the three theses of relativism to determine which theses can be denied, if any. Depending on which thesis fails, the method will yield different results.

Consider the formal requirements for relativity. Applying what I noted earlier, this thesis requires that there be several different philosophical theories and several different presuppositions to which those theories are relative. With regard to the question of philosophical methodology, all of these conditions would seem to be met by my investigations earlier in this study, though this might indeed be challenged in some cases. Of particular methodological interest is the possibility that different theories with different presuppositions may all have common features that are invariant to any presupposition.[2] Perhaps the overall theories may strictly be different, yet if I can find in those different theories certain features that are invariant, then I might be said to have provided a perspectival reduction with regard to those features. So perhaps different presuppositions may all yield a common ontology of objects, for example. The resulting invariant ontology would represent a reduction of the apparent relativity according to those presuppositions, at least with regard to their ontology, even if those presuppositions may yield differences beyond that ontology. This kind of reduction would thus represent a version of an argument by cases, discussed earlier, whereby whatever starting assumptions or presuppositions are adopted, certain uniform conclusions follow. As already noted, it appears unlikely that this kind of demonstration would solve the most intractable problems of philosophy, since if there were invariant features across a range of different presuppositions, those features should have been noticed by now. However, insofar as this search for invariant features on the basis of different presuppositions already represents a recognized feature of philosophical practice, I would simply note that the proposed method of perspectival reduction incorporates this feature as one possible outcome.

---

[2] As Nozick proposes in (Nozick, 2001).

The denial of the thesis of objective equity entails that there are common standards for theory appraisal, and that some philosophical theory along with its presuppositions evaluates better on the basis of these standards than other theories. This again is a commonly recognized feature of philosophical practice, whereby rival theories are evaluated and criticized in order to show how one theory is better than others. Of course, the thesis of objective equity requires that the criticism of rival theories be based upon standards that are shared by those rivals, and this is the aspect of this practice that has been most problematic. Any criticism of rival theories very often can be shown to depend upon the presupposition of certain standards which those rival theories do not share, and this recognition of varying standards of theory evaluation tends only to reiterate the kind of apparent relativity according to presuppositions that I have already posited. Yet I would note again that this recognized feature of philosophical practice likewise finds a place within the method proposed here. Clearly this is not an aspect of philosophical practice that will vanish.

What suggests a novel approach to philosophical practice is the denial of the thesis of incommensurability. If there is a transformation rule between rival theories, then the kind of relativity between those theories is not especially radical. It would still represent a form of relativity, but it would seem to be a more consonant form of contextualism rather than a dissonant relativism. Furthermore, the pattern of commensurability inherent in those transformation rules should help to illuminate the topic under investigation. Just as the Lorentz transformations in the special theory of relativity that provide commensurability between measurements within different inertial systems become part of the conception and analysis of space and time, so the recognition of commensurability with regard to some topic in philosophy would become part of the conception and analysis of that topic. So whereas some ethicists seek to identify invariant features of rival ethical systems, and others seek to establish one of those rivals as the best one, one might instead seek ways to transform one ethical theory into another, for example. If that were possible, then it would appear that the transformation pattern between these rival ethical theories should itself become part of the understanding and analysis of ethics.

This method is somewhat analogous to the method of triangulation in which an absolute position is computed on the basis of multiple relative perspectives.[3] The use of multiple perspectives is not adopted just for the sake of acknowledging those perspectives, but to increase the degree of objectivity and to identify something beyond mere perspectivism that still acknowledges the role of perspectives. If a perspectival reduction were accomplished by means of the identification of invariant features across perspectives, those invariant features would be inherent within each single perspective, but it might not be evident that those features were invariant unless multiple perspectives were considered. If a perspectival reduction identified a single theory that was better than its rivals, this superiority might not be recognized unless all its rivals were evaluated and shared standards between them were identified. More importantly, if a perspectival reduction yielded a transformation rule that provided commensurability between perspectives, that rule could not be derived from a single perspective, but requires the consideration and coordination of multiple perspectives.

I noted earlier that the search for invariances and the identification of an objectively preferable theory are well-recognized aspects of philosophical practice. The technique of commensurability does not seem to be very well appreciated, though there are some predecessors to this technique, as will be acknowledged later.[4] Since the search for commensurability between perspectives represents the novel aspect of the method proposed here, I will focus the remainder of this study on this technique.

Of course the question of how commensurability rules can be devised is not readily answered by what I have said thus far, nor even in my study of relativism. Indeed, perhaps commensurability rules cannot be generated by any special method, but rely upon the ingenuity of particular investigators. They might best be understood as abductive hypotheses, as Peirce had discussed, that arise from a kind of insight, but need to be tested to determine whether they indeed can transform rival theories into each other to demonstrate commensurability. Perhaps the investigation into the gener-

---

[3]The notion of triangulation in a methodological context has become common in social sciences. See for example (Tiainen & Koivunen, 2006). Sven Ove Hansson likewise invokes the notion of triangulation in the context of methodological pluralism (Hansson, 2010). Using a different metaphor, Sellars speaks of combining a manifest image with a scientific image "in one stereoscopic view" (Sellars, 1991, pp. 10–11).

[4]See Chapter 21.

ation of commensurability rules might benefit from a historical approach, by examining the way in which the example I have offered of commensurability rules was discovered. How did Lorentz work out his transformation equations, and how did Einstein come to apply them within his special theory of relativity? Perhaps a study of these questions could yield some insight into the development of commensurability rules in other areas. I am not especially qualified to answer those historical questions. In any case, I can only admit that if there is a general method for deriving commensurability rules, I do not know it, and if this method were known, that would constitute a significant achievement for philosophy and likely for other disciplines.

Yet using the Lorentz transformations as a model provides some clues for the form that such commensurability rules might take. The Lorentz transformations identify a number of dimensions across which values are adjusted between inertial frameworks, namely the three spatial dimensions and the temporal dimension. Importantly, those dimensions are linked directly to those frameworks, since inertia is understood as resistance to a change in a state of motion, and motion is understood in terms of these dimensions. Thus it seems that commensurability rules in general should likewise identify a number of dimensions across which the transformation between theories will occur, by means of shifting values across those dimensions. Further, these dimensions should be related importantly to whatever relativizing factor appears in the instance of putative relativism in question. So if something appears relative to cultures, for example, then it should be some aspects that define or differentiate cultures that could provide the potential dimensions that would form the basis for a commensurative transformation. Since the general philosophical method proposed here is occasioned by the apparent relativity of philosophical theories to presuppositions, the dimensions involved in perspectival reduction would likely relate either to the specific presuppositions identified in a particular case or possibly to the nature of presupposing in general.[5]

---

[5] So while it might be thought that commensurability is merely an instance of isomorphism between theories, it seems to me that the role of dimensions within commensurability rules suggests that something additional must be operative within commensurability. There is no restriction here that commensurability rules should preserve the number of statements or entities within a theory, for

One attempt at a criticism of this proposal can be anticipated and refuted at this point, namely the possibility of vacuous commensurability. Someone might attempt to show that commensurability rules can be identified for any set of competing theories by devising some proxy function, similar to the proxy function that Quine uses to demonstrate ontological relativity (Quine, 1969, pp. 55–58), according to which any arbitrary theory might be transformed into any other. If this were possible and commensurability could be established so easily, then the proposed method of perspectival reduction would essentially be worthless.

Suppose that such vacuous commensurability by means of some proxy function were possible. The mere fact of a transformative proxy function does not establish the kind of commensurability operative here. The method requires understanding the dimensions across which commensurability is achieved to be part of the analysis of what is being investigated. If vacuous commensurability can be completed across dimensions that are applicable to anything at all, then it would appear that the commensurability is not specific to what is being analyzed. The dimensions across which the proxy function operates may indicate that there is some commensurability operative in some way, thus indicating that the apparently vacuous commensurability may not be so vacuous after all. Rather, it might simply be directed toward a different topic of analysis than the topic to which an instance of perspectival reduction should properly address. It is in this way that I understand Quine's proxy functions to work, by directing attention toward the commensurability between the syntax of a language and its semantics, and thus justifying Quine's attribution of *ontological relativity* rather than *ontological relativism*, according to the distinction offered in (Ressler, 2013, pp. 44–50, 180–188). For perspectival reduction to succeed by virtue of commensurability, the dimensions across which commensurability is achieved must be grounded precisely in the topic of the competing theories, such that those dimensions and the resulting commensurability become part of a successful analysis of the topic in question. A proxy function that vacuously transformed any set of theories on any topic would likely be directed toward some aspect of those the-

---

example. Compare the account of commensurability in (Ressler, 2013) with Nelson Goodman's account of extensional isomorphism in (Goodman, 1966, pp. 13–22).

ories as theories, such as the language in which they are expressed, not the topic of those theories.

The proposed method of perspectival reduction does not hold that a reduction will be possible in every case, and in that respect, the proposal further represents a skeptical approach. If indeed none of the three theses of relativism can be denied in the case of the apparent relativity according to presuppositions, then it may be the case that Collingwood was correct, and that ultimately philosophy is relative to absolute presuppositions, at least in certain areas. If there is a complete failure of any commensurability rules between rival ethical systems, for example, then perhaps ethics is ultimately relativistic after all. Yet the conclusion of relativism on the basis of the inability to complete a perspectival reduction may be unwarranted or premature. After all, a perspectival reduction might eventually be possible even if no existing philosopher is capable of completing it, whether because of current widespread intellectual prejudices or simply because there is no one sufficiently ingenious to see how a reduction can be completed. In the book on relativism, I suggested that incommensurability might only be able to be demonstrated on the basis of an indirect *reductio ad absurdum* proof by assuming that some commensurability rules were possible, then demonstrating that absurd consequences follow, just as Euclid argued his incommensurability proofs in geometry (Ressler, 2013, pp. 158–160, 186–187). However, it is not clear that such demonstrations would be possible without relying on certain presuppositions that themselves could be in question. Indeed, Euclid himself relied upon certain axioms and postulates that can be seen as presuppositions, the denial of one of which yielded an important range of non-Euclidean geometries. Failing the possibility of a presuppositionless indirect proof of incommensurability, I would recommend a skeptical approach in this case by suspending judgment on whether the topic in question is truly relative to its presuppositions and would suggest that further investigation should continue until commensurability rules could be identified. So in practice, I suggest that no conclusion of relativism should be affirmed as a result of a failure of perspectival reduction, since future research may uncover the commensurability rules that would deny such relativism.

It has been a common claim that relativism is ultimately incoherent. If this claim is correct, then it would appear that the kind of perspectival reduction advocated here must always ultimately succeed, since its failure would result in incoherent relativism. I have been highly suspicious of the claims of the incoherence of relativism, particularly given that most such claims ultimately rely on certain presuppositions not shared by relativists. For that reason, I attempted to work out the logic of relativism in a way that charitably represented the claims even of global relativism, and on the basis of that logic demonstrated the formal coherence of global relativism (Ressler, 2012, 2013). While not all arguments for the incoherence of relativism can be adjudicated by an appeal to formal logic, it seems to me that all such arguments rest upon certain presuppositions that might clearly be challenged (Ressler, 2013, pp. 264–276). Consequently, I do not think that arguments for the incoherence of relativism properly guarantee the success of perspectival reduction. Again, I would recommend a measure of skepticism and continued investigation. Let the success of specific instances of perspectival reduction demonstrate the untenability of relativism, rather than a prior commitment to any putative incoherence of relativism in general.

In discussing other methodologies earlier in this study, I took great pains to point out their presuppositions, so in advocating the method of perspectival reduction over these methods, it might be thought that I am suggesting that this method has no presuppositions. However, I understand perfectly well that this method must have some presuppositions, and if I do not here point out those presuppositions, it is likely because I am too much involved in advocating this method to appreciate properly what those presuppositions are. Others will no doubt take up this task later. Yet let the presuppositions of this proposed method be what they are. I do not claim that perspectival reduction is immune to its own methods. Perspectival reduction requires the identification of the presuppositions of rival theories, followed by the attempted reduction of the apparent relativity of those theories precisely on the basis of those presuppositions. In yielding some result, this method would appear to generate yet another rival theory whose presuppositions would include the presuppositions of the method. Then let the results of this method be incorporated back into a further iteration of the method and see what emerges. Let the results of perspectival reduction be taken together with the initial set of rival theories that occasioned the first iteration of perspectival reduction, along with the presuppositions of all the methods, including perspectival reduction. Then let a further instance of perspectival reduction be performed, and indeed still further instances against the results of this new instance of perspectival reduction. As noted earlier, it seems that philosophy from the middle should be an iterative process, and perspectival reduction supports precisely such iteration.

A number of patterns of repeated application of perspectival reduction could be anticipated from these iterations:

Convergence Repeated iterations converge upon a single stable result.

Divergence Repeated iterations continually generate different, non-convergent results.

Repetition Repeated iterations do not converge upon a single result, but yield a series of different results that continually recur in some pattern.[6]

The most favorable case would be the convergence upon a single stable result, in which case it would appear that the resulting theory would have a strong claim to be the correct account of the topic of investigation. The results would seem to indicate that the use of differing perspectives has successfully triangulated upon some stable truth beyond mere perspectives. Divergence and repetition, though, would present problems in interpreting the situation. Divergence might for example suggest that the investigation has uncovered a case of anti-realism in which there is no fact of the matter, or it might suggest that the attempt to show commensurability between perspectives in the various iterations have been faulty in some way. What a pattern of repetition might suggest, I cannot now guess.

Yet at this point, some doubts might arise concerning the feasibility of this proposed method, precisely on the basis of certain conditions or presuppositions of perspectival reduction. The method would seem to require that the alternative theories that

---

[6]Note the similarity with Gupta and Belnap's Revision Theory of Truth discussed earlier, according to which stable patterns of truth assignments are sought upon subsequent revisions, but where paradoxes oscillate truth-value assignments. Whether this similarity is significant, I do not yet know, but should emerge from an application of perspectival reduction to competing theories of truth.

enter into the method are complete to the extent that the consequences of the presuppositions are worked out fully and that the theory has been adjusted to eliminate any inconsistencies. Including any incomplete theory in the application of this method would risk allowing the potential failings of those incomplete theories to undermine the quality of the results of the method. If the inputs to the method is faulty, then faulty output should be expected. However, it is not clear that any philosophical theory is complete in this sense.

A second condition appears to be that alternative theories must be adequate, in the sense that they must provide viable explanations of the topic in question. If I am concerned with ethics, it would seem that I should only be interested in alternative theories that adequately explain all aspects of ethics. Including an inadequate theory in the application of this method would likewise appear to compromise the quality of the results. However, again, it is questionable whether any philosophical theory is adequate in this sense.

A third condition seems to be required by the search for commensurability rules. The dimensions that figure in such commensurability rules need not be quantitative in nature, as in the Lorentz transformations; however, it does appear that in order to formulate commensurability rules and to verify that the rules do in fact transform one theory into another, it is necessary for the alternative theories to be formalized according to some formal system. Perhaps this is not an impossible condition to be met, but it is certainly a difficult one, particularly given that the two previous requirements of completeness and adequacy would oblige the theories in question to be quite extensive.

Given these difficult conditions, it would seem that the proposed method of perspectival reduction could not practically be conducted at all. Consequently, the method would appear merely to articulate a desired idealization, which might be useful and effective if it were possible, but given its practical infeasibility, ultimately only expresses a wish. Since the method seems to be unfeasible, it may be wondered why I should bother to articulate it at all. Worse still, it might seem perverse of me to offer a method that appears to hold so much potential, only to snatch it away immediately because that potential can never be met.

Yet I disagree with this overall assessment. By hypothesis, even if the apparent conditions of the method cannot be met, even if the method ultimately represents an over-optimistic idealization, this does not indicate that this idealization can have no practical methodological impact. Rather than focusing on the conditions for the application of the proposed method and lamenting that they seem too difficult, I suggest examining the nature of the ideal results of such an ideal application to identify the qualities that such results would have. Those qualities would then represent certain virtues that philosophical theories would have if they had resulted from the application of the method. Those virtues would represent theoretical virtues regardless of the feasibility of any actual instance of perspectival reduction. Thus if I were to encounter a philosophical theory that exemplifies those virtues, I could consider them to have the same merits as if they had been derived by perspectival reduction, even if they had in fact been generated according to some other methodology.[7] Moreover, the articulation of the full methodology, even if only an ideal, would still serve a useful function by directing the attention of philosophers to that new ideal. Perhaps in time the conditions for applying the full methodology directly will not appear as difficult as they do upon initial explication.[8]

If an application of perspectival reduction were to result in the recognition of certain invariant features or in the affirmation that one theory that was objectively preferable to the other, the ideals exemplified by these results would already appear to be fairly well understood. They exemplify the ideals inherent in the notion of objectivity.[9] Consequently, I will focus on perspectival reduction by means of commensurability rules.

Suppose then that perspectival reduction has been performed on some set of alternative theories with regard to some topic, specifically by seeking commensurability between these alternatives, and that the results of this process have been thrown back

---

[7] As will be argued regarding one theory of explanation in Chapter 14.

[8] In this way, I reinterpret Dewey's phrase "experimental logic" (Dewey, 1916), namely, let the method be attempted, rather than dismissed on *a priori* grounds. Even if philosophy is indeed an armchair enterprise, that does not mean that it should involve no work or effort.

[9] Even if there is some disagreement on the nature of objectivity, the general idea underlying them seems clear enough. See (Daston & Galison, 2007) for a study of the development of various conceptions of objectivity.

repeatedly into further iterations of the method. Suppose further for the sake of simplicity that these iterations ultimately converge upon some single resulting theory. The question now is what theoretical virtues this result would demonstrate specifically due to the application of the perspectival reduction, separate from other theoretical virtues already recognized, such as simplicity, predictive power, and so forth. I suggest that two important virtues can be identified:

Competitive subsumption Competing theories have been placed into a commensurative relation, according to the assumption, which means that each of these theories can be transformed into each other by means of the commensurability rules indicated by the results of perspectival reduction. These rules become part of the analysis of the topic in question in the resulting theory. As a consequence, then, all competing theories should be subsumed in some important way under the results of perspectival reduction such that those competing theories can be recovered from the perspectival reduction. A theory that exhibits this feature would thereby exemplify competitive subsumption.[10]

Reflexive reiteration The results of perspectival reduction have been incorporated within further iterations of perspectival reduction, according to the assumption, with the end result that the ultimate theory to which the process converges will always yield itself again, should any further iterations of the process be conducted. Because it is the result to which the process converges, any further application of the method will simply reiterate this same result. So this resulting theory should be able to reiterate itself in some important way in its articulation. A theory that exhibits this feature would

---

[10]Compare Brand Blanshard's arguments against criticisms of the coherence theory of truth (Blanshard, 1939, p. 276). Where a line of criticism suggests that two alternative systems may be equally coherent, Blanshard challenges whether that alleged coherence can be maintained when the requirement for comprehensiveness is honored, particularly comprehensiveness with regard to whether the plan for one system is included within the other. See also Huizinga: "They are all only partial solutions of the problem. If any of them were really decisive it ought either to exclude all the others or comprehend them in a higher unity" (Huizinga, 1950, p. 2).

thereby exemplify reflexive reiteration.[11]

If indeed the proposed method is sound, these two qualities would appear to merit recognition as virtues of philosophical theories. Yet rather than christen them as radically new theoretical virtues, I prefer to understand them as aspects of existing virtues that may not have been appreciated sufficiently well. I tend to see competitive subsumption as an aspect of explanatory power whereby the theory that exemplifies this virtue can explain not only the topic in question but can also explain competing theories on this topic. After all, the variance in the competing theories of some base phenomena itself appears to constitute a kind of phenomenon that would likewise need to be explained.[12] Additionally, reflexive reiteration seems to be an aspect of consistency in the form of self-consistency whereby the theory finds a place for itself within itself. Indeed, a good theory should be able to explain how its own theory is possible if the world is as the theory says it is.

What results from these considerations and proposals is a pluralistic meta-methodology, a method that acts upon other methodologies, whether in its full articulation or in the application of the two theoretical virtues it embodies. To the question concerning which methodology philosophy should employ, I would reply *any and all methodologies*, so long as their results are coordinated through perspectival reduction, whether by seeking explicit commensurability rules or by seeking theories that exemplify the theoretical virtues of competitive subsumption and reflexive reiteration. It is for this reason that I did not criticize the other methodologies explored earlier in this study by evaluating whether their presuppositions were supported or not. Given the method I propose here, such an evaluation would have been counterproductive, since perspectival reduction by means of commensurability rules does not seek to reject various presuppositions, but rather uses those presuppositions within a process of triangulation to provide greater understanding. Ultimately, it would seem

---

[11] Robert Nozick has formulated a similar idea that he calls "self-subsumption" (Nozick, 1981, pp. 199ff).

[12] The practice of making distinctions seems to embody some aspect of competitive subsumption, by showing that contrary views can be incorporated into a more comprehensive account, namely an account in which further distinctions are made. See more on distinctions in Chapter 19.

that any presupposition has the potential to reveal the nature of any topic in question, even presuppositions that are in error.

Chapter 13

Error

There are certainly many grounds for concern with the method proposed in the last chapter, particularly with regard to the imprecision surrounding the formulation of the alleged theoretic virtues of competitive subsumption and reflexive reiteration. More urgently, perhaps, is a concern with the general demand to incorporate alternative theories in the initial stages of a perspectival reduction. Some or even most of these theories may simply be in error, even if they are sufficiently comprehensive. If the search for commensurability rules must take account of these erroneous theories, then it would seem that the error infecting these alternative theories would spread their contagion throughout the entire methodology, thus yielding error in the final results. To use the metaphor of triangulation that I employed to characterize the method of perspectival reduction, if even one of the compass readings that I use to triangulate a location is in error, then the location that I compute from the method of triangulation would thereby be erroneous. While the notion of using multiple perspectives on a topic in order to increase objectivity sounds like a fruitful idea, the clear possibility of gross error distorting the results of the method ultimately would appear to make the proposal impractical. Rather than incorporating every perspective in the method, it would seem to be critical to determine which perspectives are erroneous and to eliminate those perspectives. However, the problem of determining what methodology to employ in determining erroneous perspectives appears merely to reiterate the general methodological problem of this study, so it may seem that the proposed method of the last chapter does not advance the aims of this study at all.

Briefly, my response to this concern is that even error can reveal truth.[1] There must be some grounds of truth within an error in order for an error to occur. If I mistake one thing for another, there must be something in the object of my mistake that makes me misidentify it, and this something is not an error, only the judgment based on it. The reason that I misidentify an object has something critically to do either with my perspective on that object or with myself. What the method of perspectival reduction seeks to do is to identify what is true within any perspective, even grossly erroneous perspectives, precisely on the basis of what constitutes that perspective, and to coordinate the truths of the various perspectives into a single account of the topic.[2] The elaboration of this brief response will also help to clarify the notion of competitive subsumption.

Consider the idea of an error theory as used by John Mackie in his ethical theory. Mackie's thesis is stated baldly: "There are no objective values" (Mackie, 1977, p. 9). This thesis by itself does not prompt the need for any error theory, however. The issue of error enters into Mackie's account under pressure from a version of linguistic philosophy that holds that philosophical issues can be settled in some important way by clarifying the meanings of the terms and concepts used in philosophical and ordinary discourse. Mackie does not share this vision of linguistic philosophy. Thus when philosophers of this sort claim that the concepts used in moral judgments presuppose the objectivity of values, Mackie is happy to concede that objectivity is clearly implied by such judgments. However, such presuppositions are in error, since there are no objective values. Hence, Mackie's error theory is directed toward the higher order judgments about values implied within ordinary moral discourse, not primarily toward the judgments themselves. It is those higher order judgments concerning the objectiv-

---

[1] Ortega claims "The error must contain some element of truth" (Ortega y Gasset, 1967, p. 25), likewise (Ortega y Gasset, 1946, p. 128). Dewey holds that "The existence of ignorance as well as of wisdom, of error and even insanity as well as of truth will be taken into account" (Dewey, 1958, p. 20). Likewise, Nozick claims that even falsehoods can be illuminating (Nozick, 1981, pp. 11–13).

[2] "...everyone says something true about the nature of things, and while individually they contribute little or nothing to the truth, by the union of all a considerable amount is amassed" (Aristotle, 1984, p. 1569, 993b1–4).

ity of right and wrong that are in error, not necessarily the judgments of what is right and wrong.

The notion of error theory seems primarily to consist in the imputation of error within the concepts inherent in ordinary discourse. Yet Mackie recognizes that more than a mere imputation of error is sufficient. He also demands "that we can explain how this belief, if it is false, has come to be established and is so resistant to criticisms" (Mackie, 1977, p. 42), and he accordingly provides such an explanation with regard to his error theory on the basis of Humean projectivism. Thus error theory for Mackie also includes the requirement for a theory of error, namely a theory concerning how the error in question could possibly arise. This is the aspect of error theory that is particularly relevant to the concerns surrounding error in perspectival reduction. The idea of competitive subsumption can be understood in terms of providing an explanation of competing theories on the basis of a more comprehensive theory, including an explanation of the apparent errors of competing theories.

Suppose that I were to advocate a theory on a given topic, well aware that there are competing theories on that topic. Then my theory must be such that it should be possible for competing and erroneous theories to arise on the basis of my theory, if it were true. Otherwise, the mere existence of erroneous theories would appear to count against my theory, if my theory precluded the possibility that anyone could come to formulate an erroneous theory. Therefore, any theory that I advocate must be able to explain the errors of any competing theories on the basis of my theory.[3] For example, John Locke seems to be relying on this principle in his dispute with Edward Stillingfleet, the Bishop of Worchester, concerning the question of whether there is an innate idea of some god. If there were such an innate idea, perhaps it would be possible to explain how Locke could make the mistake of denying this innate

---

[3] Aristotle acknowledges something like competitive subsumption in terms of providing an explanation of errors (Aristotle, 1984, p. 1824, 1154a22–27), also cited in (DePaul & Ramsey, 1998, p. 278). Curiously, in his *Three Dialogues Between Hylas and Philonous*, George Berkeley makes Philonous claim "It is not my business to account for every opinion of the philosophers" (Berkeley, 1906, p. 36), but then has him provide precisely such an account. Ortega claims "our newest concept has the obligation to explain the old ones" (Ortega y Gasset, 1960, p. 227).

idea while still believing in a god, but it would not seem possible to explain the case of atheists who not only deny this innate idea but also deny the existence of any god (Locke, 1823, p. 495).[4] As another example, consider the argument by Henry Sidgwick that Utilitarianism can provide an explanation for the common sense rules of ethical Intuitionism (H. Sidgwick, 1901, p. 494).[5] This argument appears to embody a claim of the competitive subsumption of Intuitionism within Utilitarianism. Unfortunately, the third method of ethics that Sidgwick considers, Hedonism, does not likewise appear to be subsumed within Utilitarianism and therefore it would seem that Utilitarianism does not exhibit full competitive subsumption.

Explanations of erroneous competitors cannot merely be given on the basis of the competing theory alone. The way in which erroneous theories may reveal the truth may not be apparent simply from those theories themselves. Someone who advocates an erroneous theory is not always acting irrationally, since the errors in question may seem perfectly rational under certain conditions. Therefore, some account must be taken of the perspective from which the competing theory is offered. This would appear to require taking into account not only the nature of the competing theory but also the nature of those who would advocate such a theory, since there would appear to be something about the condition of the advocate of the competitor that makes the wrong theory seem to be the right one. The most revealing aspect of advocates of erroneous theories is the presuppositions they adopt, whereby the particular presuppositions adopted may support an erroneous theory, while different presuppositions would reject it. Since in perspectival reduction it is precisely the presuppositions of rival theories that are used to coordinate the various perspectives, this method appears well suited to provide an explanation of erroneous theories, but only on the basis of the results of the method, not by attributing error at the outset.[6]

---

[4]Étienne Gilson recounts this case in (Gilson, 1999, p. 136).

[5]Mackie cites this case, but challenges Sidgwick's claim (Mackie, 1977, p. 126).

[6]It is for this reason that perspectival reduction should not be suspected to involve any *ad hominem* fallacy. It is not that a rival theory is rejected as erroneous because of some personal aspect of whomever advocates the theory, but that a rival theory is acknowledged as erroneous on the basis of the greater ability of a different theory to explain how someone could hold that rival theory to be true.

Note that the proposed virtue of competitive subsumption is not unique to perspectival reduction by means of commensurability rules, but is also applicable to the two other means of effecting a perspectival reduction. If there are invariances among all competing perspectives, there would seem to be some explanation needed of how those perspectives can still be different, if indeed they have invariant features. If one theory is objectively preferable over its competitors, there would seem to be some explanation needed of how those competing perspectives could be mistaken if there were an objectively superior perspective available. The virtue of competitive subsumption addresses both of these needs.

Recall that the notion of error was introduced in this chapter as part of a supposed concern or criticism of the proposed method of perspectival reduction. The concern was that some of the alternatives that form the basis of the method may simply be erroneous. From what has just been argued, it seems that perspectival reduction by means of commensurability rules tends to erode the notion of error, at least with regard to its negative connotations. Indeed, any theory that falls short of a final true theory is thereby erroneous, but insofar as errors do arise within the world that must be explained by that final true theory, the virtue of competitive subsumption exemplified by that final true theory would hold those errors not as wicked aberrations, but precisely as what would follow naturally when certain conditions are met. Those conditions would determine some perspective, and that perspective would yield a competing theory. The subsumption of that competing theory within the final true theory would ultimately support the comprehensiveness of that final theory.

Yet the notion of competitive explanation has already been disparaged by Stephen Pepper as part of his doctrine of world hypotheses. Pepper claims that differing metaphysical systems can be attributed to differences in their root metaphors, which seem to correlate very closely to Collingwood's notion of absolute presuppositions and the resulting historicism that Collingwood concludes. Pepper identifies four fundamental root metaphors that have shaped metaphysics thus far: Formism, Mechanism, Contextualism, and Organicism (Pepper, 1942), later suggesting that a fifth root metaphor might be found in Existentialism (Pepper, 1970). With regard to these root metaphors, Pepper claims, "It is illegitimate to disparage the factual interpretation of one world hypothesis in terms of the categories of another — if both hypotheses are equally adequate" (Pepper, 1942, p. 98). This illegitimacy extends precisely to the kind of competitive explanation that I have been advocating here:

> The exponents of the theories which we are about to study have in the past, almost to a man, been dogmatists. They have believed their theories implicitly, accepted their danda [evidence] as indubitable, and their categories generally as self-evident.
>
> One reason they have been so sure of themselves is that whichever of these hypotheses they have espoused, they have been able to give relatively adequate interpretations in their own terms of the danda and categories of the other hypotheses. "You see," they say, "we are able to explain what these other mistaken philosophers have thought to be facts, and to show where the errors of their observations lay, how they rationalized their prejudices, accepting interpretations for facts and missing the real facts. Our hypothesis includes theirs and is accordingly the true account of the nature of things."
>
> This would be a good argument if the other hypotheses were not equally well able to make the same argument. Among the facts in the world that a relatively adequate world theory must adequately interpret are, of course, other world theories, and a world theory that cannot reasonably interpret the errors of other world theories is automatically inadequate. By that much it lacks the requisite scope. The four world theories which we shall consider [Formism, Mechanism, Contextualism, and Organicism] have no difficulty in explaining each other's errors. (Pepper, 1942, pp. 99–100)

It is striking how Pepper apparently recognizes the virtue of competitive subsumption, yet dismisses it on the grounds that each different world hypothesis can make equal claim to competitive subsumption on the grounds of explaining the errors of its competitors. The problem with Pepper's line of reasoning here is that perhaps these four world hypotheses can indeed equally well explain the others, but that does not preclude the development a further world hypothesis with notably greater explanatory power than these four. Indeed, in presenting Existentialism as a fifth world hypothesis, Pepper suggests that it may be more adequate than the prior four (Pepper, 1970, p. 191), presumably also more adequate in terms of its explanatory power with regard to its competitors. So it appears that Pepper may have been hasty in disparaging the proposed virtue of competitive subsumption.

Still, in general there is the possibility that more than one alternative theory can provide equally strong explanations of its competitors, even if not all of them can. One interpretation of this possibility is that the topic in question truly admits of multiple adequate theories, that the topic is pluralistic in nature. While this seems a viable interpretation, the further possibility of new theories would make this interpretation premature. After all, the method of perspectival reduction is intended to be an iterative process. If multiple theories appear equally adequate and equally explanatory, then they should all be thrown back into the process for a further iteration to see whether there might be a new theory that can more adequately subsume all of these competitors and thereby to provide a more comprehensive explanation.

Chapter 14

Explanation

If the notion of competitive subsumption can be understood in terms of an adequate explanation of alternative theories, then it is important to understand the nature of explanation to determine what would count as an adequate explanation. Here as elsewhere in philosophy, there are multiple competing accounts of the nature of explanation. Consider three of the more important accounts: the causal theory, the covering law model, and the pragmatic theory.

The causal theory of explanation holds that something is explained when the causal forces responsible for its existence or occurrence have been identified. Thus to explain why a mirror broke is to identify the causes for its breaking, such as a sharp strike from a hammer. If the hammer had not struck the mirror, then the mirror would not have broken. So the cause of the mirror's breaking is precisely its explanation.

The covering law model of explanation is primarily due to Carl Hempel. In general, according to this model, something is explained when it is covered by some general law by means of which the event or occurrence can be inferred. Hempel identifies two versions of the covering law model. The first is known as the Deductive-Nomological model, according to which an occurrence can be explained if that occurrence can be deduced logically from certain initial conditions in conjunction with universal laws (Hempel, 1965, pp. 174, 232). Thus the occurrence to be explained would form the conclusion of a deduction whose premises included universal laws and initial conditions. For example, the hammer striking the mirror could be explained by a deduction from universal laws of motion and the initial conditions of the positions of the hammer and mirror as well as the forces imposed upon the hammer. However, not every hammer that strikes a mirror breaks it, so Hempel recognizes that there needs to be a version of the covering law model to apply in cases where probability is involved. This second version is known as the Inductive-Statistical model, according to which an occurrence can be explained if that occurrence is the likely result of certain initial conditions in conjunction with statistical laws (Hempel, 1965, pp. 301–2, 385–6). So given statistical laws stating that mirrors of a certain kind break with a high frequency when struck with a particular force and the initial conditions that the mirror in question was in fact struck with that particular force, the breaking of the mirror would be supported inductively by those statistical laws and initial conditions. Thus the identification of those laws and conditions would constitute the explanation of why the mirror broke.

The pragmatic theory of explanation is largely due to Bas van Fraassen on the basis of the work of Sylvain Bromberger and others on the nature of why-questions. According to van Fraassen, there are three elements in any pragmatic explanation. First, the explanation is an answer to a why-question in which there is a presupposition of certain matters of fact, which form the topic of the explanation. Second, the explanation addresses a contrast class related to the topic, in which the speaker requests an explanation of why one member of the contrast class was selected rather than another. Third, the explanation is offered in accordance with a specification of a certain form that determines the relevant kind of explanatory factor (van Fraassen, 1980, pp. 141–142). So I might take the breaking of a mirror as the topic of an explanation. The contrast class might be the mirror's breaking as opposed to the mirror's remaining intact. My request specification might be for an explanation of what reasons the person wielding the hammer had for breaking the mirror. This account is pragmatic in nature since all three elements in an explanation are subject to the interests of the one demanding an explanation. With regard to the topic, my interest might have been with the swinging of the hammer rather than the breaking of the mirror. With regard to the contrast class, my interest might have been in the breaking of the mirror as opposed to the transmutation of the mirror into gold. With regard to the request specification, my interest might have been in the causal mechanisms of the breaking of the mirror rather than in the reasons for someone breaking it.

In an early presentation of the pragmatic theory of explanation, van Fraassen suggests that the notion of a request specification could be understood in terms of Aristotle's doctrine of the four kinds of causes: material, formal, efficient, and final (van Fraassen, 1977, p. 149). So my request specification for the reasons why the person wielding the hammer broke the mirror would represent a request for a final cause or teleology, whereas a request specification for the causal mechanisms would represent a request for an efficient cause. Note that a request for efficient causes appears to be precisely the kind of explanation sought by the causal theory of explanation, so it would appear that the pragmatic theory of explanation subsumes the causal theory within its account. Yet it seems to me that the notion of a request specification need not be limited to Aristotle's four causes. For example, perhaps I am interested in the laws under which the event to be explained can be subsumed. This nomological interest should also qualify as a viable request specification according to the pragmatic theory of explanation. More specifically, I might be interested in an explanation precisely in terms of Hempel's Deductive-Nomological model or Inductive-Statistical model, so it would appear that the covering law model would likewise be subsumed within the pragmatic theory of explanation as another possible request specification. Generally, it seems to me that any competing account of explanation should count as a request specification within the pragmatic theory of explanation. Thus Mary Hesse offers a conception of explanation in terms of metaphors (Hesse, 1966), and her notion of explanation as a metaphorical re-description by means of models might just as well count as a request specification within the pragmatic theory.[1]

Consequently, it appears that the pragmatic theory of expla-

---

[1] Maria Rentetzi argues that Hesse's account of explanation can be used to overcome criticisms of van Fraassen's account (Rentetzi, 2005). If I am correct that Hesse's account can be subsumed under van Fraassen's, then it would appear that Rentetzi's argument is misplaced. Insofar as the criticisms of van Fraassen's account concern lack of constraints in what counts as an explanation, reducing van Fraassen's account to a part thereof would indeed impose some constraints, but only by losing the whole in favor of the part.

nation provides an example of the notion of competitive subsumption, since all competing theories can be subsumed under it. In this case, it seems that competitive subsumption is exhibited straightforwardly by the inclusion of alternative theories as parts of pragmatic explanation, specifically as request specifications for an explanation. Previously I characterized competitive subsumption in terms of an explanation of alternative theories, not in terms of a relation between parts and wholes. However, this is not necessarily a problem, insofar as delineating the relation between parts and wholes may itself constitute a kind of explanation and therefore would constitute a request specification within the pragmatic theory of explanation. This kind of mereological explanation would be akin to a teleological explanation. For example, one might explain the job of a corporate officer in terms of the whole corporation and the role that the officer plays within it, namely by identifying the ends and goals of the corporation and determining the part of those ends and goals that fall under the responsibility of the corporate officer. So the inclusion of alternative accounts of explanation as parts of the pragmatic account would exhibit competitive subsumption by providing a mereological explanation of its competitors and the parts or roles that they serve within the overall pragmatic account.

Furthermore, there appears to be a sense in which the theory of pragmatic explanation also exhibits reflexive reiteration. If alternate theories of explanation constitute request specifications that someone wanting an explanation may demand, then that person might want something explained causally, nomologically, teleologically, metaphorically, or even mereologically. In each case, these particular alternative theories of explanation would dictate the way in which the explanation should be offered, whether by identifying causes, deducing from general laws, or otherwise as appropriate. Suppose that a person wanted something explained pragmatically. In that case, the pragmatic theory of explanation would dictate the way in which the explanation should be offered, namely by identifying each of the three elements specified by the pragmatic theory: a topic, a contrast class, and a request specification. Of course, this merely reiterates the pragmatic theory of explanation itself, which is what is precisely involved in reflexive reiteration.[2] The point of reflexive reiteration is to ensure that there was room for the theory itself as something to be explained within that theory, to ensure a kind of consistency. Since explanation is something that might need to be explained, the theory of explanation would need to include a way to explain itself.[3] Whereas it may seem difficult to explain the causal theory of explanation causally or the Deductive-Nomological theory of explanation nomologically, the pragmatic theory of explanation provides some grounds for pragmatic explanation of explanation in a way that reasserts itself as strong candidate for the proper account of explanation in general.

Since the pragmatic account of explanation exemplifies the two theoretical virtues identified from an ideal application of perspectival reduction, it seems to me that this account should constitute an example of an application of the method of perspectival reduction. It is true that the pragmatic account did not result from an explicit application of the method, but rather from a direct analysis of the nature of explanations in general and why-questions in particular. Yet by exemplifying the theoretical virtues that fall out of an ideal case of perspectival reduction, the pragmatic account might have been formulated from precisely the kind of thinking demanded by an application of perspectival reduction. Since that kind of thinking ultimately supports the same account as van Fraassen offers on the basis of direct analysis, I am encouraged to think that the reverse might apply, namely that an explicit application of perspectival reduction could produce results that would represent a direct analysis of a topic of philosophical research. Yet since competitive subsumption and reflexive reitera-

---

[2] Certainly if pragmatic explanation continued to be indicated as a request specification, an explanation would never emerge. At some point, whoever desires a pragmatic explanation would need to designate a non-pragmatic request specification in order actually to get an explanation.

[3] It might be thought that the demand for an explanation of explanation itself is incoherent in that it initiates an infinite explanatory regress. However, there is ultimately no such regress in this case. While indeed anyone seeking a pragmatic explanation of something must eventually designate a non-pragmatic request specification, as noted in the previous footnote, this does not indicate a regress with regard to the explanation of explanation. Rather, the explanation in this case is primarily provided by the ability of the pragmatic account to provide a place for itself within its own account of explanation, along with its rivals, and this is what is required in competitive subsumption and reflexive reiteration.

tion are intended to represent theoretical virtues that are exemplified at the ideal end of a process of perspectival reduction by means of applying commensurability rules, it may be wondered whether the pragmatic account of explanation might actually provide commensurability rules as well.

I claimed earlier that commensurability rules would need to identify certain dimensions across which rival theories might be transformed into each other. These dimensions frame the fundamental structure of the ultimate theory. In the paradigm example of commensurability, the Lorentz transformations identify four temporal and spatial dimensions across which different inertial frameworks can be transformed. In identifying three elements in any explanation, namely topic, contrast class, and request specification, the pragmatic theory of explanation likewise identifies a number of dimensions that provide the fundamental structure of the ultimate theory of explanation. Of course, the pragmatic theory was not formulated according to the method of perspectival reduction and therefore was not seeking transformation dimensions in commensurability rules. However, if the pragmatic theory could be shown to provide the basis for such commensurability rules, it would appear that it could just as well have been the product of the method of perspectival reduction.

Yet there would seem to be an additional problem in finding commensurability between competing theories of explanation. There does not appear to be a clear way to transform the causal theory of explanation into the Deductive-Nomological theory, for example, whether across the three dimensions specified by the pragmatic theory or across any other dimensions. The general descriptions of the competing theories seem to be too flatly contrary to each other, with no apparent grounds for thinking that they might be transformable at all. However, this apparent difficulty reveals an important point about the kind of commensurability needed within the method of perspectival reduction. The point is that commensurability must be between first order theories and not between higher order descriptions of those first order theories.

Consider again the paradigm case of the Lorentz transformations. The commensurability these transformations provide is not between competing descriptions of the nature of space and time, but between different measurements of space and time. What are being transformed are not statements of the form "The nature of space and time is ..." but "The distance between x and y is n", namely the measurements of space and time themselves, not higher order descriptions or interpretations of those measurements.

Likewise, then, what would be subject to transformations in commensurability rules in theories of explanation are not higher order interpretations of the nature of explanation, but particular explanations. Consider the earlier example of the breaking of a mirror. Take any given proposed explanation, such as the explanation that some god willed the mirror to break. According to some theories of explanation, this proposal might not count as an explanation at all, but it may count as explanatory according to others. Thus it would appear that higher order theories serve to group proposed explanatory statements into classes according to whether those statements are truly explanatory or not. It is those classes of explanatory statements that are of primary importance to any commensurability rules between competing theories of explanation, not the statements describing the higher order theories themselves. For any given proposed explanatory statement, the pragmatic theory of explanation claims that three elements can be identified, and these three elements indeed appear to provide the necessary dimensions for commensurability between the different classes of explanatory statements associated with the various theories of explanation, and therefore an explanation of why one theory of explanation accepts that proposed statement as explanatory and others not.

Finding exact commensurability rules in the case of theories of explanation, though, requires more than merely identifying dimensions. It must be shown how those dimensions can be used to transform explanatory attributions from one first order theory to another, and this is not clear in the case of theories of explanation. The role of the topic seems to be to group together explanatory statements that could be transformed. Statements concerning the same topic should be transformable, since they clearly represent potentially rival claims. However, there may also be commensurability across different topics, for example, with regard to counterfactual statements. Suppose there had been a plate of glass where the mirror had been when it was broken, and the plate of glass was broken by the hammer rather than the mirror. An explanation of the breaking of the mirror and a hypothetical explanation of the breaking of the glass might be subject to commensurability rules even though they are not strictly on the same topic, if that topic were specifically designated to be the breaking of the mirror, not the breaking of the glass. Of course, the topic might be enlarged to encompass a more general situation comprising both the breaking of the mirror and the hypothetical breaking of the glass, given the presence of glass in certain kinds of mirrors.

In the same way, it would appear that the role of the contrast class is to group together explanatory statements that might be transformable among each other. A contrast class between the breaking of the mirror as opposed to the mirror being transmuted into gold would correlate closely with a contrast class between the breaking of the mirror as opposed to the mirror being transmuted into platinum, or indeed any kind of transmutation. The primary point of the contrast is between breaking and transmutation, in which the final material involved in the transmutation seems of lesser relevance. Similarly, it would appear that other contrast classes might be grouped together according to the relevance of the concepts involved.

The request specification seems to be the key point of difference in rival theories of explanation, as argued above, determining what counts as an explanation and what does not. The goal of commensurability rules with regard to explanation is to seek to transform a causal explanation into a Deductive-Nomological explanation, for example, assuming for simplicity that the topic and contrast class are held constant. Perhaps some specific factor may be key in providing commensurability between rival explanations. For example, it may be that identifying general laws in a Deductive-Nomological explanation could form the foundation for explanations according to different request specifications. Those general laws might determine the causes that could be identified in a causal explanation. They might even be shown to restrict the kinds of ends or goals that could be identified in a teleological explanation. This would not necessarily demonstrate that the covering law model of explanation was correct after all, though it might explain why Hempel thought that the covering law model of explanation was correct. The structure governing the transformation of explanations according to the covering law model into any other explanatory request specification would determine the ultimate theory of explanation, so if the covering law model were to provide the basis for a commensurative transformation, then it would need to identify the dimensions across which a transformation could be made, just as the pragmatic theory clearly identifies. It may be that the key factor in providing commensurability rules between different request specifications is something that has not been identified in any existing theory of explanation. For instance, van Fraassen argues that it is not laws of nature that are fundamental in science, but considerations of symmetry (van Fraassen, 1989), so perhaps commensurability rules might be devised on the basis of symmetry rather than laws.

While I am not confident that I can outline the specific commensurability rules needed to provide a transformation between the various competing theories of explanation, I can suggest the general way in which such transformation could work. Suppose that for a given topic, the various explanations that satisfy each contrast class and request specification are progressively aggregated together. So holding the topic of explanation constant, let each possible contrast class and each possible request specification be explored and let all the explanations that satisfy these be gathered together. What is thus aggregated together is a progressively more complete set of knowledge about the topic. These elements of knowledge would not be completely independent, however, since some of them could be deducible from others. Ideally, all of them would eventually be connected together into a coherent body of knowledge, and this knowledge would extend somewhat beyond the topic itself toward the inquirers about the topic, since the explanations include request specifications concerning teleology, and would therefore need to extend to the aims and interests of the inquirers. So if complete knowledge of the topic and the inquirers were given, and the connections between these items of knowledge were made explicit, it appears that any item of knowledge on the topic could be transformed into any other item by means of entailment. Note that these items of knowledge represent possible explanations in accordance with some contrast class and request specification. What needs to be understood further in order to provide full commensurability rules between various explanations is the nature of pragmatic interest in general, namely why certain pieces of knowledge satisfy certain pragmatic interests rather than others. Perhaps such an investigation is better conducted within the field of cognitive psychology than within philosophy, but in any case, I will not attempt an answer here. My suggestion is that if complete knowledge on a given topic were available, and if the nature of pragmatic satisfaction were completely understood, then it seems possible that commensurability rules could be identified to transform an explanation from one perspective to an explanation from another. This transformation would proceed by coordinating the grounds of pragmatic satisfaction with the particular items of knowledge that would satisfy a particular explanatory interest, such that when those interests shift, the explanatory items of knowledge likewise shift according to some rule.[4] The identification of commensurability rules in this way would thereby satisfy the full ideal of perspectival reduction. However, in the absence of complete knowledge and understanding of any given topic that would ground such commensurability rules, the proposed theoretical virtues of competitive subsumption and reflexive iteration could still point the way forward toward that ideal, and they point most compellingly to the pragmatic theory of explanation among currently available theories.

The question of the nature of explanation was addressed in this chapter since the notion of competitive subsumption that emerged from a discussion of perspectival reduction was presented in terms of an explanation of rival theories. If commensurability rules could be identified between request specifications within the pragmatic theory of explanation, then it would not seem to matter which kind of explanation was used to explain those rival theories, since any kind of explanation could be transformed into any other kind. If commensurability rules are impossible with regard to theories of explanation, though, then the question becomes more complicated. It may be that only one kind of explanation is appropriate to the specific pragmatic concerns of the method of perspectival reduction, such as the kind of mereological explanation noted within the pragmatic theory of explanation itself, where competing theories formed an identifiable part of the larger theory. Pending further results concerning the possibility of

---

[4]Yet items of knowledge aggregated by various conceptions of explanation might not all be mutually inferable, since there may be discontinuous clusters of knowledge, such as knowledge about two specific physical objects very widely separated in space. However, the nature of pragmatic satisfaction is what provides a bridge between these potentially discontinuous clusters, for instance by linking knowledge of physical properties to desires and actions.

commensurability rules within the theory of explanation, perhaps it would be considered sufficiently significant merely to be able to demonstrate explanatory competitive subsumption according to some conception of explanation.

Chapter 15

Intuitions

One notable feature of the method of perspectival reduction is that it appears to be unconcerned with philosophical intuitions, in contrast with other methodologies discussed earlier. In Descartes' method of first philosophy, intuitions are a fundamental source of knowledge. In experimental philosophy, intuitions are studied scientifically using surveys across various populations. In inference to the best explanation, one might think that what Peirce called abduction was really intuition, although Peirce at one time denied that there was any power of intuition (Peirce, 1998a, pp. 11–27, 28–55). In reflective equilibrium, intuitions concerning particular judgments are brought into equilibrium with general principles. In Husserlian phenomenology, the concepts that are the target of phenomenological analysis are given initially in intuition (Husserl, 2001a, p. 168). Even in what I have been calling last philosophy, it would seem that the end that is projected as the ultimate state of philosophy must be apprehended through intuition.[1] Unlike these methods, perspectival reduction does not appear to acknowledge a role for intuitions.

Yet likewise, neither does Quinean naturalism seem to be much concerned with intuitions. In fact, George Bealer argues that the absence of any role for intuition in Quine's overall epistemology leads to its incoherence, because the starting points, the epistemic norms, and the terms of epistemic appraisal employed by Quinean

---

[1] The end state might also be given by divine revelation, but if one denies any religious or mystical grounds for revelation, then what was thought to be revelation simply collapses into a form of intuition, whatever that may be.

naturalism or empiricism cannot be supported within that doctrine without an appeal to intuitions (Bealer & Strawson, 1992). I am suspicious of incoherence arguments in general, as noted in Chapter 3, and I think the problem with Bealer's argument lies in the claim that there is no room for intuitions within Quinean naturalism. While indeed Quine himself may deny the role of intuitions, the question is whether intuitions may nonetheless appear within his epistemology in another guise, understood in terms of notions that do appear within Quinean naturalism.[2]

Quine does recognize the important role of hypothesis within his naturalistic doctrine, and he outlines a number of virtues that a successful hypothesis may have. One of these virtues is conservatism:

> In order to explain the happenings that we are inventing it to explain, the hypothesis may have to conflict with some of our previous beliefs; but the fewer the better. Acceptance of a hypothesis is of course like acceptance of any belief in that it demands rejection of whatever conflicts with it. The less rejection of prior beliefs required, the more plausible the hypothesis — other things being equal. (Quine & Ullian, 1978, pp. 66–67)

However, Quine is not perfectly clear why conservatism should be a virtue, though he may rightly claim that people do in fact take conservatism to be a virtue of hypotheses. For my part, I suspect that conservatism is a theoretic virtue because there is a pragmatic investment of some kind in the hypothesis or the consequences of the hypothesis. Not only may there be an intellectual investment in terms of what is printed in textbooks and taught to students that would need to be changed if the hypothesis were abandoned, but more importantly, there may be an investment in wider practice related to the hypothesis. If I explicitly accept a given hypothesis, I typically act in accordance with that hypothesis such that the presuppositions of my actions do not conflict with the hypothesis.[3] So

---

[2] Indeed Quine himself apparently takes this approach to intuition: "Where an intuition has anything at all to be said for it, it has something making no mention of intuition to be said for it: sensory clues that may not have registered as such, long forgotten beliefs, analogies more or less vague" (Quine & Ullian, 1978, p. 92).

[3] This is not always true, of course, since in some cases the presuppositions of

if I accept a hypothesis concerning the cause of a certain disease, for example, I tend to avoid what I take to be the cause, since I do not want to contract that disease. Such avoidance may furthermore become a habit. In this way, the acceptance of a hypothesis may also tend to shape my values, if indeed in accordance with the hypothesis I come to see what I take to be the cause of the disease to be bad.

Yet if the explicit acceptance of a hypothesis may involve an investment in practice, then likewise practice in general may be understood to involve certain implicit hypotheses, since I may not perfectly well understand all the reasons for my actions. Whether formed by habit or training or empirical adjustment, my practices and their inherent values constitute a kind of investment that I tend to preserve, since they are part of a general competence I have in navigating the world and reacting to it. So given a broad range of practices and values that I have, it would seem that a number of hypotheses or presuppositions can be associated with them, whether I am explicitly aware of them or whether they are merely implicit within my actions. Occasionally, though, it may happen that even hypotheses held only implicitly may be pushed explicitly into my consciousness by some chance event or by philosophical reflection.

I suggest that this account of the virtue of conservatism with regard to hypotheses enables a reinterpretation of intuitions according to Quinean terms. Intuitions are implicit hypotheses that represent an investment in practice that become explicit to consciousness.[4] Thus if Quine takes conservatism to be a virtue of hypotheses, Bealer may indeed charge that Quine is employing intuition to establish conservatism as a virtue; yet Quine may reply that such an intuition is merely a hypothesis that represents part of general epistemological practice, not any separate faculty that has no place in Quinean epistemology. The putative intuition may represent a good hypothesis or a bad one, so it needs to be balanced against other hypotheses and other virtues as well as empirical evidence, such that the investment in practice embodied in a putative intuition would need to be abandoned. Of course,

---

my actions may conflict even with beliefs that I explicitly acknowledge.

[4] A comparably minimal conception of intuitions as inclinations to believe is developed in (Earlenbaugh & Molyneux, 2009), but without the Quinean background.

the virtue of conservatism holds that abandoning such practices should be minimized where possible. However, this process of balancing between hypotheses, epistemic virtues and evidence is part of the Quinean epistemological program. In this way, there does not seem to be any incoherence in Quinean naturalism as Bealer claims, since what is called intuition can be redescribed in terms already explicit within the Quinean account.

However, this neo-Quinean characterization of the nature of intuitions is not how Bealer understands intuitions. For him, intuitions are "intellectual seemings" of an *a priori* nature (Bealer, 1996, pp. 5–6), (Bealer & Strawson, 1992, pp. 101–102). This difference in the understanding of intuition may suggest that the neo-Quinean account of intuitions and Bealer's account are merely referring to different things. Bealer's arguments against Quine may still succeed even if something called intuitions can be identified within the Quinean doctrine, so long as there is no room for intellectual seemings in the doctrine. Yet while Bealer's arguments may have some force by appealing to the phenomenology of intuitions, the crux of the issue is rather the proper characterization of that phenomenology, whether as intellectual seemings or as implicit hypotheses. Since there is some characterization of the phenomenology of intuitions consistent with the Quinean doctrine, namely implicit hypotheses, I find it hard to see the incoherence in that doctrine in the way Bealer claims. If the doctrine is seen to be incoherent when an alien characterization of intuitions is imposed upon it, then interpretive charity should preclude such an imposition. It is precisely a Quinean interpretation of intuitions that should count in any proposed incoherence argument, not an alien interpretation imposed on Quine.

Intuitions can differ between people, so it is not surprising that intuitions concerning the nature of intuitions should differ. For example, Henri Bergson held that intuition was "the kind of intellectual sympathy by which one places oneself within an object in order to coincide with what is unique in it and consequently inexpressible" (Bergson, 1912, p. 7), which does not clearly align either with Bealer's conception or with the neo-Quinean conception I suggested. With a diversity of perspectives concerning the nature of intuitions, it seems that the method of perspectival reduction might profitably be employed to sort out the nature of intuitions. Indeed, it may be that the neo-Quinean characterization of intuitions may serve to explain its competitors, liberated from its Quinean heritage, perhaps by providing an explanation of why there should be any intellectual seemings according to Bealer's characterization. However, I am not primarily interested in arguing for the nature of intuitions here, but rather in explaining the apparent unconcern that perspectival reduction shows toward intuitions, whatever they may be.

The primary methodological concerns with intuitions are whether they can serve as evidence for philosophical argumentation and in what way.[5] Regardless of the specifics of this controversy, I think there is a minimal way in which intuitions can constitute evidence, namely as evidence that someone has had a particular intuition at a given time. While this kind of evidence may seem trivial, it has an important consequence with regard to the method of perspectival reduction. The manifestation of an intuition in a person indicates that there is something about that person such that something appears intuitively correct or even obvious. While it may be tempting to dismiss this kind of evidence merely as the psychological peculiarities of an individual person, the evidence in question may not represent the subjective idiosyncrasies of individual taste, nor indeed even the adverse affects of a neurological disorder or even the malicious influence of an evil demon, if the intuition turns out to be grossly false. Rather, this evidence may be approached philosophically with regard to the presuppositions that the individual may inherently hold in order that the intuition in question could arise in the way that it does. Understood in this way, intuitions therefore would constitute evidence of a certain perspective, the kind of perspective upon which the method of perspectival reduction operates. So it would seem that the apparent unconcern of perspectival reduction was merely apparent, since intuitions are the sorts of things that are indicators of the perspectives upon which the method relies, even though those intuitions are ultimately operative merely in the forms of presuppositions, not as the products of some distinctive faculty.

Yet it is not only intuitions that can generate perspectives. Even if the neo-Quinean characterization of intuitions as hypotheses inherent in practice is not correct, its shift from intuitions to hypotheses suggests that the role of intuitions in generating perspec-

---

[5] See for example the contributions in (DePaul & Ramsey, 1998).

tives could just as well be served by hypotheses that may not actually be held by anyone as an intuition. Nor indeed is it clear that the perspectives generated by intuitions are always the most important ones. The perspectives that happen to be adopted by actual persons might not be sufficient to represent the full scope of the topic in question, but may represent a kind of parochialism in thought constrained by the contingencies of actual intuitions. In order to fill out a full range of perspectives upon which a reduction may be performed, it may be necessary to go beyond actual intuitions and to postulate a range of counter-intuitive hypotheses. In this way, the most critical perspectives in understanding a given topic according to this method may be the ones that defy any intuitions. Therefore, perspectival reduction finds a place for intuitions, but intuitions are neither essential to the method nor privileged in it.

Accordingly, to practice perspectival reduction properly would require setting aside one's own particular intuitions and demoting them to the status of a mere perspective, rather than privileging them as evidence that must be preserved. As I understand it, this is the merit of a genealogical analysis such as the kind practiced by Friedrich Nietzsche or Michel Foucault.[6] By understanding the ways in which concepts and ideas arise, perhaps ways that seem counter to contemporary ways of thinking about them, those concepts and ideas become unhinged slightly for the genealogical analyst. For ideas that may have a dubious heritage, even if I might not abandon them entirely, they may no longer have the same power for me. Insofar as these concepts would likewise contribute to my intuitions, I should be able to bracket those intuitions in a kind of skeptical *epoché*. So the deployment of a genealogical analysis need not fall into a genetic fallacy. The genealogical method need not be interpreted as claiming that since an idea has arisen under questionable circumstance, that idea is thereby faulty and should be abandoned entirely. Rather, it constitutes a method designed to ease the grip of prejudices, precisely in order to gain a greater degree of objectivity.[7]

In this way, Nietzsche's conception of objectivity appears more

---

[6]See for example, (Nietzsche, 1994) and (Foucault, 2002).

[7]See also (Nietzsche, 2001, pp. 202–203) and (Nietzsche, 1968, p. 148), cited by (Geuss, 1994) in similar reflections.

comprehensible and compelling:

> Finally, as knowers, let us not be ungrateful towards such resolute reversals of familiar perspectives and valuations with which the mind has raged against itself for far too long, apparently to wicked and useless effect: to see differently, and to want to see differently to that degree, is no small discipline and preparation of the intellect for its future 'objectivity' — the latter understood not as 'contemplation without interest' (which is, as such, a non-concept and an absurdity), but as having in our power our 'pros' and 'cons': so as to be able to engage and disengage them so that we can use the difference in perspectives and affective interpretations for knowledge. From now on, my philosophical colleagues, let us be more wary of the tentacles of such contradictory concepts as 'pure reason', 'absolute spirituality', 'knowledge as such': — here we are asked to think an eye which cannot be thought at all, an eye turned in no direction at all, an eye where the active and interpretive powers are to be suppressed, absent, but through which seeing still becomes a seeing-something, so it is an absurdity and non-concept of eye that is demanded. There is only perspectival seeing, only a perspective 'knowing': the more affects we allow to speak about a thing, the more eyes, various eyes we are able to use for the same thing, the more complete will be our 'concept' of the thing, our 'objectivity'. But to eliminate the will completely and turn off all the emotions without exception, assuming we could: well? would that not mean to castrate the intellect? ... (Nietzsche, 1994, p. 92)

Where intuitions form the basis for various perspectives, having the power to engage or disengage those perspectives would indeed constitute a valuable kind of objectivity, while remaining within the grip of a given intuition constitutes a significantly limited kind of subjectivity, even if that intuition should turn out to be correct. Perspectival reduction likewise requires precisely this kind of objectivity, whereby perspectives can be engaged and disengaged freely in order to determine a way in which the apparent relativity of perspectival thinking might be reduced to some non-relativistic form.

Therefore intuitions play only a limited role within perspectival reduction, namely as evidence for various perspectives. This role can just as well be served by hypotheses, even counter-intuitive hypotheses, and perhaps can be served better this way.[8] If indeed the nature of intuitions themselves can be understood in terms of hypotheses that embody an investment in practice, in accordance with the neo-Quinean account of intuitions I presented above, then the greater importance of hypotheses than intuitions becomes clearer. Rather than seeking to preserve the evidential status of intuitions, perspectival reduction requires the ability both to engage with those intuitions to appreciate the full nature of individual perspectives and to disengage from them to understand how the full range of perspectives could be coordinated. Disengaging from intuitions requires suspending the force of the investment of practice that intuitions embody, thereby downgrading them to the status of mere hypotheses.[9]

Yet in order to evaluate those hypotheses correctly, perspectival reduction would appear to require the ability to engage with those mere hypotheses fully in order to appreciate the perspective that they represent, even with regard to flagrantly counter-intuitive hypotheses. This engagement with counter-intuitive hypotheses is already enshrined within philosophical practice as thought experiments.

---

[8]Thus I generally agree with the line of argument against intuitions in (Cappelen, 2012), though Cappelen's claim that "The various activities that get classified together as 'philosophy' today are so classified as the result of complex historical and institutional contingencies, not because philosophy has an essence that ties it all together as a natural kind" (Cappelen, 2012, p. 21) does not perfectly agree with my conception of philosophy presented in Chapter 4.

[9]Compare: "Philosophers might be better off not using the word 'intuition' and its cognates" (Williamson, 2007, p. 220), though Williamson's grounds for this statement do not perfectly align with my line of thinking here.

Chapter 16

Thought Experiments

Thought experiments appear to be the hallmark of philosophy. Descartes supposes that a malicious demon deceives him into thinking that he has a body (Descartes, 1985b, p. 15). John Locke supposes that a prince and a cobbler have switched memories (Locke, 1959a, p. 457). David Hume supposes that a person has experienced all shades of colors except for a particular shade (Hume, 1978, p. 6). It is rare to find a philosopher who has not used thought experiments for some purpose.

Daniel Dennett calls one form of argument using thought experiments an "intuition pump" (Dennett, 1980, 1984), since the situations invoked in such thought experiments seem designed mainly to elicit certain intuitions from the readers or listeners of those experiments. One is supposed to think about the experimental situation and let one's intuitions guide the conclusion of the argument, preferably to the conclusion intended by the author of the thought experiment.

However, there is no guarantee that any given thought experiment will elicit the same intuitions and therefore the same conclusions from every one considering the experimental situation, even from trained philosophers. Every situation within a thought experiment is subject to multiple interpretations, and there are at least two points at which interpretation enters into thought experiments. The point first is obviously the interpretation of the situation itself. Given the state of affairs described in the thought experiment, the interpretation of that situation is supposed to have some philosophical consequences. Differing interpretations of that situation will thus lead to different conclusions.

The second point is less obvious, but equally important. Thought experiments typically suppose certain counterfactual situations, particularly situations that cannot feasibly be attained in order to perform an actual experiment. As those situations become increasingly fanciful and exotic, it is not perfectly clear that those situations are still strictly relevant to the philosophical topic for which the situation was invoked. Thus the second point of interpretation lies in the evaluation of whether an interpretation of the situation properly applies to its intended philosophical purpose. For example, I am free to suppose that a certain stretch of empty space is conscious, but if I intend to draw from this supposition any philosophical conclusions concerning the nature of consciousness, I need to consider first whether my supposition itself precludes consciousness before I continue to consider what the supposed consciousness of empty space would mean with regard to the nature of consciousness. This evaluation not only requires interpretation, but interpretation specifically concerning the topic for which the situation was invoked. I need to understand consciousness well enough in order to determine whether empty space is the sort of thing that can be conscious in the first place. Without such a preliminary evaluation, I could certainly continue to analyze the notion of consciousness as applied to empty space, but it would no longer be clear whether I am analyzing the original notion of consciousness I sought to clarify or whether I am analyzing some different, purely fictional notion of consciousness.[1]

The interpretations that enter thought experimentation at both of these points rely critically on some body of background information. Where that information is shared and well established, the likelihood of differing interpretations and therefore differing conclusions would appear to be reduced. However, philosophical argumentation often concerns topics regarding which the necessary background information itself is controversial. This is certainly the case in the example just given where a certain amount of understanding of the nature of consciousness is required in order to evaluate whether I can properly suppose that empty space is conscious in any meaningful way. Perhaps there are conceptions of consciousness that would permit empty space to be conscious,

---

[1] These points are also raised in (Fodor, 1964) and (Quine, 1972).

but to suppose this situation in order to argue for a particular conception of consciousness would constitute an instance of begging the question to a considerable degree.

The potential for differing interpretations and the characterization of thought experiments as intuition pumps suggests that the role of thought experiments with regard to perspectival reduction is the same as intuitions themselves, namely as means for constituting different perspectives that might be reduced. Perhaps one thought experiment might make one perspective seem particularly plausible, as its author had intended, where a different perspective would seem more compelling in a different thought experiment, though each experimental situation would be subject to contrary interpretation. In any case, the deployment of thought experiments prompts intuitions and interpretations that ultimately count merely as differing perspectives of the sort that invite the application of perspectival reduction.

Indeed, one function of thought experiments might be precisely to expose the presuppositions of the one proposing a given thought experiment. Given the conclusions that the proposer of a thought experiment draws, someone with a contrary interpretation of that thought experiment would be in a position to identify what presuppositions ground those conclusions, whether these presuppositions are considered to be intuitions or perspectives or otherwise. Such presuppositions in the proposer's argument might not have been clear without the deployment of the thought experiment to tease them out.[2]

Yet few thought experiments are intended by their authors simply to prompt intuitions, certainly not to prompt contrary intuitions that would constitute different perspectives. Insofar as any given thought experiment does prompt contrary intuitions, it would seem to have failed in some important way. Thought experiments are typically intended to be decisive in arguing for the correctness of some particular perspective or the incorrectness of other perspectives or both. Thus in the example of the supposed consciousness of empty space, I might deploy such a thought experiment explicitly to argue against some proposed conception of consciousness that did permit empty space to be conscious as part

---

[2]Compare: "Thought experiments do provide evidence, in the shape of mainly non-psychological facts. That philosophers sometimes disagree as to what evidence they provide is only to be expected" (Williamson, 2007, p. 246).

of a *reductio ad absurdum*. By making such a supposition, I might be able to demonstrate that some absurd conclusion would follow and thereby to argue that the proposed conception of consciousness is defective or false. This kind of deployment of a thought experiment would thereby appear designed to constrain intuitions by demonstrating that some of them are incoherent or improper in certain ways. Of course, insofar as such demonstrations will still rely on certain background information that may itself be subject to contrary interpretations, they may not be as decisive as their authors may have intended and may still represent occasions for prompting differing perspectives.

Another way that thought experiments may seek to constrain intuitions and corresponding perspectives is to deploy a series of thought experiments. Whereas a single thought experiment may indeed prompt contrary intuitions though differing interpretations of one situation, it would be much harder for a single line of interpretation to apply equally well to a coordinated series of different thought experiments on the same topic. A good example of this is the group of thought experiments that David Chalmers deploys with regard to the question of qualia, the alleged subjective quality of conscious experience. Where prior thought experiments sought to show that qualia might be absent from a functionally cognitive system, or that the one person's qualia with regard to the experience of a red thing may be the same as another person's qualia with regard to the experience of a green thing, Chalmers poses two additional thought experiments to test the intuitions regarding the two earlier thought experiments. He considers first a case in which neurons in a conscious person are gradually replaced with functionally equivalent silicon chips, and second a case in which a functionally equivalent chip providing significantly different qualia is installed in a conscious person with a toggle switch (Chalmers, 1996, pp. 247–275). The point of these additional thought experiments is to constrain the intuitions that govern the prior thought experiments, since intuitions that succeed in the earlier cases may fail in these two new cases. Of course, there is still a considerable amount of interpretation involved in these additional thought experiments, as Chalmers himself notes (Chalmers, 1996, p. 251), and there is no guarantee that there will be one and only one interpretation that fits all of these thought experiments perfectly.

Still, the pressure that a series of thought experiments puts on interpretations to constrain the intuitions governing them suggests that as the number of thought experiments on a given topic increases, the likelihood of narrowing the various interpretations down to a single valid one should increase. Thus the consequence would appear to be that thought experiments should be increased as a methodological expedient. Yet this general strategy seems roughly similar to the strategy employed in perspectival reduction, namely to increase the number of perspectives as a means of triangulating on a single best perspective. The question now to explore is whether this similarity is merely apparent or whether this strategy of deploying thought experiments is more closely linked with the principles of perspectival reduction.

If indeed only a single interpretation can adequately apply to a series of thought experiments, that would satisfy one of the three means of achieving a perspectival reduction, namely by showing that one of the perspectives is objectively to be preferred over all of the others. There would appear to be two main ways that a series of thought experiments could achieve such a result. One way would be to devise one thought experiment for each of the competing perspectives to demonstrate that they were all internally incoherent by supposing a situation condoned by a particular perspective, then showing that the situation is untenable in some way. This way effectively uses thought experiments as part of *reductio ad absurdum* arguments against each faulty perspective. The main challenge with this approach is to ensure that no such thought experiment could likewise be deployed against the preferred perspective, else no adequate perspective would emerge from the process of perspectival reduction if all perspectives were ultimately untenable.

The other way to demonstrate the objective preference for one perspective over the others would be to pose a series of neutral thought experiments, neutral insofar as they are not explicitly directed against any particular perspective in the way just mentioned, and then to demonstrate that one perspective can better interpret all of the thought experiments than any other perspective. The main challenge with this approach is to show that the way that each perspective is interpreted in this approach is in fact the best interpretation for those perspectives. Thought experiments, as already emphasized, require considerable background information in order to interpret the experimental situation. It is not always made clear what background information properly corresponds to which perspective. While I have suggested that differences in background are what constitute various perspectives with regard to thought experiments, where the perspectives are initially taken to be existing philosophical positions on some topic, those positions themselves are subject to interpretation, yielding perspectives on perspectives. For example, there are many interpretations of what constitutes realism, and many interpretations of what constitutes anti-realism. So if the aim is to perform a perspectival reduction on a series of existing philosophical positions including these two general positions, a considerable amount of philosophical charity would be required according to this approach to ensure that the best interpretation of those philosophical positions is applied to the situations posed in the series of thought experiments, else the best overall perspective may be obscured behind a poor interpretation. The problem in this case is that the argument works only when the best possible interpretation for each perspective is available, else the argument would be limited by the ability of the arguer to imagine feasible interpretations of those perspectives. Where the imagination of the arguer is weak or biased, the argument is accordingly faulty.[3]

This last point suggests a further challenge with regard to both of these approaches. The strategy of demonstrating one perspective to be better than the others requires that standards of evaluation applied in the demonstration are shared between the perspectives. If standards are not shared, then different standards associated with differing perspectives may show that each perspective is preferred over the others according to its own standards, which merely propagates another form of relativism and perspectivism, rather than reducing the perspectives.[4] Of course, understanding which standards are demanded by each perspective is a matter of interpretation of those various perspectives, but despite all of these challenges and problems, there does seem to be a clear role for thought experiments in this aspect of perspectival reduction, if these challenges can be met.

---

[3]As suggested in my suspicions concerning incoherence arguments presented in Chapter 3.

[4]See Chapter 7 of (Ressler, 2013).

The question of shared standards further suggests that thought experiments can likewise serve a role in a second means for achieving perspectival reduction, namely by demonstrating invariances between perspectives. Since thought experiments can function only on the grounds of background information, it may happen that all perspectives share background information, and this invariant information between perspectives would emerge as a conclusion from the process of perspectival reduction. This invariance might be revealed precisely by means of a thought experiment. Although again it appears that understanding what background information should properly be associated with which perspective would be a matter of interpretation and therefore would be subject to multiple interpretations, it may be that for each perspective there is some interpretation of it that shares background information with some interpretation of every other perspective. While this kind of invariance would not properly constitute an instance of absolute invariance, but only relative invariance according to interpretations, where the perspectives in question may be existing philosophical positions that are subject to interpretation, this kind of invariance not only seems to be the best that could be expected, but likewise represents a significant result. If each competing perspective has an interpretation that contains invariant features across the entire range of interpreted perspectives, then those invariant features would constitute the basis for an explanation of how competing perspectives on the same thing could arise. Of course, this is precisely the kind of explanation involved in the third means for achieving perspectival reduction, namely by devising commensurability rules between perspectives.

Yet with regard to such commensurability rules, what is fundamentally important is the transformations between perspectives, so it is not clear how such transformations could properly be demonstrated using thought experiments. Insofar as thought experiments suppose some particular situation, even if transformations across perspectives could be demonstrated with regard to that situation, it would not constitute a demonstration that the transformation rule would be adequate to all situations. Nor does it seem likely that a series of thought experiment could demonstrate this kind of adequacy, since there does not appear to be any limit to the fanciful situations that a thought experiment might suppose. Consequently, it would seem that such thought experiments would merely constitute illustrations of commensurability rules in certain imagined situations, if indeed commensurability rules were possible with regard to the topic in question.

Yet in arguing for the possible commensurability between competing conceptions of explanation, I myself employed a thought experiment by supposing that the explanations corresponding to different request specifications were aggregated together. The role of this thought experiment was not to demonstrate certain commensurability rules in the particular situation posited by the experiment, however. Nor did the kind of commensurability ultimately asserted with regard to explanation depend upon this thought experiment. The claim of commensurability might just as easily have been asserted without the accompanying thought experiment. Still, the thought experiment did appear to serve a useful role in making the proposed commensurability seem plausible, whether it ultimately succeeded in that role or not. Thus with regard to the strategy of seeking commensurability rules in perspectival reduction, thought experiments appear primarily to serve an auxiliary role, whether in identifying relative invariances that can serve as a basis for a claim of commensurability, in illustrating the proposed commensurability rule in certain situations, or in arguing for the plausibility of commensurability rules.

In these ways, thought experiments can serve certain roles within perspectival reduction, whether in articulating perspectives by prompting contrary intuitions or in contributing to the reduction of those competing perspectives. While Bertrand Russell claimed that puzzles in logic and philosophy serve a comparable function to experiment in science (Russell, 1905, pp. 484–485), none of these auxiliary roles for thought experiments in perspectival reduction seem to correspond to the critical role of actual experimentation in science. Some philosophers may consider this to represent an unfortunate demotion of the status of thought experiments in philosophy. However, I would emphasize a different aspect of experimentation within the core structure of perspectival reduction that I think more than compensates for the shift in emphasis away from exotic thought experiments.

Experimentation in science is often employed to confirm or to disconfirm a certain hypothesis, where the experiment is deliberately designed in such a way that the results of the experiment should either support or challenge the hypothesis. Yet sometimes experiments are performed simply as a means of exploring what would happen under certain conditions, without any prior hypothesis in mind. This exploratory aspect of experimentation typically occurs at early stages of an investigation when phenomena tend to outstrip available theories, and the aim of this kind of experimentation is to increase the range of phenomena that should ultimately be explained by an adequate theory.

Whereas the aim of using thought experiments in philosophy is typically to contribute to the confirmation or disconfirmation of some position, I would emphasize the exploratory aspect of perspectival reduction precisely in the proliferation of alternative perspectives that become subject to the process of reduction. As noted in the chapter on intuitions, relying on existing intuitions to form perspectives may not provide a sufficient base of perspectives to reveal the full nature of the topic being investigated. An adequate range of perspectives therefore might be attained only by developing the consequences of counter-intuitive hypotheses, much as the exploration of the denial of Euclid's parallel postulate developed a series of non-Euclidean geometries. Furthermore, where the kinds of perspectives in philosophy can be generated by differing methodologies, perspectival reduction would benefit from the devising of new methodologies and developing the consequences of their application to traditional problems of philosophy.

This exploratory aspect of perspectival reduction in philosophy therefore seems the reverse of exploration in science in a sense. Where scientific experimentation seeks to multiply the empirical data in order to decide between competing theories, experimentation through the multiplication of perspectives in philosophy according to perspectival reduction seeks to multiply competing theories in order to isolate the underlying phenomenon. In this sense, the early stages of perspectival reduction represent a temporary suspension of simplicity and other theoretical virtues in the proliferation of hypotheses and their resulting perspectives, since even extremely complex hypotheses may provide useful perspectives on a philosophical topic, whether simplicity and other virtues can be identified within invariant features of those perspectives, whether those virtues are subsequently reinstated in identifying a best perspective, or whether those virtues are invoked in evaluating commensurability rules.

Thus boldness and imagination in philosophy would serve to

benefit perspectival reduction, where timidity and traditionalism can only undermine it. For example, consider the attitude adopted by Nelson Goodman in his introduction to *The Structure of Appearances*:

> We shall find that systems of logical philosophy, which I call "constructional" to distinguish them from uninterpreted formal systems and from amorphous philosophical discourses, may be founded on many different bases and constructed in different ways. And several quite different programs may be equally correct and offer equal if different advantages. An impartial survey of alternative programs, however, will not by itself realize any of them. A passionate effort at construction is likewise needed and is wholly compatible with the dispassionate appraisal of results. To seek to develop a system is not to argue for its superiority to other systems. Perhaps the day will come when philosophy can be discussed in terms of investigation rather than controversy, and philosophers, like scientists, be known for the topics they study rather than by the views they hold. (Goodman, 1966, p. xviii)

Here Goodman advocates actually creating systems, rather than arguing in advance whether the proposed systems will be adequate, before even having the fully developed system available for appraisal. This is the same attitude that perspectival reduction requires.

When philosophers tend to prejudge the feasibility of certain hypotheses before developing them further, certain perspectives get abandoned before they can show their worth. Where the methods for investigating philosophical topics rely mainly on the establishment of invariances or of a single best alternative, this preliminary culling of hypotheses may seem somewhat plausible. However, if the topic in question can ultimately best be understood in terms of commensurability among alternatives, a wide range of perspectives is essential, requiring a passionate effort to develop those perspectives even when their underlying hypotheses appear radically counter-intuitive. What is required is a sense of experimentation to see what can be made of those hypotheses.

Chapter 17

Necessity

According to one conception of philosophy that has been influential throughout the twentieth century and beyond, the subject matter of philosophy is necessary *a priori* statements. It seems likely that this conception developed primarily as a reaction to the increasing success of modern science overshadowing philosophy. Science is concerned with finding natural laws that are fundamentally contingent, since those laws might have been otherwise, and that are *a posteriori*, since they must be established by empirical investigation. Given the increasing importance of science, if there is to be a role for philosophy, it would appear that philosophy must be concerned with something different than science, namely that which is necessary and *a priori*.

I do not share this conception of philosophy. Philosophy predates modern science, so I would strongly resist any conception of philosophy that primarily represents a reactionary redefinition of the field against the ascendancy of modern science, assuming that I am correct in this attribution. I neither think that this conception of philosophy properly matches the practice of philosophy throughout its history, nor that it should ground the practice of philosophy in its future.

Furthermore, while it might indeed be claimed that what science studies is both contingent and *a posteriori*, it is not clear that everything that is contingent or *a posteriori* can be investigated by scientific methodology. This is not a criticism of science by any means, but rather a criticism of philosophical characterizations of the relations between philosophy and science. If there is a gap between scientific methodology and what is contingent and *a posteriori*, then either some other discipline must investigate these matters, or they will remain unexplored. According to the conception of philosophy that I favor, philosophy is concerned with all knowledge, though study of some subject matters may become sufficiently advanced with their own particular methodologies that they constitute specializations within the overall range of knowledge, as presented in Chapter 4. This does not mean that philosophy is no longer concerned with those subject matters. It means that philosophy is primarily concerned with reconciling the results of those specializations with the rest of the body of knowledge. So anything that falls outside of the methodologies of the various specialized disciplines and sciences would belong to philosophy to investigate. This would apply not only to anything contingent and *a posteriori* that may fall outside of scientific methodology, but also to anything contingent and *a priori* or necessary and *a posteriori*.

Yet I have strong doubts whether these categories are fundamentally important to philosophy at all. The concern with both sets of categories, necessity and contingency, *a priori* and *a posteriori*, is very ancient, dating at least back to Aristotle and brought into prominence in the work of Kant. Insofar as these categories have been identified and investigated, they are part of the overall philosophical heritage that must be understood. However, I am not convinced that either set of categories is critical for understanding the fundamental issues in metaphysics or epistemology. It is true that many issues that are currently understood to be fundamental are framed precisely in terms of these categories, but my suspicion is that the issues thus framed will not prove to be fundamental issues in the end, but rather represent historical issues that have arisen mainly because these categorical distinctions have been made. A proper investigation of these suspicions exceeds the scope of this study. What is important here is whether these categories have any constitutive or methodological importance to the nature and practice of philosophy.

I will restrict myself here to the category of necessity, partly because the role of experience embodied in the distinction between what is *a priori* and what is *a posteriori* is entangled in specific methodological questions surrounding empiricism in general, but primarily because the enthusiasm for possible worlds arguments had come to dominate the tradition of analytic philosophy, at least at the time that the research for this book was begun, although the trends in philosophical fashion seem to be changing at the time of publication. The appeal to possible worlds had become so widespread that it might be thought that a concern with necessity and possibility must be fundamental to philosophy and that the proper philosophical method must include arguments based upon possible worlds, as claimed by many defenders of conceptual analysis.[1] By contrast, this study has intentionally not made much mention of possible worlds at all. While there are certainly philosophical concerns about the metaphysical status of possible worlds themselves, my main concern is rather with the methodological importance of necessity and possible worlds arguments. The question here is whether the method of perspectival reduction presented in this study can be understood in terms of necessity and possible worlds and whether it should be so understood.

Perspectival reduction depends on the nature of relativism, and the logic of relativism closely parallels the modal logic of necessity and possibility,[2] so it might be thought that the notion of necessity would be operative somewhere within perspectival reduction. Yet a successful perspectival reduction represents a denial of relativism in the case of the presuppositions of various competing philosophical positions, so it is not clear whether the parallel with the logic of necessity should ultimately be maintained within perspectival reduction, depending upon how the relativism in question is ultimately denied. I propose then to investigate the role of necessity within each of the three ways that a successful perspectival reduction might be accomplished, namely by means of invariances, objective preferability, or commensurability.

The identification of invariances across perspectives seems very much like the assertion of invariances across possible worlds, so it might be thought that this kind of invariance precisely represents necessity within perspectival reduction. Yet in order to assimilate perspectival invariance to necessity, perspectives would need to be assimilated to possible worlds, and this is not at all clear.

---

[1] For example, Frank Jackson in (Jackson, 1998). Williamson takes a different approach in (Williamson, 2007), but is thereby obliged to account for modal knowledge under his approach. Nozick aims to "shrink necessity in order to make room for veridicality" (Nozick, 2001, p. 119), but it is not clear how influential Nozick has been in this case.

[2] See (Ressler, 2012) and (Ressler, 2013) for details of this logic.

In the logic of relativism, theories are made relative to some particular relativizing factor, such as a culture or a conceptual scheme, and it is the indexing of a theory to such a factor that constitutes a perspective. Possible worlds are not indexed in this way at all. Note that in developing his logical analysis of relativism, Steven D. Hales models the modality of relativity concurrently with the modality of necessity (Hales, 1997, 2006). So Hales allows that necessity is perspectival (Hales, 1997, p. 47). I would additionally suggest that perspectives might merely be possible, so that whatever invariances can be established among the various perspectives might possibly have been otherwise. So there is a conceptual distinction made between perspectives and possible worlds. There may indeed be perspectival invariances recognized among a particular set of relativizing factor on topics that are purely contingent and not necessary at all.

Nor does the denial of objective equity among perspectives indicate any necessity. If one perspective is objectively to be preferred above all the rest, this does not mean that whatever that perspective asserts is thereby necessary, nor does it indicate that the perspective is necessarily objectively preferable. Objective preference has no clear link with necessity. Suppose that it did. Then whatever is objectively true would appear to be part of some perspective that is objectively preferable over others that would contain falsehoods or at least half-truths. If this objective preference were to establish necessity, then it would seem that every truth would involve some necessity, thereby leaving little room for contingency in the world, which does not represent the actual world properly.

Still less does the identification of commensurability rules indicate any necessity. Commensurability between perspectives indicates a form of contextualism between them, so none of those perspectives would be shown to be necessary by means of a commensurability rule, since there are contextual differences. Nor does the new perspective that asserts commensurability between the original perspectives indicate any necessity, at least by means of the commensurability rules alone. If the original perspectives had been different, for example, then different commensurability rules might be required, or those perspectives might in fact be incommensurable. So nothing about commensurability rules suggests much of a role for necessity.

Therefore, the method of perspectival reduction does not seem to indicate any important methodological role for necessity or any constitutive role in understanding the nature of philosophy as embodied within the method. Nothing about perspectival reduction indicates that it is only appropriate or even best suited for the investigation of necessary truths.

Of course, the indifferent attitude of perspectival reduction toward necessity does not indicate that that there is no role for necessity in philosophy. Certainly the concepts of necessity and possibility themselves demand philosophical investigation just as other concepts do. Furthermore, assuming that there are necessary truths,[3] they should be easily identifiable within the practice of perspectival reduction. Those necessary truths should prove to be invariant across perspectives, at least perspectives that are not grossly erroneous, though as argued earlier, they are not the only truths that could be invariant across perspectives. Likewise, those necessary truths should prove to be objectively preferable above the errors and half-truths contained in some perspectives, thereby making the search for commensurability rules unnecessary. However, the way in which necessary truths behave within perspectival reduction still does not suggest in any way that necessity is especially important to perspectival reduction. The method would function just as well with regard to anything that is merely contingent and indeed in a world in which nothing was necessary.

There are certainly philosophical methodologies according to which necessity is important, such as some varieties of conceptual analysis, and there are methodologies whose presuppositions hold that the subject matter of philosophy is necessary *a priori* truths. The indifferent attitude of perspectival reduction toward necessity does not indicate that those methodologies should automatically be rejected. After all, perspectival reduction is intended for application to any number of methodologies and their presuppositions. Yet methodologies that hold necessity to be of prime importance to philosophy must be considered to be merely perspectives among other perspectives, against which the process of perspectival reduction would operate. The necessity operative within these methodological perspectives would be relegated to the status of

---

[3] I do not make this assumption, at least with regard to absolutely necessary truths that do not rely upon some system within which necessity can be established.

presuppositions that need to be coordinated within that perspectival reduction.

I have been curious why the notion of necessity has gained such importance in philosophy. It is not clear to me what is gained in asserting that p is necessarily q over the simple assertion that p is q. Certainly there does not seem to be any practical difference, since if p is q, then it is true in the actual world that I inhabit, and there does not seem to be any practical risk that I would suddenly be transported to some fanciful possible world where p is not q such that I should be concerned with what would be necessary in any possible world.[4] I had wondered briefly whether the obsession with necessity was primarily an effort to insert something eternal or transcendent back into philosophy to compensate for the banishment of gods from the bulk of philosophy, or perhaps whether it was an attempt to prop up the dignity of a profession overshadowed by the success of science. Perhaps there may be some truth to these suspicions, but they are only suspicions.

However, if some necessary truth could be established, then it should count as something foundational in the architecture of knowledge on which other truths could be based. If some truth is necessary, then it would seem to be more secure than truths that were merely contingent, and therefore any system built on such a necessary truth would appear to be stronger than one that was established on a contingent basis or on the mutually coherence of its statements. So perhaps the concern with necessity in philosophy is ultimately a manifestation of an inherent yearning for foundationalism leading toward first philosophy. Certainly if such foundationalism were the proper course for philosophy to take, and if necessary truths could be established, then the practice of philosophy would have a much clearer direction than it does now, so perhaps a hope for a foundational grounding in necessary truths is at least understandable. This study, however, expressed method-

---

[4]Some might claim that the formulations of laws governing p and q would justify a concern with necessity, since those laws would indicate an instance of nomological necessity, and that necessity is best expressed in terms of possible worlds. Yet it is not clear that regular occurrences require the formulation of universal laws, rather than understanding that regularity in terms of symmetry as van Fraassen argues (van Fraassen, 1989). Nor is it clear to me that possible worlds semantics are the best way to understand necessity in general, though these semantics do provide a convenient way of modeling necessity.

ological suspicions concerning first philosophy and continued to investigate a way for philosophy to proceed without either firm foundations or a clear end state. Perhaps these initial suspicions are misplaced, and some first philosophy will ultimately be established. Yet the approach of this study suggests that if such will be the case, a first philosophy cannot merely be assumed at the beginning, but must be established on the basis of some form of median philosophy such as perspectival reduction, although that first philosophy may ultimately dispense with perspectival reduction as a mere methodological expedient in a context of discovery, if indeed it can establish its justification independently.

In any case, perspectival reduction does not require necessary truths in order to proceed, nor does it specifically aim for the establishment of necessary truths. If philosophers continue to place such high methodological value on the quest for necessary truths, they may not fully appreciate the way in which perspectival reduction functions and what it might achieve. If indeed perspectival reduction is a valid and valuable method for philosophy to adopt, then it would seem that other philosophical values besides necessity would need to be readjusted as well.

Chapter 18

Language

Philosophy in the twentieth century has been dominated by a fundamental concern with language.[1] This concern has taken different forms, but in general it appears that there has been a general presupposition in recent philosophical practice that closer attention to language would be able to solve, dissolve, or simply reject the outstanding problems of philosophy. It seems clear that the attention that has been focused on language has yielded important results, certainly with regard to the study of language itself. It is not clear, though, that a fundamental concern with language has succeeded in resolving very many traditional problems of philosophy or any new problems that have arisen. Yet insofar as linguistically oriented philosophy has expanded philosophy in some directions, its results should not be devalued. Perspectival reduction aims to subsume alternative methodologies, so it would seem that any important linguistic results should be preserved within a broader application of perspectival reduction.

However, it is not clear that perspectival reduction itself gives language any special methodological importance. Of course, to determine whether something is invariant across various perspectives, the languages used within those perspectives need to be understood, if those perspectives imply any difference in language, and questions of translation may arise to determine whether what is said within different languages is the same. Yet it is not clear that the differences between perspectives are fundamentally lin-

---

[1] I am tempted to say that this concern has been something like an unholy obsession.

guistic differences such that a concern with language and translation would always sort out such differences.

Nor is it clear that the objective preferability of one perspective over another depends critically on linguistic considerations, since this preferability should be grounded in standards for theory appraisal that do not seem to be linguistically grounded. Understanding the language employed by various perspectives may be required for identifying precisely what those standards may be, but it is not clear that the adherence to different standards of theory appraisal nor differences in the application of those standards depends specifically on linguistic concerns.

With commensurability, though, it appears that language may indeed be important, primarily since commensurability has commonly been understood in terms of translation between the languages of different perspectives.[2] However, I have argued in the book on relativism that this interpretation of commensurability is not an adequate one with regard to the kind of commensurability that is part of the claims of relativism (Ressler, 2013, pp. 163–165). Translation understood as the preservation of meanings between different languages may indeed count as a kind of commensurability with regard to relativism, but not all commensurability and incommensurability in relativism must be understood in terms of this kind of translation. Rather, commensurability is best understood more generally as a transformation between perspectives, and this transformation may occur where there is no difference in language and where translation would therefore not be required. For example, in the paradigm instance of commensurability, the Lorentz transformations in the special theory of relativity, the differing spatial and temporal measurements given according to different inertial frameworks are not understood to occur in different languages associated with those frameworks. Likewise, in my attempts to find commensurability between the different perspectives on the nature of explanation in Chapter 14, it is not clear that those who hold different theories of explanation are speaking different languages. Rather, what emerged from that discussion was that it was the difference in pragmatic interests that govern differing theories of explanation, and these pragmatic interests were not obviously concerned with the pragmatics of language use as such.

---

[2] Most notably by Donald Davidson (Davidson, 1973).

Yet even if those conceptions of philosophy where concern with language is fundamental are subordinated to the status of mere perspectives within the process of perspectival reduction, there is a fundamental connection between philosophy and language that appears to justify the twentieth century concern with language. It seems that all philosophy must be presented in language in order to qualify as philosophy. Suppose, for example, that I contemplate a philosophical issue in a deep meditative trance, intentionally seeking to avoid framing my thoughts in language. I might thereby gain some form of insight or enlightenment, but I would not thereby be engaged in philosophy, unless I were to attempt subsequently to frame that insight in language. The problem in this case appears to be communicability. If my insight cannot be communicated, it would seem to count merely as a form of mysticism rather than philosophy.

Not just any kind of communicability is sufficient for philosophy either. Suppose that I could formulate a series of nonsensical syllables as an incantation that could reliably induce in someone else the same insight that I had revealed to myself in meditation, ignoring the problematic question of what would count as the same insight. Again, this would seem to represent an instance of mysticism rather than philosophy. The problem in this case is the impossibility of defense and analysis of that insight. Philosophy apparently requires that whatever insight I may have should be able to be defended against objections, rather than merely be transferred to others by some linguistic means. Philosophical insight must be understood, not merely possessed, and this understanding seems to require that I can analyze that insight both for myself and for others, and these requirements can best be met by framing philosophical insight in some language, whether formal or informal.

This strong connection between philosophy and language does not thereby indicate that philosophical problems can be solved or dissolved by paying close attention to language. Rather, a more likely conclusion would be that language poses a special problem for philosophy, perhaps by limiting philosophy to what language can achieve. Philosophy may seek to reveal all knowledge, but if philosophy must be expressed within language, then philosophy can only reveal what is capable of being expressed in language.³ However, I am not entirely comfortable with this suggestion, primarily because it is not clear precisely what the limits of language are, or even if there are any. To argue for the limitations of philosophy on the grounds of its connection with language requires a prior conception of the nature of language, and therefore the argument would only be as good as this conception is adequate.⁴ Furthermore, it seems clear that philosophy has enhanced the capacity of language, rather than being limited by it, by forcing various languages to express concepts that may not have been available originally within that language, and it seems likely that the expressive needs of philosophy in the future may push the very nature of language still farther. So it may be that any supposed limit of language will eventually be transcended precisely under the needs to express increasingly more adequate philosophical understanding.

Still, there is a troubling question in philosophy that is grounded in its strong connection with language, namely the extent to which philosophical results might be influenced by this connection, which I take to be one of the aspects of the debate between realists and anti-realists in various areas of philosophy. If language influences the results of philosophical investigation, then it may be wondered whether the topics of philosophical investigation are truly independent of language and merely expressed in it, or whether those topics are fundamentally dependent upon language itself. As a general methodology, perspectival reduction should be applicable to this debate as to any other philosophical question. Yet it is not clear prior to this application how the results of perspectival reduction to the question of realism or anti-realism would affect the understanding of the connection between philosophy and language, and indeed how it would affect the methodological understanding of this connection with regard to the process of perspectival reduction. What it suggests at this

---

[3] This seems to be the opinion of John Locke in Books III and IV of his Essay Concerning Human Understanding (Locke, 1959b), as well as Ludwig Wittgenstein in his Tractarian period (Wittgenstein, 1922).

[4] Consider in this regard Colin McGinn's arguments for the limitations of philosophical inquiry (McGinn, 1993), which are grounded in a conception of human faculties deriving from the work of Noam Chomsky. If Chomsky's views or McGinn's conceptions of those views are faulty, then so are McGinn's arguments for the limits of philosophy. However, McGinn's arguments are grounded more generally in cognitive capacities rather than specifically in the nature of language.

point, though, is mainly that philosophical perspectives that take a special concern with language should be important to understanding the question of realism and anti-realism within an application of perspectival reduction, even if those perspectives alone do not provide the royal road to philosophy in general.

Chapter 19

Distinctions

The three general techniques of accomplishing perspectival reduction include two techniques that are already well-known in philosophical practice, namely the search for invariances among the various perspectives, and the search for one perspective that is objectively preferable to all the others. The third general technique, namely the search for commensurability rules between perspectives, is presented here as a technique that has not yet been well appreciated in philosophical practice. However, there is another general technique in philosophical practice that has not been represented within the account of perspectival reduction thus far, namely making distinctions. This technique appears so fundamental to philosophical practice that its absence in any proposed philosophical methodology would seem to be an unacceptable omission. In fact, at least one author has claimed that the practice of making distinctions counts as the defining method for philosophy (Sokolowski, 1998, p. 516).

Yet the use of distinctions is not restricted to philosophical practice. One such use is the generation of categorizations and taxonomies, in which a general category is subdividing by making distinctions within that category in order to isolate qualities among members instantiating that category where those qualities are not shared among the entire general category. For instance, not all animals have wings, so it would appear that one could say that animals are both winged and non-winged, which might be taken to represent a contradiction. However, no single animal is both winged and non-winged, so a distinction between the subcategory of birds within the category of animals resolves this apparent contradiction. Yes, some animals are winged, namely birds, but there are also other kinds of animals besides birds, and most of these kinds do not have wings. If on further reflection some of these other kinds include members that do have wings, yet are not properly classified as birds, for example bats, then other distinctions will generate further sub-categories within the taxonomy. There would seem to be nothing particularly profound about this use of distinctions, which is part of nearly every scientific discipline.

The use of distinctions within philosophy likewise is designed to resolve apparent contradictions or other apparent problems in philosophical theories. Sometimes these distinctions are used to generate systems of categories, even with regard to distinctions among the various kinds of distinctions themselves (Suarez, 1976). Yet the role of distinctions in philosophy is not restricted to taxonomic purposes. The apparent contradictions or other problems for which distinctions are invoked to resolve are not only problems with regard to the qualities attributed to various categories, but may include problems with the formulation of a given theory, or problems with the degree to which certain evidence bears upon a theory, or problems in evaluating a theory with regard to some test case, for example.

Thus, in Plato's *Theaetetus* dialogue, Socrates considers the question whether knowledge is perception, and raises the issue of a foreign language (Plato, 1961, pp. 867–868, 162c–163c). One certainly perceives the foreign language, whether as sounds made by a speaker of the language or as characters written in an alphabet, but it does not seem that such perception should count as knowing the language. Here a test case is being evaluated to determine its bearing on a philosophical theory. By characterizing the language as foreign one, one that is by hypothesis unknown to someone, this test case raises a problem for the theory that knowledge is perception with regard to the evidential value of this situation, since one can clearly perceive the foreign language, but it is not clear that one thereby knows that language in any relevant sense. Theaetetus resolves the problem by making a distinction between knowing what is presented within perception, namely the sounds and the shapes of the characters, and knowing the meaning of the language. So in a minimal sense one knows a foreign language just by perceiving it, but not in the full sense of knowing a language.

As Nicholas Rescher expresses it, "Distinctions are the instruments we use in the (potentially never-ending) work of rescuing our assertoric commitments from inconsistency while yet salvaging what we can" (Rescher, 2001, p. 119). Yet Rescher does not see this as a fundamentally conservative activity, but rather a creative one that drives the development of philosophy, eventually linking it to Hegelian dialectic. "Distinctions are the doors through which philosophy moves on to new questions and problems. They bring new concepts and new theses to the fore" (Rescher, 2001, p. 120).

This characterization suggests that distinctions serve a function within perspectival reduction both to clarify existing perspectives and to generate new ones. If there is any ambiguity within a philosophical perspective, that ambiguity will likely be resolved by making distinctions in the terms it uses. Likewise, as Rescher indicates and the example from the *Theaetetus* illustrates, distinctions can save a perspective from inconsistencies that might otherwise suggest that the perspective should be rejected on the grounds of incoherence. In Chapter 3, I argued for the methodological value of apparently incoherent positions as opportunities for philosophy to expand, and the function of distinctions that Rescher identifies is a key way in which an apparently incoherent position might be shown not be incoherent after all.

Yet this same practice of making distinctions can serve an additional function within perspectival reduction, since the clarification of philosophical perspectives by means of distinctions also clarifies each perspective's difference with other perspectives. Where initially two perspectives might seem to share common features, this commonality might be merely apparent, before the full consequences of each perspective are made explicit, and made explicit specifically by means of distinctions. Such clarification might make the difference between both perspectives appearing to meet evaluative standards equally well and one perspective demonstrating itself to be objectively preferable.

More importantly, the clarification of perspectives by means of distinctions may serve to identify the dimensions across which a perspectival reduction might be achieved by means of commensurability rules. In the example from the *Theaetetus*, the distinction within language of the sounds and shapes of the characters as opposed to the meaning of the language, roughly aligning to the modern distinction between syntax and semantics, identifies dimensions to which competing theories of language might be aligned, and once aligned in this way, the commensurability across these perspectives might become evident. In fact, it seems likely that the search for commensurability rules itself would prompt the development of additional distinctions whose need might not have been appreciated otherwise.

In short, since perspectival reduction is a meta-methodology acting on the results of other philosophical methodologies, whatever functions distinctions serve in existing philosophical practice, they continue to serve in perspectival reduction. Additionally, distinctions appear to serve a vital role in establishing the dimensions across which a perspectival reduction might be accomplished by means of commensurability rules.

Chapter 20

Constraint

There is one aspect of perspectival reduction that continues to concern me, namely its apparent lack of constraint. I should note in advance that this chapter will not completely solve this concern, but will rather seek to develop this concern most fully and to explore some of the solutions I have contemplated thus far. Clearly I think that perspectival reduction offers significant promise for progress within philosophy, but I will not be so dishonest as to attempt to hide problems with this method that I have not yet been able to resolve.

Perspectival reduction requires a multitude of different perspectives on a given topic, but there does not appear to be any limit on how many perspectives the method will accommodate. Ideally, it would seem that all perspectives should be incorporated into the method, whether in its initial stages of investigation in seeking commensurability rules, or at some later state whereby the results of a perspectival reduction should be found capable of explaining all of the various perspectives that may arise with regard to the topic.

However, this lack of constraint on the perspectives involved in perspectival reduction presents a problem. On the one hand, if every possible perspective is incorporated into the method, including perspectives that may admittedly be in gross error, it may be wondered whether any commensurability rules could ever be devised to coordinate this vast proliferation of perspectives. If commensurability could be demonstrated between two given perspectives, the addition of a further perspective would apparently decrease the probability that the commensurability rules between the first two perspectives would be applicable to the third. As further perspectives are added, the probability that those commensurability rules could apply to all the perspectives would seem to decrease sharply. With regard to all possible perspectives, then, it would appear that the probability of finding any commensurability rules may even approach zero.

On the other hand, if constraints are introduced to reduce the number of perspectives that any instance of perspectival reduction would need to consider, then the problem of the criterion seems to reassert itself. Those constraints would constitute criteria that either need to be supported by other criteria or are completely unsupported. Furthermore, certain presuppositions could be identified within any given set of constraints proposed within perspectival reduction, such that different constraints may be relative to different presuppositions. Yet the method of perspectival reduction was introduced precisely as a means to overcome the problem of the criterion and the relativity of presuppositions. So, for example, suppose that a criterion were proposed whereby perspectival reduction should only consider those perspectives that are not clearly in error. The proposal seems to be a reasonable one; however, if there were a clear method whereby erroneous perspectives could be identified, one that was not troubled by any relativity according to presuppositions, then it would appear that the method of perspectival reduction would not really be needed. Rather, it would seem that the proposed method of determining erroneous perspectives should be embraced and enhanced as the proper method for philosophy. Yet any proposed method for determining errors would depend upon certain presuppositions, and the identification of various presuppositions in contemporary philosophical methods was what prompted the search for an alternative method in the form of perspectival reduction.

This problem with constraint is mirrored in the anarchism embraced by Paul Feyerabend, in his use of the slogan "anything goes" (Feyerabend, 2010, p. 7).[1] Feyerabend is concerned about the improper limitation of scientific practice according to any restrictive theory about scientific method. His epistemic anarchism is in-

---

[1] Feyerabend's use of the slogan itself is problematic, as he himself recounts. See (Feyerabend, 2010, pp. xii–xiii, xvii).

tended to free scientific practice from such intrusive restrictions on the part of theoretically inclined philosophers of science. Yet it might be wondered, if indeed anything goes, whether anything can come of it. My intention in this study is not to argue against method, as did Feyerabend, but to argue for a meta-methodology that would provide some constraints for the kind of anarchism he espouses, by seeking a way to coordinate the various perspectives that are engendered by differing methods. However, at this point there is some concern that the proposed coordination of the various perspectives is undermined by the very proliferation of perspectives, that there need to be further constraints on the kinds of perspectives that enter into the method in order to achieve any results at all.

Of course, it is important to note that as presented in this study, there are indeed some constraints on perspectives, precisely by virtue of what constitutes a perspective with regard to the method, and these constraints are dictated by the apparent relativity of philosophical theories to presuppositions. Recall that this apparent relativism was accepted merely as a methodological expedient, subject to the subsequent reduction of the apparent relativism by the denial of one of the main theses of relativism, either by identifying invariances, by determining one perspective to be objectively preferred over the others, or by devising commensurability rules to coordinate the various perspectives. The nature of the apparent relativity thereby determines what can enter into the method as a perspective.

Perspectives within a system of relativism are not freestanding theories or conjectures, but are indexed to something according to a non-arbitrary relation. The entities to which relativized theories are indexed constitute a set of relativizing factors, such as cultures in an instance of cultural relativism, or languages in an instance of linguistic relativism, and this set must constitute a kind.[2] Thus, in order to enter into a relativistic system, theories must be linked with some relativizing factor. For example, a theory cannot appear within cultural relativism without being linked with some culture. In relativity, there must be something that can answer the question: to what is it relative? So the requirement that perspectives involve a non-arbitrary relation to some relativizing factor provides

---

[2] See (Ressler, 2013) for more extensive discussion of these requirements.

some constraints on the perspectives that enter into perspectival reduction, since any putative perspective that is not indexed to a relativizing factor can safely be excluded from consideration.

However, since the relativizing factors are always presuppositions in perspectival reduction, it is not clear that this constraint counts for much. Given any wild conjecture or erroneous theory on a topic, a number of presuppositions of those positions could always be identified, and it is the dubious validity of such presuppositions that would make the theory erroneous or the conjecture wild. Since those positions can be linked with presuppositions, they would meet the constitutive constraints concerning relativizing factors and would therefore qualify for consideration within perspectival reduction. Since any position has presuppositions, every position would qualify for inclusion within perspectival reduction, meaning that anything goes after all, despite the constitutive constraint.

Yet even if this constraint does not limit the number of perspectives that enter into perspectival reduction, it does indicate the way in which this apparent explosion of perspectives could be managed. As noted in the book on relativism, the kind of commensurability rules that would provide an instance of perspectival reduction must utilize something about the relativizing factors as dimensions constituting the basis for transformation from one perspective to another.[3] So in the paradigm case of commensurability, the Lorentz transformations in the special theory of relativity, spatial and temporal measurements are relative to inertial frameworks. The Lorentz transformations operate upon measurements within each perspective across the three spatial dimensions and the temporal dimension, and these dimensions constitute something important about the very nature of an inertial framework. Thus I have suggested that any identification of commensurability rules with regard to an instance of apparent relativism should identify certain dimensions associated with the relativizing factors against which the commensurability transformation would operate. In perspectival reduction, where the relativizing factors are presuppositions, then, any proposed commensurability rules must identify certain dimensions of those presuppositions and operate upon them to effect a transformation between perspectives. While

---

[3] (Ressler, 2013, Section 6.6).

it might be thought that those dimensions should be sought within the nature of presuppositions themselves, and therefore these dimensions would be the same for any application of perspectival reduction, it seems to me that the dimensions should properly be identified with regard to the topic in which those presuppositions appear. Perhaps those dimensions would not fall directly within the scope of the topic itself, but may relate to other topics that interrelate with the topic. So, for example, if I am attempting to implement perspectival reduction within metaphysics, the dimensions may not necessarily be essentially metaphysical in nature, but may be found within a field that coordinates with metaphysics, such as epistemology.

Consider the contentious question of personal identity, to offer a speculative example of such commensurability dimensions. Currently, the question of personal identity appears to be investigated primarily according to the following methodology: First, devise a series of test cases composed of stories according to which someone's body, brain, or psychology are altered in increasingly fantastic ways. Second, determine the identity of the resulting monstrosities, whether they constitute the original person or some different person, basing this assignment of identities upon one's own intuitions. Third, assert that most people would share those intuitions. Fourth, claim that contrary intuitions are incomprehensible. Clearly, this methodology has not yielded a consensus with regard to the question of personal identity, but seems rather simply to have spawned a range of contrary intuitions. As I have suggested, a topic in which contrary intuitions are operable is a topic that appears ideally suited to treatment by perspectival reduction.

Most helpfully in this regard, Derek Parfit has compiled a table correlating various test cases against a range of various criteria for personal identity (Parfit, 2008, p. 182). The table specifies how each criterion would assign personal identity according to each test case, whether the result would be original person *A*, original person *B*, a new person, or whether the result is indeterminate. See Table 20.1 below for a schematic of this table. Each criterion assigns personal identity differently and therefore constitutes a distinct position. Yet such a table might be made complete by adding further criteria for every distinct combination of assignments of

	Criteria			
Case	1	2	3	...
A's brain and psychology, but B's body	A	B	A	...
A's brain and psychology, but a new body	A	A	B	...
A's body, but a new brain and psychology	A	A	A	...
...	...	...	...	...

Table 20.1: Schematic table of personal identity criteria, adapted from Parfit

personal identity for each test case.[4] While it might not be clear how to characterize every resulting criterion for personal identity, let it be supposed that there is some characterization that yields that particular pattern of personal identity assignments, even if it is beyond anyone's ability to understand the rationale behind the criterion. By making such a list of criteria complete by combinatorial means, I would thereby appear to enunciate every possible perspective on personal identity with regard to the test cases listed.[5] So if I recognize each possible criterion as a valid perspective, it would seem that anything goes. I think it is clear why Parfit does not consider such a complete list of criteria, namely that he likely thinks that most such criteria are clearly false or even incoherent and therefore unworthy of any consideration. Yet it appears that there should be some clear criterion for determining which criteria of personal identity are clearly false and which are at least worthy of consideration, preferably not based upon the blunt intuitions of those who address the question of personal identity, since intuitions concerning personal identity vary considerably, which is why there is a philosophical problem of personal identity. The method of perspectival reduction takes the problem of the criterion very seriously, and seeks to avoid blunt appeal to intuitions, particularly intuitions that may differ.

Yet without imposing arbitrary constraints on the criteria for

---

[4]This technique should be familiar from the method of generating truth tables in elementary symbolic logic. Here, instead of truth-values, four possible assignments of personal identity are used. Of course, if there are other candidates for personal identity assignments other than these four, then a different table could be devised with more valuation options.

[5]Obviously, if more distinct test cases are devised, then the complete list of perspectives will grow accordingly.

personal identity, the method of perspectival reduction would appear to accept every possible criterion for personal identity. Thereby the method faces the problem of how it could be possible to devise commensurability rules for this complete list of criteria, where there is such radical disagreement between these criteria, specifically fostered by combinatorial means. Perspectival reduction requires the identification of the presuppositions for each criterion and the use of these presuppositions in the formulation of commensurability rules.[6] Indeed by making the list of criteria for personal identity complete, I have thereby made it much harder to accomplish even the identification of the presuppositions for each criterion, since it will be difficult to understand why anyone might assign personal identity according to many of these criteria, and if the criteria cannot even be understood, then it would seem hopeless to expect that presuppositions could be identified in these cases. One might consider imposing a constraint upon this complete list of criteria, limiting the list only to those criteria that could be understood. However, I would strongly resist such an imposition in principle, since the apparent incomprehensibility of these criteria might primarily be due to a problem in one's own comprehension, not a problem with the criteria themselves. Some of these criteria may later prove to be important to appreciating the commensurability rules between perspectives on personal identity, if such rules are even available, so excluding them from consideration may be improper.

Practically, though, perspectival reduction might be performed by seeking an account that exemplifies the theoretical virtues of competitive subsumption and reflexive reiteration, as noted in Chapter 12, projecting to the ideal end of the iterative process, rather than actually performing a reduction by means of identifying commensurability rules. Yet this practical short-cut does not alleviate the theoretical concern with constraints identified here, particularly with regard to competitive subsumption, since the proliferation of competitors is precisely the problem contemplated here.

---

[6]Again, I am here considering only the novel aspect of perspectival reduction in terms of commensurability, rather than the two other means of attaining perspectival reduction, namely by invariances or objective preferability, since it is with regard to commensurability rules that the problem with the apparent lack of constraint seems most acute.

Having thus made the problem seem as difficult as possible, I can suggest the general approach that I would take to understand various criteria of personal identity according to perspectival reduction, even if I do not attempt to solve the problem of personal identity here. First, there do not appear to be any invariances identifiable among the various criteria, particularly since I have extended the perspectives to a complete list of criteria representing every possible difference in assignments of personal identity. Second, so long as the question of personal identity continues to rely upon individual intuitions, it appear that no definitive judgment that one perspective is objectively preferable to the others is forthcoming, though there may be widespread agreement that a large number of perspectives are objectively worse than others. Consequently, I would seek for commensurability rules based on the presuppositions of the various criteria. To that end, I think it is productive to consider the question why any assignment of personal identity is important, and it seems to me that there is no single reason why personal identity is important, but rather several.

First, there is the issue of phenomenology. In some of the test cases for personal identity, the phenomenology of persons before and after the modifications imposed by the cases will be radically different than others, for example, if I wake up from an operation with a significantly different body, assuming that it is clear who *I* am. Second, there are a number of legal issues. If I am subjected to a brain transfer operation, there may be legal questions concerning the ownership of the property I had in my possession before the operation, concerning my accrued social benefits, possibly even concerning my citizenship, if I am combined in some important way with a citizen of another country. Third, there are issues surrounding personal relationships, not only legal questions about marriage if I were married before the situation in the test case occurs, but also basic issues of how I interact with others and how I would want others to interact with me. This last point further suggests that there are perspectival aspects to some of these issues as well. With regard to personal relationships, there is the question of those relationships from my perspective, and the separate question of those relationships from the perspective of others. What I might want in my relations from my perspective with regard to attributions of personal identity, however I determine what my perspective would be in each of the test cases, might not match what others might want from their perspective, or even might not match what I might want were I to consider the issue from their perspective. Likewise, with regard to legal issues, there is the question of what rights I would want to have assigned to me according to whatever perspective I determine to be mine in each test case, but if I were to consider the matter more objectively from the perspective of overall public policy, the question may indeed be quite different.

There may indeed be more issues than these three concerning why the question of personal identity is important. However many issue there are, I would claim that each issue constitutes a dimension of analysis according to which certain presuppositions concerning personal identity could be aligned, and these presuppositions in turn underlie the various criteria for personal identity. Adopting different stances with regard to these dimensions may take the simple form of prioritizing one dimension over the other when there are conflicts in attributions of personal identity, perhaps preferring phenomenology over legal considerations, for example. Alternatively, the way in which these dimensions relate to presuppositions may be more complex than simple prioritization, possibly involving additional categories from ethical theory and metaphysics, and thereby possibly increasing or refining the dimensions. Yet whatever dimensions are ultimately determined to underlie the various presuppositions related to each criterion of personal identity, those same dimensions should be critical in the identification of commensurability rules between the various criteria. If indeed commensurability is possible across the various perspectives on personal identity, there should be some means of transforming the assignments of personal identity from one perspective to the assignments in another, according to the alignment of the various perspectives across the dimensions associated with their presuppositions. Of course, it may be that no commensurability is possible with regard to personal identity at all, in which case it may be that the issue is fundamentally a relativistic one after all. If commensurability is possible, it is my proposal that the underlying dimensions for such commensurability could be found by considering the reasons why personal identity should matter at all, admittedly a distinctly pragmatic approach.

Even if one were to agree that this approach might be profitable with regard to the question of personal identity, it does not completely satisfy the underlying concern in this chapter about constraints. It still seems that anything goes with regard to the number of perspectives that this method considers, and the proposal with regard to identifying dimensions does not make the process of perspectival reduction significantly easier, given the combinatorial proliferation of perspectives. Nevertheless, it is mainly my argument thus far that if perspectival reduction is possible without any initial constraints about which perspectives should be considered, then it should proceed according to the kind of dimensional analysis that I have suggested with regard to the question of personal identity. There is no guarantee that a perspectival reduction is possible in any given case, particularly with regard to such a thorny issue as personal identity.[7] Further, it is not my intention to minimize or waive away the concern with constraints here. As I noted at the beginning of this chapter, the concern is one that still exercises me.

So assuming that the process of perspectival reduction will require the identification of certain dimensions underlying the presuppositions of the various perspectives, the question is still how perspectival reduction by means of commensurability rules is possible in cases where the number of perspectives is allowed to increase without constraint. One suggestion that I have contemplated is to attempt to reduce the proliferation of perspectives to some essential conflict. The idea is that perspectival reduction works best in cases in which there is a clear disagreement between two or more perspectives such that there is an apparent instance of relativism involved. Yet it may be the case that given a disagreement between two perspectives, the consideration of additional perspectives may not add anything substantial to that disagreement. So the suggestion is that enough perspectives should be considered such that there is a substantial disagreement between perspectives, but that further perspectives that do not add anything to that substantial disagreement can safely be ignored.

---

[7] I note here an argument from Matti Eklund "that it is our concept of personal identity that itself breaks down in fission cases. Then, insofar as a proposed criterion of personal identity gives incoherent verdicts about fission cases, it merely reflects a feature of the concept, and this is of course a point in favor of the criterion" (Eklund, 2002, p .465). I would agree that there is no reason to think that every concept must be completely coherent. Likewise, there is no reason to expect that every attempt at perspectival reduction will result in a successful reduction.

This kind of constraint therefore does not seem completely arbitrary and might make the implementation of perspectival reduction much easier.[8]

One way to identify an essential conflict on a given topic is based on Nicholas Rescher's account of the aporetic method.[9] An apory is a "collective inconsistency among individually plausible contentions" (Rescher, 2006, p. 19). The following is one example of an apory that Rescher offers:

1. All knowledge is grounded in observation (empiricism).

2. We can only observe matters of empirical fact.

3. From empirical facts we cannot infer values (the fact-value divide).

4. Knowledge about values is possible (value cognitivism). (Rescher, 2006, p. 19)

These four contentions are inconsistent considered together, but the rejection of one of these contentions would make the remaining three consistent. Therefore, rejection of these contentions would yield four different consistent positions: (1) value intuitionism, (2) value-sensibility theories, (3) values-as-facts theories, and (4) positivism or value-skepticism (Rescher, 2006, pp. 19–20). Ultimately Rescher endorses a cost-benefit analysis in order to identify the best resulting position from the consideration of an apory.

It seems to me, though, that the aporetic method may be a plausible way to develop a series of perspectives on an issue, and the perspectives it develops are thereby constrained to a very tight essential conflict. Fewer contentions would not have yielded a collective inconsistency, whereas additional contentions might not

---

[8]Similarly (Hiah, Poll, & van der Burg, 2025, p. 517) proposes the notion of perspectival saturation with regard to a point in an iterative application at which adding new perspectives does not change the result of the reduction. However, such perspectival saturation depends critically on where one starts. It is possible that starting from different places in an iterative application could result in clusters of perspectives that provide different results. This is not necessarily problematic for perspectival reduction, since these different results would simply constitute further perspectives that would initiate further iterations of perspectival reduction, though this solution is still not completely satisfactory, as noted below.

[9]See (Rescher, 2001, pp. 93–102) and (Rescher, 2006, pp. 17–26).

have added anything substantial to this essential conflict. The resulting set of conflicting perspectives appears to be precisely the kind of situation for which perspectival reduction was designed. Where Rescher would seek a perspectival reduction by showing that one perspective is objectively preferable to the other by means of a cost-benefit analysis, I would be more inclined to seek commensurability rules between these perspectives, in the way outlined above in Chapter 12.

Yet I think there are two concerns with the use of the aporetic method to constrain perspectives within the method of perspectival reduction. One is that Rescher notes that apories are generated from statements that are each plausible. I have been strongly resistant to imposing constraints of plausibility on perspectival reduction, since I think there may be very important perspectives that are not especially plausible at all, at least initially. The importance of such implausible perspectives would consist in the ability of those perspectives to reveal aspects of a topic that might not be apparent from a consideration of only those perspectives that are plausible. Of course, the plausibility constraint in the aporetic method is imposed not directly on perspectives, but on a set of statements that generate those perspectives, so the plausibility constraint might not be problematic in the way that concerns me. Yet if what is most important is merely an essential conflict between perspectives, then it is not clear that the plausibility constraint is important in generating apories and perspectives. Rather, any inconsistent group of contentions should be sufficient to indicate an essential conflict between perspectives, whether the contentions that generate those perspectives are plausible or not.

The second concern follows from the latter consideration. Even restricting contentions within apories to plausible contentions, it is not clear that there will be only one apory associated with any given philosophical issue. If there are several apories on a topic, and several perspectives generated from those apories, then it is not clear that the perspectives generated by the aporetic method form such an essential conflict as I had hoped. The possibility envisioned here is that an apory is itself only one perspective on the topic, and that other apories on the same topic would constitute different perspectives. Of course, by characterizing the possibility of multiple apories as perspectives, that does not pose a problem for perspectival reduction. Rather, it would suggest several stages of application of perspectival reduction. First, for each set of putatively essentially conflicting perspectives generated by an apory, a perspectival reduction is performed. Second, where there are multiple apories on a topic, the results of each perspectival reduction in the first stage are taken together as conflicting perspectives, and a second perspectival reduction is attempted on them. Yet especially if the constraint on the plausibility of contentions in apories is relaxed, it is not clear whether the proposal to limit perspectives to essential conflicts derived from apories succeeds in usefully constraining the number of perspectives within perspectival reduction, or whether the proliferation of perspectives is merely replaced by a proliferation of apories that ultimately reinstate an unmanageable proliferation of perspectives.

In the end, I think the real constraints in perspectival reduction will be the practical limits of the ability of any given philosopher to imagine every perspective and to identify properly the presuppositions and dimensions involved in those perspectives, though I have criticized this kind of lack of imagination in Chapter 3. I suspect that this limitation will ultimately skew the results of perspectival reduction, such that the results must be viewed with some suspicion. This practical limitation is not hopeless, however, since one aspect of median philosophies noted earlier is that they tend to represent iterative processes that should eventually converge upon stable results. Even a faulty application of perspectival reduction limited by a given philosopher's perspectival imagination could bootstrap a process that may ultimately overcome my present concerns about constraints, either by finding a way whereby all possible perspectives may be managed within further applications of perspectival reduction, or by finding a better methodology to replace perspectival reduction altogether. Likewise, since philosophy is a collaborative effort, the particular limitations of any given philosopher are not fatal to the overall effort. If my own limitations as a thinker should skew the results of an instance of perspectival reduction that I might make based upon the restrictions that I place upon the perspectives I include in the process, other thinkers may not be limited in the way that I am, or at the very least, may skew the results of perspectival reduction in a different way. What thus emerges is a set of differing perspectives arising from out of differing approaches to perspectival reduction, and such a difference in perspectives would represent the starting point for another iteration of perspectival reduction.

So while I continue to be troubled by the lack of constraint in perspectival reduction, the limitations of the imaginations of actual philosophers to conceive perspectives, including the limitations of my own imagination, may provide some practical constraints on the implementation of any particular instance of perspectival reduction, however faulty the initial results may be. It seems to me that any results from an instance of perspectival reduction should count as a significant achievement. The hope is that they would constitute sufficient progress to bootstrap the next phase of investigation. Perhaps the development of those initial results may help expand philosophical imagination such that further perspectives might be contemplated. Given the iterative nature of perspectival reduction, the faults of these initial results could be corrected over time.

Chapter 21

Predecessors

The proposed method of perspectival reduction was developed primarily in response to Husserl's phenomenological investigations and his attitude toward presuppositions, as described earlier. However, it is clear that there have been important predecessors developing the idea of methodological pluralism, which I will briefly acknowledge here. I have already described Nietzsche's perspectivism with regard to his notion of objectivity, and would acknowledge him as an important predecessor to perspectival reduction. The following discussion seeks to acknowledge other predecessors, many of whom only came to my attention after I began developing and researching the idea of perspectival reduction. There may indeed be others of which I am not aware. Although their concerns do not always coincide with mine perfectly, I should like to think that the method of perspectival reduction would contribute to the aims of many of these predecessors.

Nicholas Rescher cites a predecessor whose work is not readily available, so I will simply quote Rescher's citation:

> And the 1796 prize essay of the undeservedly neglected philosopher August Ludwig Huelsen (1776-1810) was a seminal work that maintained the gradual emergence of an increasingly clearly distinguishable Science that grasps the real truth across the conflict of systems. The strife of systems simply represents the transitory birth pangs of a gradually emerging cognitive order in which this conflict is progressively transcended. (Rescher, 1994, pp. 208–9, n. 18)

From the perspective of this study, Huelsen would seem to be undeservedly neglected indeed. The method of perspectival reduction likewise represents a process that emerges from the strife of systems. "The Strife of Systems" provides the title for two later books, one by Wilmon Henry Sheldon (Sheldon, 1918), and one by Rescher himself (Rescher, 1985). Consequently, both Sheldon and Rescher likewise represent predecessors in the tradition of Huelsen.

The way that perspectival reduction seeks to develop a new theory on the basis of prior alternative theories clearly suggests the kind of dialectic that features in the work of G. W. F. Hegel and J. G. Fichte, in which a new notion emerges from out of the contradiction of two prior notions, or in the terminology of Fichte, a thesis and an antithesis resolve themselves into a synthesis. This dialectical movement relies upon just two contradictory notions, though, whereas in a case of perspectival reduction, not only are more than two alternative theories permitted, but it appears that the method works better when increasingly more alternatives are considered. In the work of Fichte and Hegel, it may seem somewhat mysterious and even mystical how a synthesis is supposed to emerge from contradictory notions. Richard Dien Winfield discusses Hegelian phenomenology as a starting point for philosophy that overcomes the reliance on presuppositions that characterize first philosophy (Winfield, 2011), also citing a book by William Maker discussing the question of presuppositions with regard to Hegel's methods (Maker, 1994).[1] Perhaps Winfield and Maker would challenge my characterization of Hegel's method as "last philosophy". Yet I think that these studies primarily affect the appraisal of Hegel with regard to the method of perspectival reduction presented here, without affecting the exposition or advocacy of the method itself.

Arthur Schopenhauer enunciates a form of perspectivism that approaches the principles underlying perspectival reduction:

> No view of the world can be entirely false which has sprung from an objectively intuitive apprehension of things and has been logically and consistently maintained. On the contrary, such a view is in the worst

---

[1] Feuerbach, on the other hand, critiques the claim that philosophy does not begin with presuppositions, and evaluates Hegel's own presuppositions (Feuerbach, 2012, pp. 59, 69).

case only one-sided as, for example, thorough materialism, absolute idealism, and others. They are all true, but they are all this simultaneously; consequently, their truth is only relative. Thus every such conception is true only from a definite standpoint just as a picture presents a landscape only from one point of view. If, however, we raise ourselves above the standpoint of such a system, we recognize the relative nature of its truth, that is, its one-sidedness. Only the highest standpoint that surveys and takes into account everything can furnish us with absolute truth. (Schopenhauer, 2000, pp. 12–13)

Indeed, Schopenhauer claims to have supplemented Kantian philosophy in this way by deducing the objective from the subjective standpoint and the subjective from the objective (Schopenhauer, 2000, p. 34), thereby providing the kind of higher standpoint that he advocates. However, it should be noted that the passage quoted is perhaps the only one in which Schopenhauer acknowledges the truth of absolute idealism, even if only as relative truth. For the most part, Schopenhauer regularly heaps scorn and abuse on the work of Fichte, Schelling, and especially Hegel, rather than attempting to see the truth in them.

Working later in the tradition of absolute idealism, Bernard Bosanquet attempts to identify a consensus on certain topics between the apparently opposed positions of realism and idealism. Thus both the realist and idealist "with an open mind, and his eye upon the object, may, or rather must, be led to investigations and appreciations which will carry him to seek completeness in regions within his opponent's spiritual home" (Bosanquet, 1921, p. vi). Reminiscent of the metaphor of triangulation applied in this study with regard to commensurability rules, Bosanquet claims that by adopting his approach, "You are no longer taking a single bearing with a single compass, but are covering a whole region with a systematic survey" (Bosanquet, 1921, p. ix). By seeking a meeting of extremes, Bosanquet seems to be working toward the identification of invariant features of alternative theories, once they are brought to a sufficient level of completeness and adequacy. While this approach represents one way to complete a perspectival reduction, the way that I have been emphasizing in this study is rather the development of commensurability rules.

Also apparently in the tradition of absolute idealism,[2] F. H. Bradley argues in *Appearance and Reality* that the Absolute must contain appearances as aspects of reality (Bradley, 1916, pp. 127–132). "All differences, we have urged repeatedly, come together in the Absolute" (Bradley, 1916, p. 203), much in the same way that all competing perspectives are subsumed within the results of a successful application of perspectival reduction. Indeed, Bradley seems to recognize the virtue of competitive subsumption:

> Show us an idea, we can proclaim, which seems hostile to our scheme, and we will show you an element which really is contained within it. And we will demonstrate your idea to be a self-contradictory piece of our system, an internal fragment which only through sheer blindness can fancy itself outside. We will prove that its independence and isolation are nothing in the world but a failure to perceive more than one aspect of its own nature. (Bradley, 1916, p. 519)

Yet Bradley appears to leap from the contradictory nature of appearances directly to the postulation of an Absolute, whereas at least Hegel progresses through many stages of the dialectic before reaching the Absolute. In this sense, Bradley's work seems to exemplify an instance of last philosophy, rather than a median philosophy.[3]

What has become known as "Ramsey's Maxim" embodies a comparable approach to perspectival reduction. Frank P. Ramsey wrote with regard to different arguments concerning universals:

> Evidently, however, none of these arguments are really decisive, and the position is extremely unsatisfactory to any one with real curiosity about such a fundamental question. In such cases it is a heuristic maxim

---

[2] While counted among the British Idealists, it is not clear how much of an idealist Bradley truly was, despite his adherence to a Hegelian Absolute. Collingwood claims that while Bertrand Russell and G. E. Moore seem to have developed their doctrines of realism in opposition to Bradley, it turns out that Bradley may represent precisely the kind of realism that they were seeking (Collingwood, 2005, pp. 245–248).

[3] See also (Bradley, 1914, pp. 258ff).

that the truth lies not in one of the two disputed views but in some third possibility which has not yet been thought of, which we can only discover by rejecting something assumed as obvious by both the disputants. (Ramsey, 1990, pp. 11–12)

While Ramsey seeks truth in a third position that denies some common assumption of two disputed views, perspectival reduction recognizes all three of these views as perspectives that embody various presuppositions, wherein truth cannot easily be identified quite so easily. Thus Ramsey's maxim is a useful heuristic in generating new perspectives by focusing attention on assumptions and presuppositions, but it is no guarantee that the third possibility that Ramsey seeks will provide a decisive argument with regard to any philosophical question, merely by rejecting the common presuppositions of two other positions. For perspectival reduction, the third possibility must additionally demonstrate the virtues of competitive subsumption and reflexive reiteration.

Karl Mannheim explicitly argues for transformation formulas as a way to reduce differences between perspectives as a way to achieve objectivity "in a more roundabout fashion": "An effort must be made to find a formula for translating the results of one into those of the other and to discover a common denominator for these varying perspectivistic insights" (Mannheim, 1960, p. 270). This common denominator clearly aligns to the dimension for commensurability rules within perspectival reduction. However, Mannheim does not link the search for translational formulas to the presuppositions that underly differing perspectives.

José Ortega y Gasset articulates a vision of philosophy that is strongly perspectival in his "Doctrine of the Point of View" (Ortega y Gasset, 1961, pp. 86–96) as well as his broader reflections on the nature and origin of philosophy (Ortega y Gasset, 1960, 1967). For example, he bluntly asserts "Knowledge ... is perspective" (Ortega y Gasset, 1967, p. 44) and suggests "Since knowledge is a matter between men and things, it will sometimes have to be viewed from the position of men and at other times from that of things" (Ortega y Gasset, 1967, p. 45, n9). He offers four steps as part of dialectical series, although these steps are not sufficiently detailed to be constitutive of a methodology:

1. *Pause* before each *aspect* and obtain a view of it.

2. *Continue* thinking of move on to a contiguous aspect.
3. Not abandon — that is, *preserve* — the aspects already "viewed."
4. *Integrate* them in a sufficiently "total" view for the purposes of the subject under consideration in each particular instance. (Ortega y Gasset, 1967, p. 48)

Yet Ortega does not link this perspectivism to his reflections on presuppositions, for example in (Ortega y Gasset, 1975, p. 81) and (Ortega y Gasset, 1987, p. 77), else he might have approached a methodology similar to perspectival reduction.

In the late nineteenth century, the geologist Thomas Chamberlin advocated "The Method of Multiple Working Hypotheses" (Chamberlin, 1890). He argues that there is a risk that relying on a single initial plausible explanation will introduce an unacceptable bias into scientific investigation whereby better explanations simply are not explored. Even treating this single initial explanation merely as a working hypothesis does not always eliminate the risk of such bias. Only by considering multiple working hypotheses can the scientist survey the full range of hypotheses. In this way, not only is it more likely that the correct hypothesis will be identified, but the method of multiple working hypotheses enables the recognition that multiple causes might be operative in some case, where the concentration on a single working hypothesis might only bring one of the causes to light. Of course, Chamberlin advocates multiple hypotheses as part of a single overall scientific methodology, whereas perspectival reduction advocates multiple methodologies, but the ultimate aim seems to be the same in both cases, namely greater objectivity.[4]

Likewise, Paul Feyerabend argues for proliferation of alternative hypotheses in science, particularly those that contradict established theories in order to provide better explanations of facts than those established theories can provide (Feyerabend, 2010, pp. 13–25). Feyerabend notoriously advocates a form of anarchism in epistemology and philosophy of science (Feyerabend, 2010, pp. 1–2), as noted in Chapter 20. Consequently, it is not clear that he

---

[4] My thanks to Howard Sankey for bringing Chamberlin's ideas to my attention.

would have approved any of the three ways for providing a perspectival reduction, which seek to provide some constraints on this anarchy.

Robert Nozick advocates a form of philosophical pluralism as a way of avoiding "philosophical parochialism": "We can keep track of the different philosophical views that have been put forth and elaborated; we can pay attention to foreign traditions and their diverse viewpoints, to the special slant of these traditions on our questions, both the different ways they pose their nearly equivalent questions, and the different answers they offer" (Nozick, 2001, p. 19). Yet Nozick only considers the denial of objective equity as a way of avoiding relativism in this context, namely by producing views that are ranked in order of preference (Nozick, 2001, p. 20), whereas this study considers two additional ways of avoiding relativism in the interest of advancing philosophical analysis, in particular emphasizing the search for commensurability rules.

Additionally, I think one can count John Rawls as a predecessor to perspectival reduction, given his characterization of wide reflective equilibrium in terms of the demand to account for all reasonable alternative conceptions (Rawls, 2001, p. 31), which approaches the ideal of competitive subsumption. Indeed, many of his discussions of utilitarianism and other competing theories of justice tend to argue how the basic utilitarian intuitions can be recovered on the basis of Rawls' theory of justice as fairness and thereby could be subsumed under it. His aim of achieving an overlapping consensus appears likewise to seek invariances underlying alternative theories. Of course, as I have noted previously in Chapter 8, Rawls is not perfectly clear concerning how alternative conceptions should be taken into account in wide reflective equilibrium. If indeed he aims for the kind of commensurability which features in perspectival reduction, it is not clear to what extent the variety of reflective equilibrium he adopts in devising his theory of justice is perfectly consonant with such a method. After all, the aim of perspectival reduction is not the preservation of any particular intuitions or general judgments. If certain intuitions happen to be preserved in the results of the method, that preservation would be a secondary matter, not a primary methodological concern.

A closer predecessor is Hector-Neri Castañeda, who likewise advocates a pluralistic methodology. "The main desideratum of our time is systematic pluralistic symphilosophical activity, that is:

the construction of many different and very comprehensive theories. The main aim is the comparative study of maximal theories in order to establish, through isomorphisms among them, a system of invariances" (Castañeda, 1980, pp. 14–15). These invariances for Castañeda seem best to represent common phenomenological ontologies between rival theories (Castañeda, 1980, pp. 18–20). The search for invariances likewise features in perspectival reduction, but Castañeda does not clearly acknowledge a role specifically for commensurability between alternative theories as another kind of structural isomorphism. Unfortunately, he acknowledges that his proposed method remains a "visionary dream" (Castañeda, 1980, p. 105), since present theories are insufficiently comprehensive, just as I have acknowledged that perspectival reduction may not be practically feasible when rival theories on a topic are incomplete or inadequate. Interestingly, Castañeda likewise traces the assumptions and presuppositions of alternative approaches, such as ordinary language philosophy, and indeed acknowledges the presuppositions of his own approach (Castañeda, 1980, p. 52), but he uses these presuppositions merely to criticize competing approaches and does not explicitly incorporate them into his proposed method.

Lastly, outside of the tradition of western philosophy, I note that the Jain doctrine of syādvāda bears considerable similarity to perspectival reduction. The Jains hold a seven-valued logic based on the application of the word 'syāt' "meaning *in some aspect* or *somehow*" (Burch, 1964, p. 82). Yet it is not primarily in the application of Jain logic that I see similarity, but in their overall epistemology. For the Jains, karma is a particle that attaches to the soul, thereby obscuring one's knowledge. Enlightenment is the state of perfect knowledge attained by the elimination of all such karmic particles. So it appears that the use of the word 'syāt' represents an acknowledgement of different perspectives resulting from various patterns of karmic obstruction. However, the perspective of perfect knowledge would also appear to include the knowledge of how particular patterns of karmic obstruction yield certain perspectives. For this reason it seems that Jains can assert of any statement from an alternative perspective that it is so in some respect, since, in effect, if one had the same karmic obstruction as those in that alternative perspective, one would see that statement to be true, even if from one's own perspective one sees that it is false.

Only someone with perfect knowledge can see truth or falsity without qualifying it with the word 'syāt'. Of course, in Jainism, the path to the kind of perfect knowledge that reconciles various alternative perspectives is specifically religious practice rather than philosophical. For epistemically imperfect and religiously skeptical philosophers, I would recommend the path employing perspectival reduction through commensurability rules.[5]

---

[5] Much of the foregoing is of course interpretation on my part, but I trust that it is not completely contrary to Jain doctrine. In any case, I expect that a Jain would claim that my account is correct "in some way" ('syāt'), given my level of karmic obstruction. My sources for this interpretation were (Burch, 1964; Dundas, 2002; Malliṣeṇa, 1957; Matilal, 1981; Soni, 2000; Umāsvāti, 1994).

Chapter 22

Conclusion

This study has proposed an addition to the overall methodology of philosophy. However, unlike the methodological meditations of Descartes, for example, this study has not argued for the abandonment of prior methods of philosophy and the institution of a completely new approach. Rather, the method of perspectival reduction is notably conservative in the sense that it tends to preserve the philosophy that has preceded it. This conservatism is manifest in two ways.

First, all of the preceding methods of philosophy and their results are retained within perspectival reduction, but they are downgraded somewhat to the status of mere perspectives, in order that their presuppositions may be identified and coordinated with all the other perspectives. Thus philosophical naturalism, inference to the best explanation, reflective equilibrium, as well as phenomenology, first philosophy and last philosophy all have their place within perspectival reduction, but their results are held in suspense until they can be coordinated with regard to their presuppositions, and until the apparent relativity of those results to their presuppositions can be reduced according to the three ways in which a perspectival reduction might be accomplished.

Second, the three techniques of perspectival reduction include two that are already known and used by philosophy, namely the search for invariances between perspectives and the identification of one objectively preferable perspective over the others. What constitutes a novel result from this study is the third technique of seeking commensurability rules between perspectives, though some predecessors have been noted in Chapter 21. So the proposal of perspectival reduction does not demand that philosophers cease arguing that one theory or account of some topic is better than others. Rather, it suggests that such arguments need not be the only way or even the best way to proceed with regard to any particular philosophical topic. Given the novelty of the technique of reducing perspectives by means of commensurability, at least once commensurability is recognized to consist in more than mere translation between different languages, this study has emphasized the role of commensurability within perspectival reduction, but it is important to reiterate that this technique is only one of three techniques that might be employed in perspectival reduction.

This emphasis may be justified also by the relation between the search for commensurability rules and the other two techniques of perspectival reduction. If there are invariances between perspectives, those invariances should become manifest within any set of commensurability rules that can be established between those perspectives, since those commensurability rules would show that no transformation is needed between perspectives to establish those invariances. Further, if one perspective is objectively preferable over the others, then that perspective ought to be the one that provides commensurability rules between all of the others, since the objectively preferable perspective should be able to explain why all of the other perspectives are deficient in some way, according to the presuppositions that they hold. Thus the search for commensurability rules tends to subsume the other two techniques of perspectival reduction, at least in practice.

Two very important issues have been left unaddressed until this point, namely the questions of truth and of justification. It would seem that a philosophical methodology ought properly to be endorsed because of its ability to identify truths and to provide justification for believing those truths. However, this study has not discussed truth or justification in any systematic way, so it may seem that the argument for perspectival reduction is fundamentally incomplete. Indeed, I agree that it is incomplete, but such incompleteness is inevitable at this point. Any argument for the ability of a methodology to identify truths and to provide justification must presuppose some notions of truth and justification, but those notions would in turn need to be established on the basis of some method, whether the brute acceptance of some intuition or otherwise. The approach of this study is to seek some way of conducting philosophical research from the middle, namely without firm foundations or a clear end state, without relying on brute intuitions, so I cannot simply presuppose some notion of truth and justification in order to argue for perspectival reduction. Rather, it would be more consistent to establish those notions by means of perspectival reduction, by identifying the presuppositions of the various rival accounts of truth and justification and attempting to reduce the apparent relativity of those accounts to those presuppositions. That task must be reserved for future studies. Once they are completed, and some notions of truth and justification emerge from the process of perspectival reduction, though, the question concerning the ability of perspectival reduction to attain truth and provide justification must be answered. It is hoped that whatever notion truth and justification that emerges from an application of perspectival reduction, the method can be shown to provide precisely that kind of truth and justification. If for some reason there is some tension or inconsistency between the method and the notions of truth and justification that are established by it, then it is hoped that the deployment of perspectival reduction could bootstrap some further methodological inquiry that would be adequate to its own notions of truth and justification. However, the question of this kind of adequacy with regard to perspectival reduction is premature at this point, pending further study.

Yet I think an argument can be made here concerning the adequacy of perspectival reduction to support the nature of philosophical inquiry, at least according to one conception. This study proposed a particular broad conception of the nature of philosophy according to which philosophy has two major functions: (1) the coordination and reconciliation of all other fields of study, and (2) the investigation of anything not covered under any of those fields. I claim that perspectival reduction helps to meet those roles very well.

First, any special field of study is defined by a certain set of presuppositions and methods. According to perspectival reduction, that set would thereby define a perspective. Where different fields clearly study different things, there would seem to be no room for conflict. Yet different fields tend to intersect at various points, and at these points some coordination and reconciliation are required.

This study has argued that since this kind of coordination and reconciliation falls outside the methods of the various special fields of study, this task should properly belong to philosophy. Once the presuppositions and methods of various fields are recognized as providing perspectives, though, the process of perspectival reduction appears perfectly well suited to address this function of philosophy. The conflicts between different fields would be resolved by reducing the apparent relativity of their differing perspectives according to their presuppositions.

Second, if philosophy is to investigate whatever falls outside the presuppositions and methods of the various special fields of study, apparently without having any special presuppositions or methods that would define a new special field of study, at least prior to the investigation, then it would seem problematic how even to begin. In this case, the very aspect of the unknown that pervades this function thrusts the question of methodology into prominence. How does one approach the unknown? Cautiously, to be sure, but caution is not much of a methodology. Yet it would seem that the general notion of philosophy from the middle and the particular method of perspectival reduction are well suited to this kind of investigation. One can approach the unknown by deploying a series of hypotheses about it and by deducing the consequences to form a theory. Once a series of rival theories are developed, those alternatives can be coordinated precisely by means of perspectival reduction. This process represents a distinctive sort of experimental method, as suggested earlier.[1]

This study started with the question of progress in philosophy. If the argument of this study is correct that there is general technique of philosophy that has not yet been appreciated and adequately deployed by philosophers, namely the search for commensurability rules, then it would seem that further progress should be expected once this technique is more widely applied to various open problems in philosophy. Everything that is old might indeed be new again, given different ways of thinking and different ways of working.

Yet if the question of progress is understood to apply not simply to the results that philosophy offers and the widespread accep-

---

[1] Similar to Dewey's proposals for a reconstruction of philosophy as an endeavor that is active and experimental (Dewey, 1919, 1958). Kitcher's reading of Dewey seems to miss this aspect completely (Kitcher, 2023).

tance of those results, then I think a case can be made that philosophy has already made great progress. According to this study, different methodologies represent different perspectives on a given topic, and according to the method of perspectival reduction, a topic can be understood better when there are increasingly more perspectives available. So in this sense, philosophy makes progress when it develops new methodologies and new ways of thinking. I propose that except for some periods of relative stagnation, the business of philosophy has always been to seek out new methods and to establish new perspectives. This study has sought to extend that search and to make it more fruitful with the proposal of the method of perspectival reduction.

References

Achinstein, P. (1962, 06). The circularity of a self-supporting inductive argument. *Analysis, 22*(6), 138-141. Retrieved from https://doi.org/10.1093/analys/22.6.138

Agassi, J. (1974). Criteria for plausible arguments. *Mind, 83*(331), 406–416. Retrieved from https://doi.org/10.1093/mind/LXXXIII.331.406

Almeder, R. F. (1998). *Harmless naturalism: The limits of science and the nature of philosophy.* Chicago: Open Court.

Anderson, D. R. (1986). The evolution of Peirce's concept of abduction. *Transactions of the Charles S. Peirce Society, 22*(2), 145–164. Retrieved from https://www.jstor.org/stable/40320131

Aristotle. (1984). *The complete works of Aristotle* (Vol. 2; J. Barnes, Ed.). Princeton, New Jersey: Princeton University Press.

Aronson, E. (2004). *The social animal* (Ninth ed.). New York: Worth Publishers.

Bacon, F. (1902). *Novum organum* (J. Devey, Ed.). New York: P. F. Collier & Son.

Baggini, J., & Fosl, P. S. (2020). *The philosopher's toolkit: A compendium of philosophical concepts and methods* (3rd ed.). Hoboken, NJ: Wiley-Blackwell.

Baynes, K., Bohman, J., & McCarthy, T. (Eds.). (1986). *After philosophy: End or transformation?* Cambridge, Massachusetts: The MIT Press.

Bealer, G. (1996). A priori knowledge and the scope of philosophy. *Philosophical Studies, 81*(2-3), 121–142. Retrieved from https://doi.org/10.1007/BF00372777

Bealer, G., & Strawson, P. F. (1992). The incoherence of empiricism. *Aristotelian Society Supplementary Volume, 66*(1), 99–138. Retrieved from https://doi.org/10.1093/

aristoteliansupp/66.1.99

Beaver, D. I. (1997). Presupposition. In J. F. A. K. V. Benthem, J. van Benthem, & A. G. B. T. Meulen (Eds.), *Handbook of logic and language*. Elsevier.

Belnap, N. D. (1982). Gupta's rule of revision theory of truth. *Journal of Philosophical Logic, 11*(1), 103–116. Retrieved from https://doi.org/10.1007/BF00302340

Bergson, H. (1912). *An introduction to metaphysics.* New York: G. P. Putnam's Sons.

Berkeley, G. (1906). *Three dialogues between Hylas and Philonous.* Chicago: Open Court.

Black, M. (1954). Inductive support of inductive rules. In *Problems of analysis* (pp. 191–208). London: Routledge & Kegan Paul.

Black, M. (1958). Self-supporting inductive arguments. *Journal of Philosophy, 55*(17), 718–725. Retrieved from https://doi.org/10.2307/2022113

Blanshard, B. (1939). *The nature of thought* (Vol. 2). London: Allen & Unwin.

Bosanquet, B. (1920). *Implication and linear inference.* London: Macmillan and Co.

Bosanquet, B. (1921). *The meeting of extremes in contemporary philosophy.* London: Macmillan and Co.

Boyd, R. (1983). On the current status of the issue of scientific realism. *Erkenntnis, 19*(1-3), 45–90. Retrieved from https://doi.org/10.1007/BF00174775

Bradley, F. H. (1914). *Essays on truth and reality.* Oxford: Cambridge University Press.

Bradley, F. H. (1916). *Appearance and reality* (Second ed.). London: George Allen & Unwin, Ltd.

Briskman, L. (1987). Historicist relativism and bootstrap rationality. In J. Agassi & I. C. Jarvie (Eds.), *Rationality: The critical view* (pp. 317–338). Dordrecht: Springer Netherlands. Retrieved from https://doi.org/10.1007/978-94-009-3491-7_21

Brueckner, A. (2013). Bootstrapping, evidentialist internalism, and rule circularity. *Philosophical Studies, 164*(3), 591–597. Retrieved from https://doi.org/10.1007/s11098-012-9876-9

Burch, G. B. (1964). Seven-valued logic in Jain philosophy. *International Philosophical Quarterly, 4*(1), 68–93. Retrieved from https://doi.org/10.5840/ipq19644140

Burtt, E. A. (1925). *The metaphysical foundations of modern science*. London: Kegan Paul, Trench, Trubner & Co., Ltd.

Cappelen, H. (2012). *Philosophy without intuitions*. Oxford: Oxford University Press.

Cappelen, H., Gendler, T. S., & Hawthorne, J. (Eds.). (2016). *The Oxford handbook of philosophical methodology*. Oxford: Oxford University Press.

Castañeda, H.-N. (1980). *On philosophical method*. Bloomington, Indiana: Noûs Publications.

Chalmers, D. J. (1996). *The conscious mind: In search of a fundamental theory*. Oxford: Oxford University Press.

Chamberlin, T. C. (1890, February). The method of multiple working hypotheses. *Science*, *15*(366), 92–96. Retrieved from https://www.jstor.org/stable/30060433

Collingwood, R. G. (1998). *An essay on metaphysics* (Revised ed.). Oxford: Oxford University Press.

Collingwood, R. G. (2005). *An essay on philosophical method* (Revised ed.). Oxford: Oxford University Press.

Daniels, N. (1979). Wide reflective equilibrium and theory acceptance in ethics. *Journal of Philosophy*, *76*(5), 256–282. Retrieved from https://doi.org/10.2307/2025881

Daston, L., & Galison, P. (2007). *Objectivity* (P. Galison, Ed.). New York: Zone Books.

Davidson, D. (1973). On the very idea of a conceptual scheme. *Proceedings and Addresses of the American Philosophical Association*, *47*, 5–20. Retrieved from https://doi.org/10.2307/3129898

Dennett, D. C. (1980). The milk of human intentionality. *Behavioral and Brain Sciences*, *3*(3), 428–430. Retrieved from https://doi.org/10.1017/S0140525X0000580X

Dennett, D. C. (1984). *Elbow room: The varieties of free will worth wanting*. Cambridge, Massachusetts: The MIT Press.

DePaul, M. R. (1986). Reflective equilibrium and foundationalism. *American Philosophical Quarterly*, *23*(1), 59–69. Retrieved from https://www.jstor.org/stable/20014125

DePaul, M. R., & Ramsey, W. M. (Eds.). (1998). *Rethinking intuition: The psychology of intuition and its role in philosophical inquiry*. Lanham, Maryland: Rowman & Littlefield Publishers.

Descartes, R. (1985a). Discourse on the method. In J. Cottingham, R. Stoothoff, & D. Murdoch (Eds.), *The philosophical writings of Descartes* (Vol. 1, pp. 111–151). Cambridge: Cambridge University Press.

Descartes, R. (1985b). Meditations on first philosophy. In J. Cottingham, R. Stoothoff, & D. Murdoch (Eds.), *The philosophical writings of Descartes* (Vol. 2, pp. 1–62). Cambridge: Cambridge University Press.

Descartes, R. (1985c). Rules for the direction of the mind. In J. Cottingham, R. Stoothoff, & D. Murdoch (Eds.), *The philosophical writings of Descartes* (Vol. 1, pp. 9–78). Cambridge: Cambridge University Press.

Dewey, J. (1916). *Essays in experimental logic.* Chicago: The University of Chicago Press.

Dewey, J. (1919). *Reconstruction in philosophy.* Boston: The Beacon Press.

Dewey, J. (1958). *Experience and nature.* New York: Dover Publications.

Diogenes Laertius. (1972). *Lives of the eminent philosophers, books i-v.* Cambridge, Massachusetts: Harvard University Press.

D'Oro, G., & Overgaard, S. (Eds.). (2017). *The Cambridge companion to philosophical methodology.* Cambridge: Cambridge University Press.

Dundas, P. (2002). *The Jains.* London: Routledge.

Earlenbaugh, J., & Molyneux, B. (2009). Intuitions are inclinations to believe. *Philosophical Studies, 145*(1), 89–109. Retrieved from https://doi.org/10.1007/s11098-009-9388-4

Ebertz, R. P. (1993). Is reflective equilibrium a coherentist model? *Canadian Journal of Philosophy, 23*(2), 193–214. Retrieved from https://doi.org/10.1080/00455091.1993.10717317

Eklund, M. (2002). Personal identity and conceptual incoherence. *Noûs, 36*(3), 465–485. Retrieved from https://doi.org/10.1111/1468-0068.00380

Essay: What (if anything) to expect from today's philosophers. (1966, January). *Time, 87*(1). Retrieved from https://time.com/archive/6628742/essay-what-if-anything-to-expect-from-todays-philosophers/

Feuerbach, L. (2012). *The fiery brook: Selected writings.* London and New York: Verso.

Feyerabend, P. (2010). *Against method* (Fourth ed.). London: Verso.

Fodor, J. A. (1964). On knowing what we would say. *Philosophical Review*, 73(2), 198–212. Retrieved from https://doi.org/10.2307/2183336

Foley, R. (1994). Quine and naturalized epistemology. *Midwest Studies in Philosophy*, 19(1), 243–260. Retrieved from https://doi.org/10.1111/j.1475-4975.1994.tb00288.x

Foucault, M. (2002). *The archaeology of knowledge*. London: Routledge.

Freundlich, Y. (1980). Theory evaluation and the bootstrap hypothesis. *Studies in History and Philosophy of Science*, 11, 267–277.

Fritzman, J. M. (1992). Against coherence. *American Philosophical Quarterly*, 29(2), 183–191. Retrieved from http://www.jstor.org/stable/20014412

Fumerton, R. (1980). Induction and reasoning to the best explanation. *Philosophy of Science*, 47(4), 589–600. Retrieved from https://doi.org/10.1086/288959

Fumerton, R. (1992). Skepticism and reasoning to the best explanation. *Philosophical Issues*, 2, 149–169. Retrieved from https://doi.org/10.2307/1522860

Fumerton, R. (1994). The incoherence of coherence theories. *Journal of Philosophical Research*, 19, 89–102. Retrieved from https://doi.org/10.5840/jpr_1994_16

Fumerton, R. (1995). *Metaepistemology and skepticism*. Lanham, Maryland: Rowman & Littlefield.

Gadamer, H.-G. (1989). *Truth and method* (Second revised ed.). New York: Continuum.

Geuss, R. (1994). Nietzsche and genealogy. *European Journal of Philosophy*, 2(3), 274–292. Retrieved from https://doi.org/10.1111/j.1468-0378.1994.tb00015.x

Gilson, Étienne. (1999). *The unity of philosophical experience*. San Francisco: Ignatius Press.

Glymour, C. (1980a). Bootstraps and probabilities. *Journal of Philosophy*, 77(11), 691–699. Retrieved from https://doi.org/10.5840/jphil198077118

Glymour, C. (1980b). *Theory and evidence*. Princeton, New Jersey: Princeton University Press.

Glymour, C. (1983). Revisions of bootstrap testing. *Philosophy of Science*, *50*(4), 626–629. Retrieved from https://doi.org/10.1086/289143

Goodman, N. (1966). *The structure of appearance* (Second ed.). Indianapolis: The Bobbs-Merrill Company.

Goodman, N. (1978). *Ways of worldmaking*. Indianapolis: Hackett Publishing Company.

Goodman, N. (1983). *Fact, fiction, and forecast* (Fourth ed.). Cambridge, Massachusetts: Harvard University Press.

Grice, P. (1986). Reply to Richards. In R. E. Grandy & R. Warner (Eds.), *Philosophical grounds of rationality: Intentions, categories, ends* (pp. 45–106). Oxford: Clarendon Press.

Gupta, A. (1982). Truth and paradox. *Journal of Philosophical Logic*, *11*(1), 1–60. Retrieved from https://doi.org/10.1007/BF00302338

Gupta, A., & Belnap, N. D. (1993). *The revision theory of truth*. Cambridge, Massachusetts: The MIT Press.

Hales, S. D. (1997). A consistent relativism. *Mind*, *106*(421), 33–52. Retrieved from https://doi.org/10.1093/mind/106.421.33

Hales, S. D. (2006). *Relativism and the foundations of philosophy*. Cambridge, Massachusetts: The MIT Press.

Hankinson, R. J. (1995). *The sceptics*. New York: Routledge.

Hansson, S. O. (2010). Methodological pluralism in philosophy. *Theoria*, *76*(3), 189–191. Retrieved from https://doi.org/10.1111/j.1755-2567.2010.01076.x

Harman, G. H. (1965). The inference to the best explanation. *Philosophical Review*, *74*(1), 88–95. Retrieved from https://doi.org/10.2307/2183532

Hegel, G. W. F. (1969). *Hegel's science of logic*. Amherst, New York: Humanity Books.

Heidegger, M. (1962). *Being and time*. New York: Harper & Row, Publishers.

Heidegger, M. (1977). The end of philosophy and the task of thinking. In D. F. Krell (Ed.), *Basic writings* (pp. 373–392). Harper & Row, Publishers.

Hempel, C. (1965). *Aspects of scientific explanation*. New York: The Free Press.

Herzberger, H. (1982a). Naive semantics and the liar paradox. *Jour-*

nal of Philosophy, 79(9), 479–497. Retrieved from https://doi.org/10.2307/2026380

Herzberger, H. (1982b). Notes on naive semantics. *Journal of Philosophical Logic*, 11(1), 61–102. Retrieved from https://doi.org/10.1007/BF00302339

Hesse, M. B. (1966). *Models and analogies in science*. Notre Dame, Indiana: University of Notre Dame Press.

Hiah, J., Poll, R., & van der Burg, W. (2025). Saturation as a methodological principle for philosophical research. *Metaphilosophy*, 56(5), 508-522. Retrieved from https://doi.org/10.1111/meta.70016

Hintikka, J. (1998, Summer). What is abduction? the fundamental problem of contemporary epistemology. *Transactions of the Charles S. Peirce Society*, 34(3), 503–533. Retrieved from https://www.jstor.org/stable/40320712

Horvath, J., Koch, S., & Titelbaum, M. G. (Eds.). (2025). *Methods in analytic philosophy: A primer and guide*. London, Ontario: PhilPapers Foundation. Retrieved from https://philpapers.org/rec/HORAPA-2

Huizinga, J. (1950). *Homo ludens: A study of the play-element in culture*. New York: Roy Publishers.

Hume, D. (1978). *A treatise of human nature* (Second ed.; L. A. Selby-Bigge & P. H. Nidditch, Eds.). Oxford: Oxford University Press.

Husserl, E. (1965). Philosophy as a rigorous science. In Q. Lauer (Ed.), *Phenomenology and the crisis of philosophy* (pp. 71–147). New York: Harper & Row, Publishers.

Husserl, E. (1970). *Cartesian meditations: An introduction to phenomenology*. The Hague: Martinus Nijhoff Publishers.

Husserl, E. (1982). *Ideas pertaining to a pure phenomenology and to a phenomenological philosophy: First book: General introduction to a pure phenomenology*. The Hague: Martinus Nijhoff Publishers.

Husserl, E. (2001a). *Logical investigations* (New ed., Vol. 1). New York: Routledge.

Husserl, E. (2001b). *Logical investigations* (New ed., Vol. 2). New York: Routledge.

Huxley, A. (1952). *The devils of Loudun*. London: Chatto & Windus.

Jackson, F. (1998). *From metaphysics to ethics: A defence of conceptual analysis*. Oxford: Oxford University Press.

James, W. (1911). *Some problems of philosophy*. London: Longman, Green, and Co.

Joachim, H. H. (1906). *The nature of truth*. Oxford: Oxford University Press.

Kant, I. (1965). *Critique of pure reason*. New York: St. Martin's Press.

Kitcher, P. (2023). *What's the use of philosophy?* Oxford: Oxford University Press.

Knobe, J., & Nichols, S. (Eds.). (2008). *Experimental philosophy*. Oxford: Oxford University Press.

Kornblith, H. (Ed.). (1985). *Naturalizing epistemology*. Chicago: University of Chicago Press.

Kuhn, T. S. (1996). *The structure of scientific revolutions* (Third ed.). Chicago & London: The University of Chicago Press.

Laruelle, F. (2012). *Struggle and utopia at the end times of philosophy*. Minneapolis: Univocal Publishing.

Laruelle, F. (2013a). *Dictionary of non-philosophy*. Minneapolis: Univocal Publishing.

Laruelle, F. (2013b). *Philosophy and non-philosophy*. Minneapolis: Univocal Publishing.

Laruelle, F. (2017). *Principles of non-philosophy*. London and New York: Bloomsbury Academic.

Lawler, I., Dellsén, F., & Norton, J. (2025). Progress and disagreement in philosophy: A brief introduction. In J. Horvath, S. Koch, & M. G. Titelbaum (Eds.), *Methods in analytic philosophy: A primer and guide* (pp. 221–233). London, Ontario: PhilPapers Foundation. Retrieved from https://philpapers.org/rec/LAWPAD

Lehrer, K. (1974). *Knowledge*. Oxford: Clarendon Press.

Lipton, P. (2004). *Inference to the best explanation*. New York: Routledge.

Locke, J. (1823). Mr. Locke's reply to the Bishop of Worcester's answer to his second letter. In *The works of John Locke* (Vol. IV, pp. 191–498). printed for Thomas Tegg [and others].

Locke, J. (1959a). *An essay concerning human understanding* (Vol. 1). New York: Dover Publications.

Locke, J. (1959b). *An essay concerning human understanding* (Vol. 2). New York: Dover Publications.

Lowe, E. J. (1998). *The possibility of metaphysics: Substance, identity, and time*. Oxford: Oxford University Press.

Mackie, J. L. (1964). Self-refutation – a formal analysis. *Philosophical Quarterly*, *14*(56), 193–203. Retrieved from https://doi.org/10.2307/2269633

Mackie, J. L. (1977). *Ethics: Inventing right and wrong*. London: Penguin Books.

Magee, B. (2009). My conception of philosophy. *Royal Institute of Philosophy Supplement*, *65*, 57–70. Retrieved from https://doi.org/10.1017/S1358246109990051

Maker, W. (1994). *Philosophy without foundations: Rethinking Hegel*. Albany, New York: State University of New York Press.

Malliṣeṇa. (1957). Syādvādamañjarī. In S. Radhakrishnan & C. A. Moore (Eds.), *A source book in Indian philosophy* (pp. 260–268). Princeton, New Jersey: Princeton University Press.

Mannheim, K. (1960). *Ideology and utopia: An introduction to the sociology of knowledge*. London: Routledge & Kegan Paul Ltd.

Marcuse, H. (1964). *One-dimensional man*. Boston: Beacon Press.

Marion, J. (1999). The other first philosophy and the question of givenness. *Critical Inquiry*, *25*(4), 784–800. Retrieved from https://doi.org/10.1086/448946

Marx, K., & Engels, F. (1976). *Collected works* (Vol. 5). New York: International Publishers Company.

Matilal, B. K. (1981). *The central philosophy of Jainism*. Ahmedabad: L. D. Institute of Indology.

McGinn, C. (1993). *Problems in philosophy: The limits of inquiry*. Oxford: Blackwell Publishers.

Meinong, A. (1960). The theory of objects. In R. M. Chisholm (Ed.), *Realism and the background of phenomenology* (pp. 76–117). Glencoe, Illinois: The Free Press.

Mellor, D. H. (2005). *Probability: A philosophical introduction*. London and New York: Routledge.

Milgram, S. (1963). Behavioral study of obedience. *Journal of Abnormal and Social Psychology*, *67*(4), 371–378. Retrieved from https://doi.org/10.1037/h0040525

Mironov, V. V. (2013, January). On progress in philosophy. *Metaphilosophy*, *44*(1–2), 10–14. Retrieved from https://doi.org/10.1111/meta.12011

Nietzsche, F. (1968). *The will to power* (W. Kaufmann, Ed.). London: Weidenfeld and Nicolson.

Nietzsche, F. (1994). *On the genealogy of morals* (K. Ansell-Pearson, Ed.). Cambridge: Cambridge University Press.

Nietzsche, F. (2001). *The gay science* (B. Williams, Ed.). Cambridge: Cambridge University Press.

Nilsson, J. (2005). A bootstrap theory of rationality. *Theoria, 71*(2), 182–199. Retrieved from https://doi.org/10.1111/j.1755-2567.2005.tb01012.x

Nozick, R. (1981). *Philosophical explanations.* Cambridge, Massachusetts: Belknap Press of Harvard University Press.

Nozick, R. (2001). *Invariances: The structure of the objective world.* Cambridge, Massachusetts: Harvard University Press.

Ortega y Gasset, J. (1946). *Concord and liberty.* New York: W. W. Norton & Company.

Ortega y Gasset, J. (1960). *What is philosophy?* New York & London: W. W. Norton & Company.

Ortega y Gasset, J. (1961). *The modern theme.* New York: Harper & Brothers.

Ortega y Gasset, J. (1967). *The origin of philosophy.* New York: W. W. Norton & Company.

Ortega y Gasset, J. (1971). *The idea of principle in Leibnitz and the evolution of deductive theory.* New York: W. W. Norton & Company.

Ortega y Gasset, J. (1975). *Phenomenology and art.* New York: W. W. Norton & Company.

Ortega y Gasset, J. (1984). *Historical reason.* New York & London: W. W. Norton & Company.

Ortega y Gasset, J. (1987). *Psychological investigations.* New York & London: W. W. Norton & Company.

Parfit, D. (2008). Persons, bodies, and human beings. In T. Sider, J. P. Hawthorne, & D. W. Zimmerman (Eds.), *Contemporary debates in metaphysics* (pp. 177–208). Malden, Massachusetts: Blackwell.

Passmore, J. (1961). *Philosophical reasoning.* New York: Basic Books, Inc.

Peirce, C. S. (1998a). *The essential Peirce* (Vol. 1). Bloomington, Indiana: Indiana University Press.

Peirce, C. S. (1998b). *The essential Peirce* (Vol. 2). Bloomington, Indiana: Indiana University Press.

Pepper, S. C. (1942). *World hypotheses: A study in evidence.* Berkeley, California: University of California Press.

Pepper, S. C. (1970). Existentialism. In J. Bobik (Ed.), *The nature of philosophical inquiry* (p. 189-211). Notre Dame, Indiana: University of Notre Dame Press.

Plato. (1961). *The collected dialogues of Plato*. Princeton, New Jersey: Princeton University Press.

Postow, B. C. (1976). Husserl's failure to establish a presuppositionless science. *Southern Journal of Philosophy*, *14*(2), 179–187. Retrieved from https://doi.org/10.1111/j.2041-6962.1976.tb01276.x

Priest, G. (2006). *In contradiction* (Second ed.). Oxford: Oxford University Press.

Prinz, J. J. (2008). Empirical philosophy and experimental philosophy. In J. Knobe & S. Nichols (Eds.), *Experimental philosophy* (pp. 189–208). Oxford: Oxford University Press.

Quine, W. V. O. (1969). *Ontological relativity and other essays*. New York: Columbia University Press.

Quine, W. V. O. (1972). Review: Identity and individuation. *Journal of Philosophy*, *69*(16), 488–497. Retrieved from https://doi.org/10.2307/2025325

Quine, W. V. O., & Ullian, J. S. (1978). *The web of belief* (Second ed.). New York: Random House.

Ramsey, F. P. (1990). *Philosophical papers* (D. H. Mellor, Ed.). Cambridge: Cambridge University Press.

Rawls, J. (1974). The independence of moral theory. *Proceedings and Addresses of the American Philosophical Association*, *48*, 5–22. Retrieved from https://doi.org/10.2307/3129858

Rawls, J. (1999). *A theory of justice* (Revised ed.). Cambridge, Massachusetts: Harvard University Press.

Rawls, J. (2001). *Justice as fairness: A restatement* (Second ed.). Cambridge, Massachusetts: Belknap Press of Harvard University Press.

Raz, J. (1982). The claims of reflective equilibrium. *Inquiry: An Interdisciplinary Journal of Philosophy*, *25*(3), 307–330. Retrieved from https://doi.org/10.1080/00201748208601970

Reale, G. (1980). *The concept of first philosophy and the unity of the metaphysics of Aristotle*. Albany, New York: State University of New York Press.

Rentetzi, M. (2005). The metaphorical conception of scientific explanation: Rereading Mary Hesse. *Journal for General Phi-*

losophy of Science, *36*(2), 377–391. Retrieved from https://doi.org/10.1007/s10838-006-0091-2

Rescher, N. (1973). *The coherence theory of truth*. Oxford: Oxford University Press.

Rescher, N. (1985). *The strife of systems: An essay on the grounds and implications of philosophical diversity*. Pittsburgh: University of Pittsburgh Press.

Rescher, N. (1994). *Metaphilosophical inquiries* (Vol. 3). Princeton, New Jersey: Princeton University Press.

Rescher, N. (2001). *Philosophical reasoning: A study in the methodology of philosophizing*. Malden, Massachusetts: Blackwell Publishers.

Rescher, N. (2006). *Philosophical dialectics: An essay on metaphilosophy*. Albany, New York: State University of New York Press.

Ressler, M. (2012). Thoroughly relativistic perspectives. *Notre Dame Journal of Formal Logic*, *53*(1), 89–112. Retrieved from http://dx.doi.org/10.1215/00294527-1626545

Ressler, M. (2013). *The logic of relativism*. Increasingly Skeptical Publications.

Ressler, M. (2024). *Authentic technological engagement*. Increasingly Skeptical Publications.

Ricœur, P. (1996). *A key to Husserl's Ideas I*. Milwaukee: Marquette University Press.

Rorty, R. (1980). *Philosophy and the mirror of nature*. Princeton, New Jersey: Princeton University Press.

Rosenberg, A. (2015). *Philosophy of social science* (Fifth ed.). New York & London: Routledge.

Russell, B. (1905). On denoting. *Mind*, *XIV*(4), 479–493. Retrieved from https://www.jstor.org/stable/2248381

Russell, B. (1912). *The problems of philosophy*. New York: Henry Holt and Company.

Schopenhauer, A. (2000). *Parerga and paralipomena: Short philosophical essays* (Vol. 2). Oxford: Oxford University Press.

Schroeter, F. (2004). Reflective equilibrium and antitheory. *Noûs*, *38*(1), 110–134. Retrieved from https://doi.org/10.1111/j.1468-0068.2004.00464.x

Schwitzgebel, E. (2009). Do ethicists steal more books? *Philosophical Psychology*, *22*(6), 711–725. Retrieved from https://doi.org/10.1080/09515080903409952

Sellars, W. (1991). *Science, perception, and reality.* Atascadero, California: Ridgeview Publishing Company.
Sextus Empiricus. (1936). *Against the physicists, against the ethicists.* Cambridge, Massachusetts: Harvard University Press.
Sextus Empiricus. (2000). *Outlines of scepticism* (J. Annas & J. Barnes, Eds.). Cambridge: Cambridge University Press.
Sextus Empiricus. (2005). *Against the logicians* (R. Bett, Ed.). Cambridge: Cambridge University Press.
Sheldon, W. H. (1918). *Strife of systems and productive duality: An essay in philosophy.* Cambridge, Massachusetts: Harvard University Press.
Sidgwick, A. (1884). *Fallacies: A view of logic from the practical side.* New York: D. Appleton and Company.
Sidgwick, H. (1901). *The methods of ethics* (Sixth ed.). London: Macmillan and Co., Ltd.
Siegel, H. (1984). Goodmanian relativism. *The Monist, 67*(3), 359–375. Retrieved from https://doi.org/10.5840/monist198467323
Siegel, H. (1986). Relativism, truth, and incoherence. *Synthese, 68*(2), 225–259. Retrieved from https://doi.org/10.1007/BF00413833
Sokolowski, R. (1998). The method of philosophy: Making distinctions. *Review of Metaphysics, 51*(3), 515–532. Retrieved from https://www.jstor.org/stable/20130246
Soni, J. (2000). Basic Jaina epistemology. *Philosophy East and West, 50*(3), 367–377. Retrieved from https://www.jstor.org/stable/1400179
Stack, M. (1983). Self-refuting arguments. *Metaphilosophy, 14*(3-4), 327–335. Retrieved from https://doi.org/10.1111/j.1467-9973.1983.tb00318.x
Stalnaker, R. (1973). Presuppositions. *Journal of Philosophical Logic, 2*(4), 447–457. Retrieved from https://doi.org/10.1007/BF00262951
Stich, S. P. (1990). *The fragmentation of reason.* Cambridge, Massachusetts: The MIT Press.
Stich, S. P., & Nisbett, R. E. (1980). Justification and the psychology of human reasoning. *Philosophy of Science, 47*(2), 188–202. Retrieved from https://doi.org/10.1086/288928
Stout, G. F. (1908). Immediacy, mediacy and coherence. *Mind,*

17(65), 20–47. Retrieved from http://www.jstor.org/stable/2248207

Strawson, P. F. (1950). On referring. *Mind*, *59*(235), 320–344. Retrieved from https://doi.org/10.1093/mind/LIX.235.320

Suarez, F. (1976). *On the various kinds of distinctions*. Milwaukee: Marquette University Press.

Sytsma, J. (2025). Experimental philosophy: A brief introduction. In J. Horvath, S. Koch, & M. G. Titelbaum (Eds.), *Methods in analytic philosophy: A primer and guide* (pp. 185–197). London, Ontario: PhilPapers Foundation. Retrieved from https://philpapers.org/rec/HORAPA-2

Thagard, P. R. (1978). The best explanation: Criteria for theory choice. *Journal of Philosophy*, *75*(2), 76–92. Retrieved from https://doi.org/10.2307/2025686

Tiainen, T., & Koivunen, E. (2006). Exploring forms of triangulation to facilitate collaborative research practice: Reflections from a multidisciplinary research group. *Journal of Research Practice*, *2*(2), Article M2.

Umāsvāti. (1994). *Tattvārtha sūtra*. New York: HarperCollins Publishers.

Umphrey, S. (1990). *Zetetic skepticism*. Wakefield, New Hampshire: Longwood Academic.

Unamuno, M. d. (1921). *The tragic sense of life in men and in peoples*. London: Macmillan and Co., Ltd.

van Fraassen, B. C. (1977). The pragmatics of explanation. *American Philosophical Quarterly*, *14*(2), 143–150. Retrieved from https://www.jstor.org/stable/20009661

van Fraassen, B. C. (1980). *The scientific image*. Oxford: Clarendon Press.

van Fraassen, B. C. (1989). *Laws and symmetry*. Oxford: Clarendon Press.

Vogel, J. (2000). Reliabilism leveled. *Journal of Philosophy*, *97*(11), 602–623. Retrieved from https://doi.org/10.2307/2678454

Walton, D. N. (2004). *Abductive reasoning*. Tuscaloosa, Alabama: University of Alabama Press.

Weinberg, J. M., Nichols, S., & Stich, S. (2001). Normativity and epistemic intuitions. *Philosophical Topics*, *29*(1-

2), 429–460. Retrieved from https://doi.org/10.5840/philtopics2001291/217

Whitehead, A. N. (1925). *Science and the modern world.* New York: The Macmillan Company.

Williamson, T. (1994). *Vagueness.* New York: Routledge.

Williamson, T. (2007). *The philosophy of philosophy.* Malden, Massachusetts: Blackwell Publishing.

Williamson, T. (2020). *Philosophical method: A very short introduction.* Oxford: Oxford University Press.

Wilson, D. J. (1987). Science and the crisis of confidence in American philosophy, 1870–1930. *Transactions of the Charles S. Peirce Society, 23,* 235–262. Retrieved from https://www.jstor.org/stable/40320176

Winfield, R. D. (2011). Is phenomenology necessary as introduction to philosophy? *Review of Metaphysics, 65*(2), 279–298. Retrieved from https://www.jstor.org/stable/23055745

Wittgenstein, L. (1922). *Tractatus logico-philosophicus.* London: Routledge.

Wittgenstein, L. (2001). *Philosophical investigations* (Third ed.). Malden, Massachusetts: Blackwell Publishing.

Woolfolk, R. L. (2013). Experimental philosophy: A methodological critique. *Metaphilosophy, 44*(1-2), 79–87. Retrieved from https://doi.org/10.1111/meta.12016

Worrall, J. (1982). Review: Broken bootstraps. *Erkenntnis, 18*(1), 105–130. Retrieved from https://doi.org/10.1007/BF00179246

www.ingramcontent.com/pod-product-compliance
Lightning Source LLC
Chambersburg PA
CBHW030137170426
43199CB00008B/103